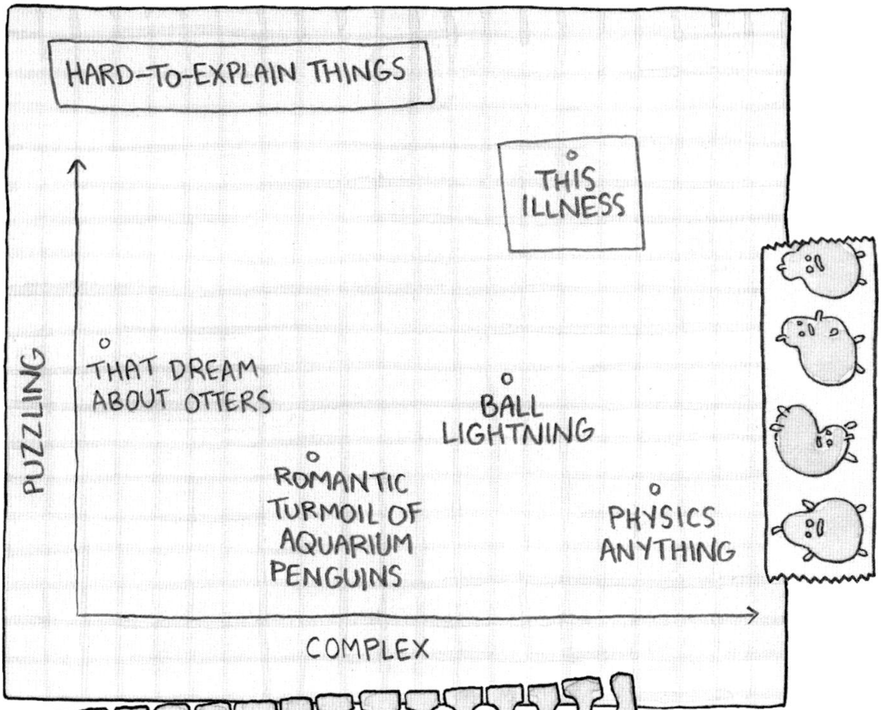
HARD-TO-EXPLAIN THINGS
THIS ILLNESS
THAT DREAM ABOUT OTTERS
BALL LIGHTNING
ROMANTIC TURMOIL OF AQUARIUM PENGUINS
PHYSICS ANYTHING
PUZZLING
COMPLEX

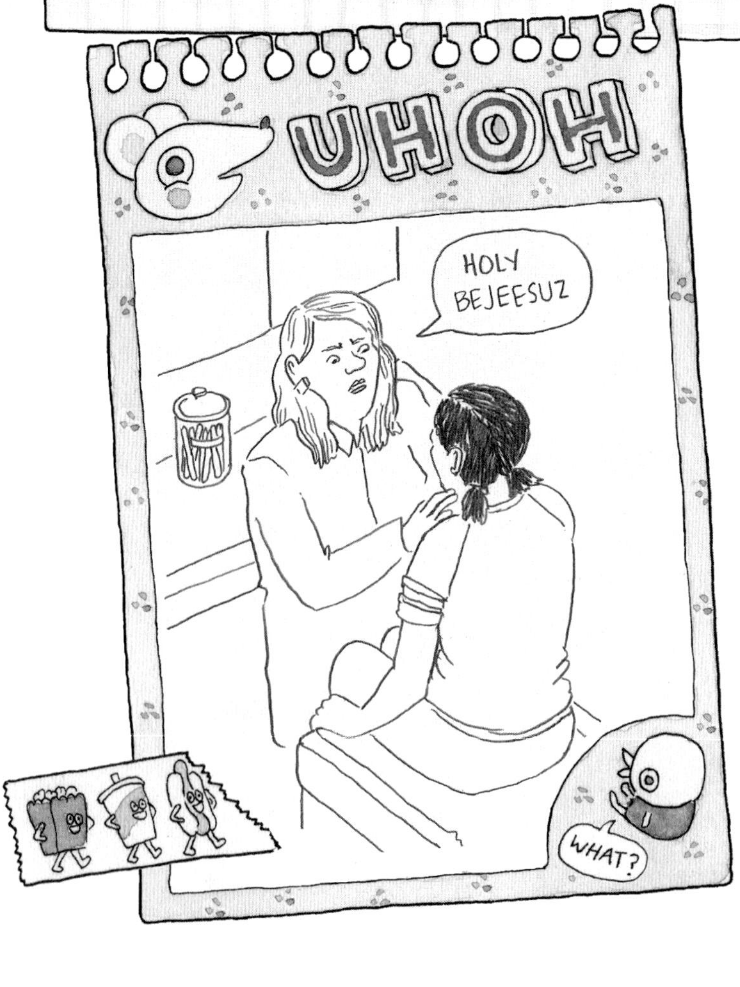
UHOH
HOLY BEJEESUZ
WHAT?

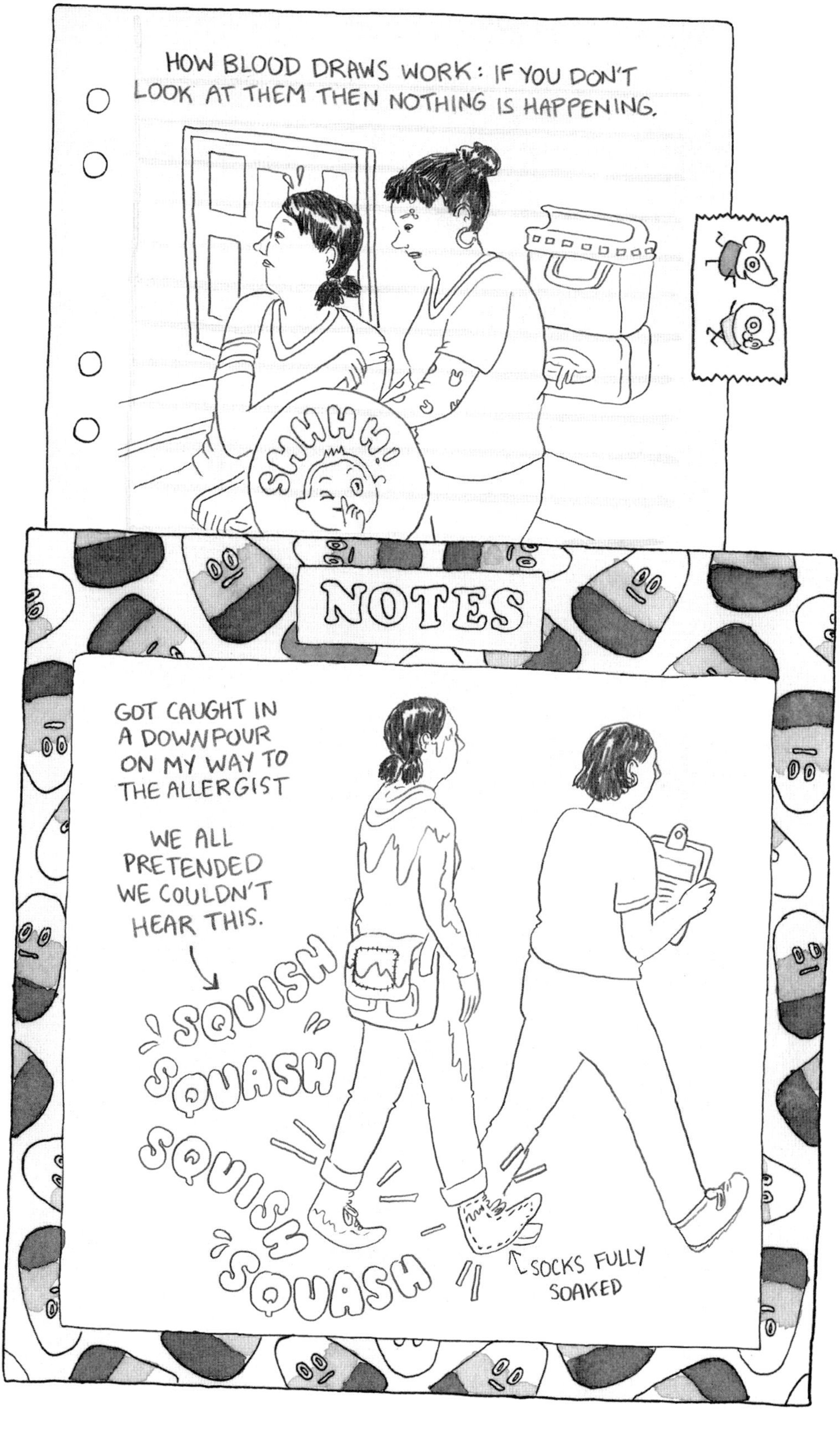
HOW BLOOD DRAWS WORK: IF YOU DON'T LOOK AT THEM THEN NOTHING IS HAPPENING.
SHHHH!
NOTES
GOT CAUGHT IN A DOWNPOUR ON MY WAY TO THE ALLERGIST
WE ALL PRETENDED WE COULDN'T HEAR THIS.
SQUISH
SQUASH
SQUISH
SQUASH
SOCKS FULLY SOAKED

Advance praise for
Notes from a Sickbed

"Tessa's intimate, surreal, and impeccably composed diary comics invite you in and wrap around you like a warm quilt. Her work is a soothing balm for the chronic frustrations of living in a human body."

—LISA HANAWALT, creator of *Tuca & Bertie*

"Tessa Brunton generously shares with us not only her struggle of living with a chronic, little-understood disease, but also her go-to skills for coping: a sharp wit and a rich, fabulously intricate inner life. And her drawings are gorgeous!"

—ROB KIRBY, author-artist, *Marry Me a Little*

"Being stuck at home on the couch with an endless illness should be an absolute nightmare, but somewhere between Tessa's unruly imagination and her dark sense of humor, she's created a surprisingly exciting, funny, and strangely uplifting world. A truly unique and wonderful book."

—JULIA WERTZ, author-artist, *Tenements, Towers & Trash: An Unconventional Illustrated History of New York City*

"This book is a gorgeous and necessary addition to the canon of graphic medicine."

—NICOLE GEORGES, author-artist, *Calling Dr. Laura: A Graphic Memoir*

For Viv

Graphic Universe™ is a trademark of Lerner Publishing Group, Inc.

Graphic Universe™
An imprint of Lerner Publishing Group, Inc.
241 First Avenue North
Minneapolis, MN 55401 USA

For reading levels and more information, look up this title at www.lernerbooks.com.

Library of Congress Cataloging-in-Publication Data

Names: Brunton, Tessa, artist, author.
Title: Notes from a sickbed / Tessa Brunton.
Description: Minneapolis : Graphic Universe, [2022] | Summary: "In 2009, Tessa Brunton experienced the first symptoms of myalgic encephalomyelitis. Notes from a Sickbed recalls the next eight years of her life—largely housebound—with honesty, a pointed wit, and a lively visual imagination" —Provided by publisher.
Identifiers: LCCN 2022005187 (print) | LCCN 2022005188 (ebook) | ISBN 9781728419480 (library binding) | ISBN 9781728462936 (paperback) | ISBN 9781728460994 (ebook)
Subjects: LCSH: Brunton, Tessa—Comic books, strips. | Cartoonists—United States—Biography—Comic books, strips, etc. | Chronic fatigue syndrome—Patients—Biography—Comic books, strips, etc. | Myalgicencephalomyelitis—Patients—Biography—Comic books, strips, etc. | LCGFT: Autobiographical comics. | Psychological comics. | Medical comics. | Graphic novels.
Classification: LCC PN6727.B7844 Z46 2022 (print) | LCC PN6727.B7844 (ebook) | DDC 741.5/973 [B]—dc23/eng/20220204

LC record available at https://lccn.loc.gov/2022005187
LC ebook record available at https://lccn.loc.gov/2022005188

Manufactured in the United States of America
2-1009104-49270-11/30/2022

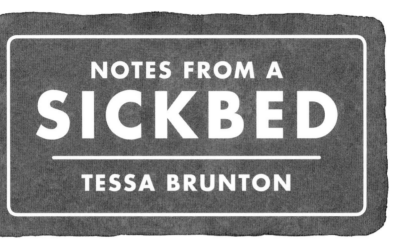

NOTES FROM A
SICKBED

TESSA BRUNTON

Graphic Universe™ • Minneapolis

Introduction

THESE COMICS ARE ABOUT MY LIFE with chronic illness. Specifically, they are about how I fumbled around trying to figure out how to live with my chronic illness, often failed, improvised solutions, distracted myself, tried not to panic, and got by.

Like many chronically ill people, it took me a long time to get correctly diagnosed, and these comics take place in the period before I knew what I was sick with. As you read them, you might wonder what that turned out to be. I eventually learned that I'd been muddling through myalgic encephalomyelitis (ME), sometimes called chronic fatigue syndrome. ME is a complex, debilitating, long-term disease with a grim record of stigma and neglect. It has no cure and remains poorly understood despite how common it is and how devastating it can be.

The diagnosis brought me community and some useful tools, but it was not a ticket out of trying to figure out how to live with the illness. Even now, after I've found some strategies that improve my symptoms, I'm still doing that work.

Life with a chronic illness doesn't have to be a struggle, and for some, it isn't. But I struggled, and thinking up these notes helped me when I was in my darker moments. If you're in a darker moment, I wish you so much good luck, and if you write down some notes, I look forward to reading them.

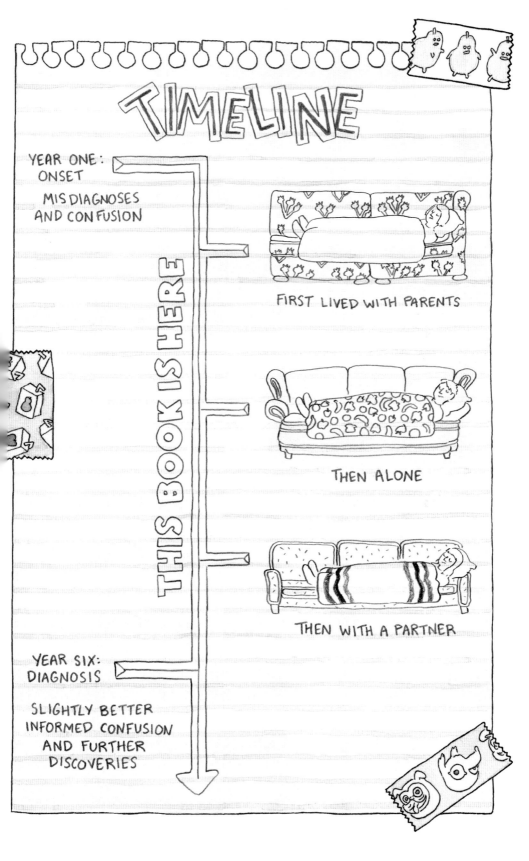

TIMELINE

YEAR ONE:
ONSET

MISDIAGNOSES
AND CONFUSION

FIRST LIVED WITH PARENTS

THIS BOOK IS HERE

THEN ALONE

THEN WITH A PARTNER

YEAR SIX:
DIAGNOSIS

SLIGHTLY BETTER
INFORMED CONFUSION
AND FURTHER
DISCOVERIES

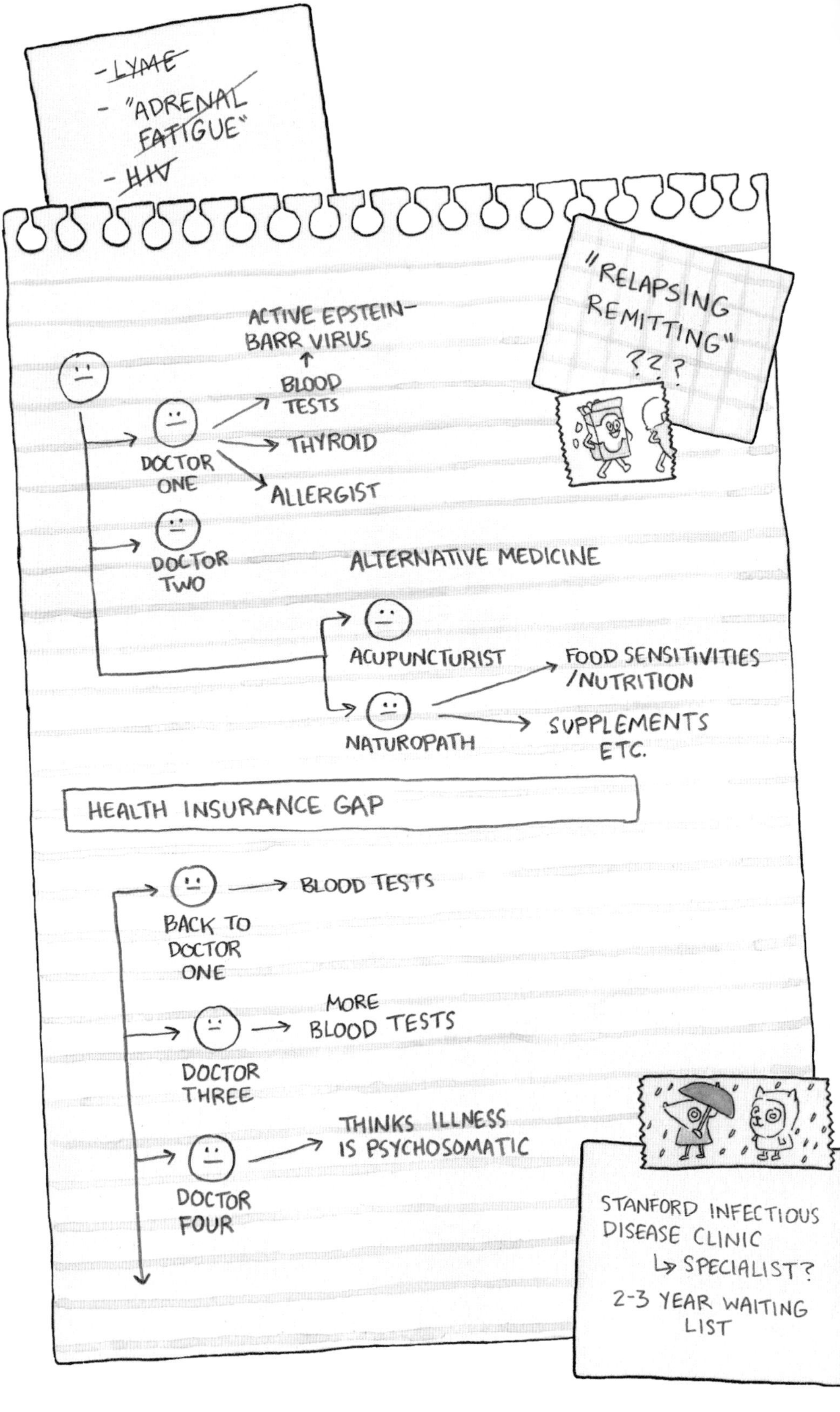
- ~~LYME~~
- ~~"ADRENAL FATIGUE"~~
- ~~HIV~~
"RELAPSING REMITTING"
???
ACTIVE EPSTEIN-BARR VIRUS
BLOOD TESTS
DOCTOR ONE
THYROID
ALLERGIST
DOCTOR TWO
ALTERNATIVE MEDICINE
ACUPUNCTURIST
NATUROPATH
FOOD SENSITIVITIES /NUTRITION
SUPPLEMENTS ETC.
HEALTH INSURANCE GAP
BACK TO DOCTOR ONE
BLOOD TESTS
DOCTOR THREE
MORE BLOOD TESTS
DOCTOR FOUR
THINKS ILLNESS IS PSYCHOSOMATIC
STANFORD INFECTIOUS DISEASE CLINIC
↳ SPECIALIST?
2-3 YEAR WAITING LIST

KNICK KNACKS

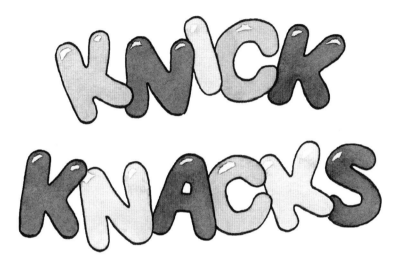

When it comes to sickrooms, I try to be like those scientists looking for habitable planets in outer space - planets that are in the Goldilocks Zone, which means they're th right distance from a star to meet some of the basic requirements for sustaining life.

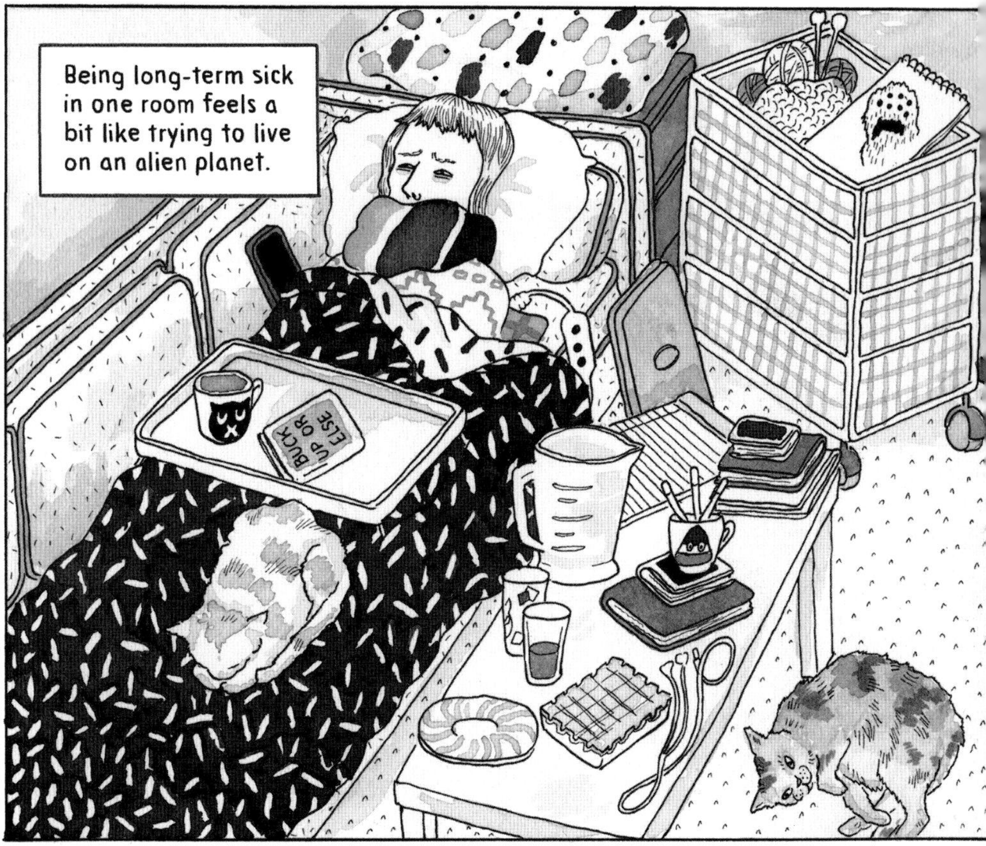
Being long-term sick in one room feels a bit like trying to live on an alien planet.
BUCK UP OR ELSE

So the features of a sickroom are key to survival, or at least key to not getting as depressed as I did the winter I foolishly stayed in a small, dark, mostly empty room because it was cheap to heat.

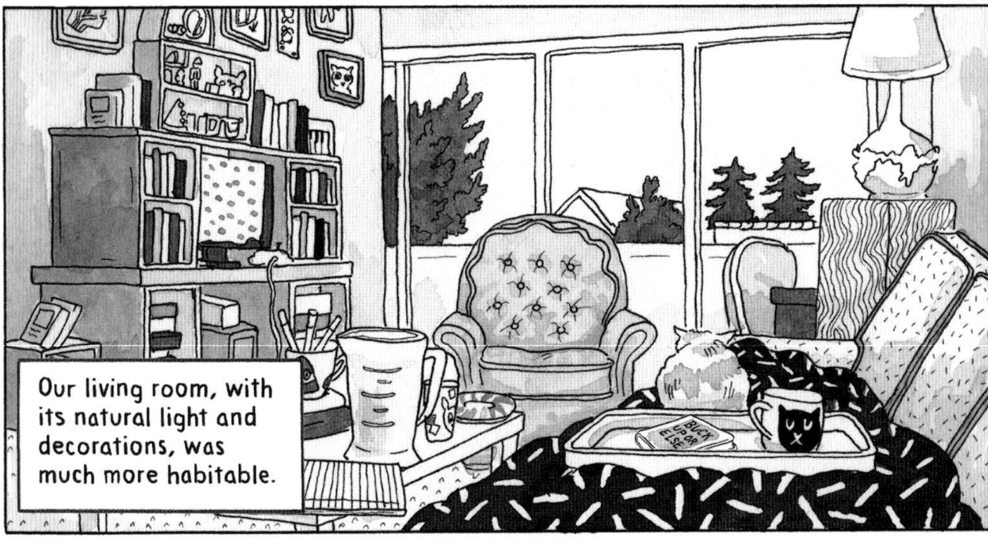
Our living room, with its natural light and decorations, was much more habitable.
BUCK UP OR ELSE

ut when you're solitary, sedentary, bored, nd ill the better part of every week, is ny room really in the Goldilocks Zone?

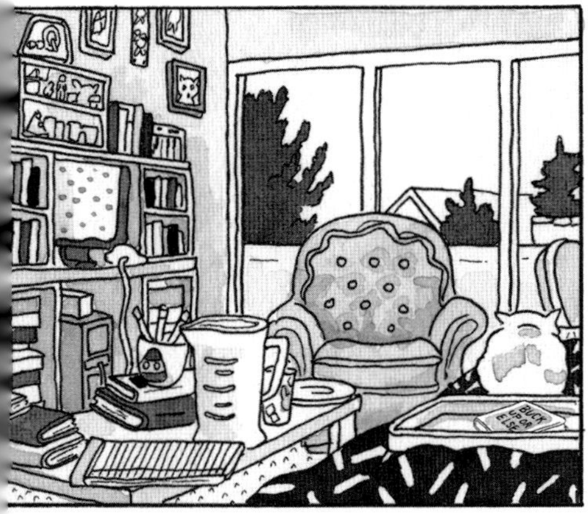
BUCK UP OR ELSE

Some days you can sort of accept that you are stuck in this room, staring eternally at your friend Jennie's cast-off gold armchair.

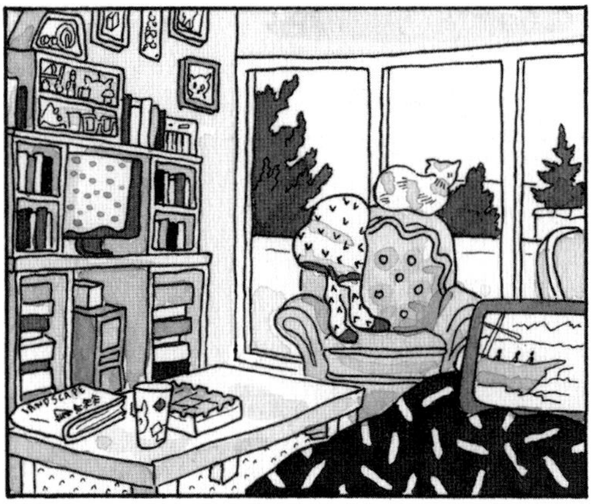
LANDSCAPE

nd some days it's a stone-cold nightmare. hen everything about the room becomes ightmarish too.

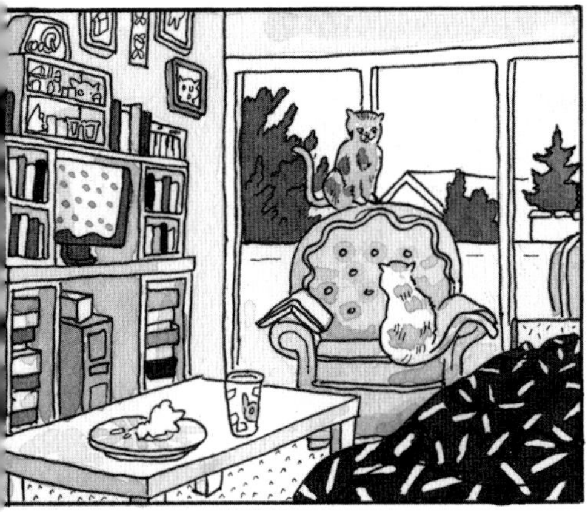

I've thought about whether I could fix this. What if instead of looking for habitable sickrooms, I created an enhanced one?

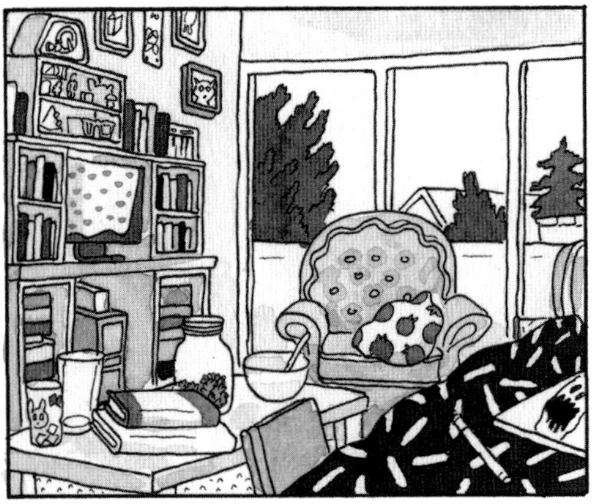

What if I somehow installed a giant aquarium? Or turned the room into a mini botanical garden of plants and flowers?

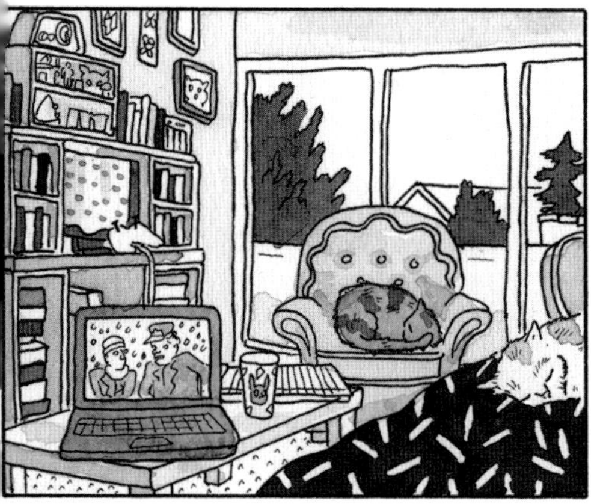

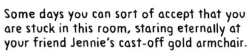

Or maybe I could put together some lively arrangement of knick knacks?

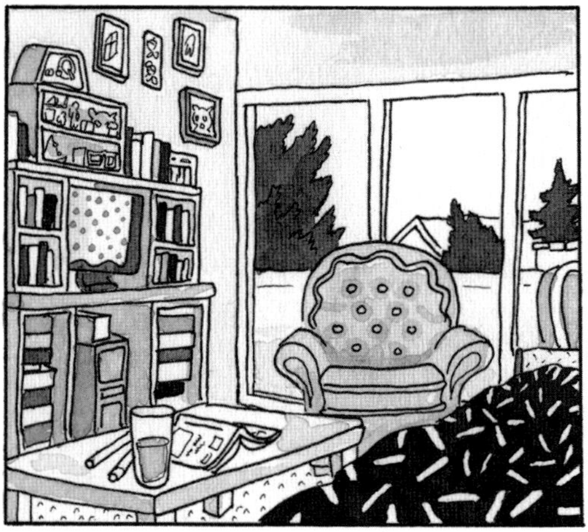

I'd start by moving my current knick knacks over to the couch to arrange around mysel

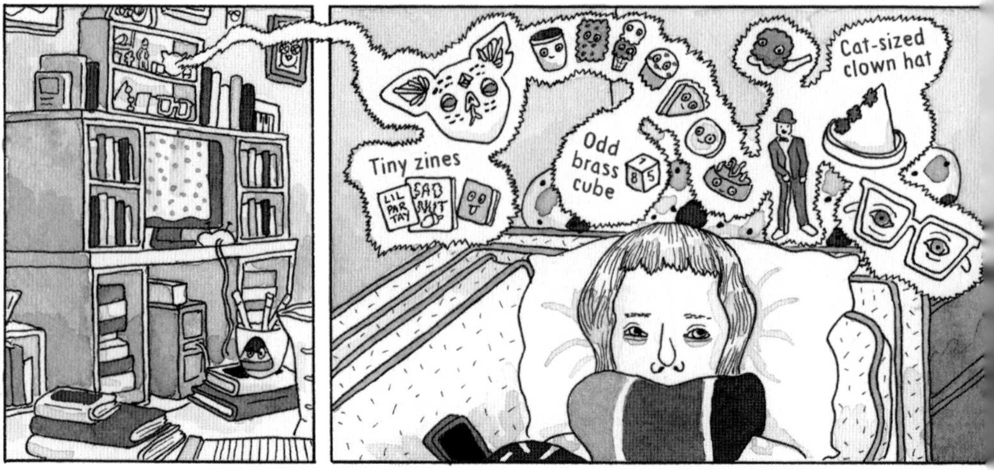
Tiny zines
Odd brass cube
Cat-sized clown hat

Then I'd add my 1980s childhood treasures, stored in a Keds shoebox these many years

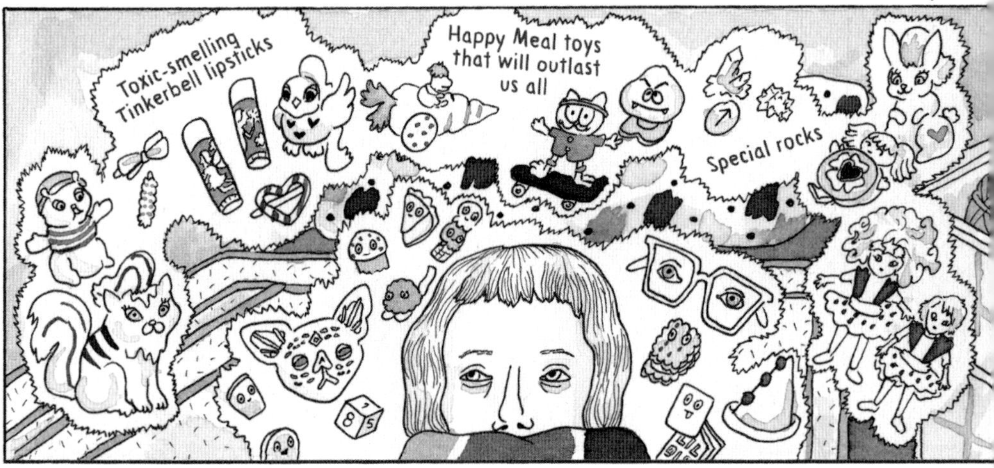
Toxic-smelling Tinkerbell lipsticks
Happy Meal toys that will outlast us all
Special rocks

And then instead of buying my monthly supply of health powders and supplements, I'd use that money for a spree, ordering all the hand-painted ponies and tin cat heads and extravagantly priced knick knacks that I covet online.

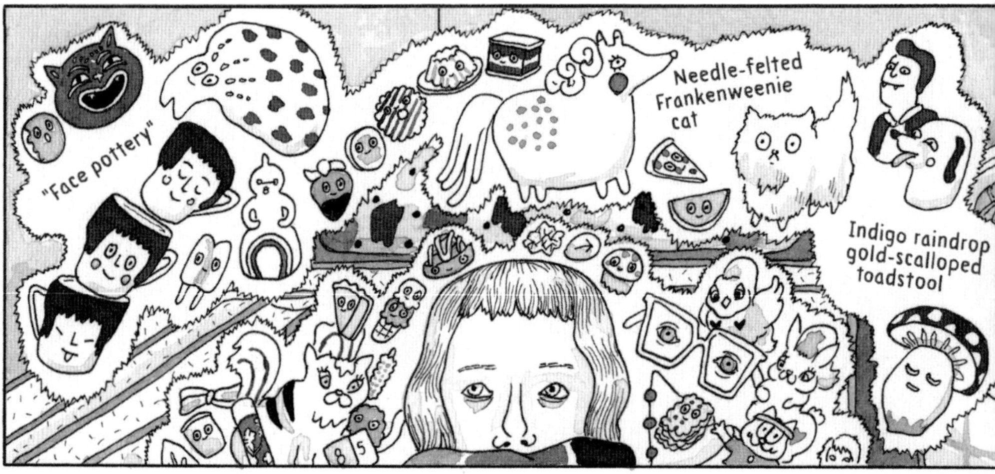
"Face pottery"
Needle-felted Frankenweenie cat
Indigo raindrop gold-scalloped toadstool

nd who needs to pay rent...

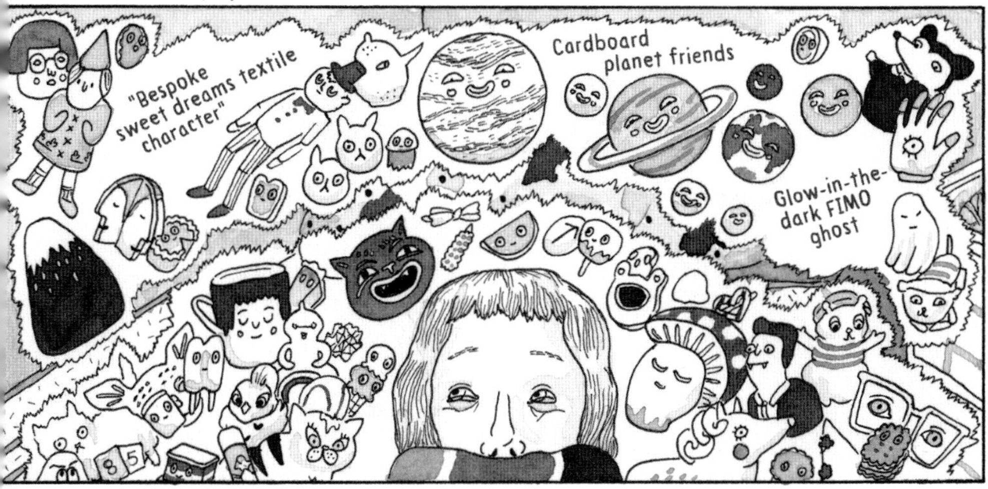
"Bespoke sweet dreams textile character"
Cardboard planet friends
Glow-in-the-dark FIMO ghost

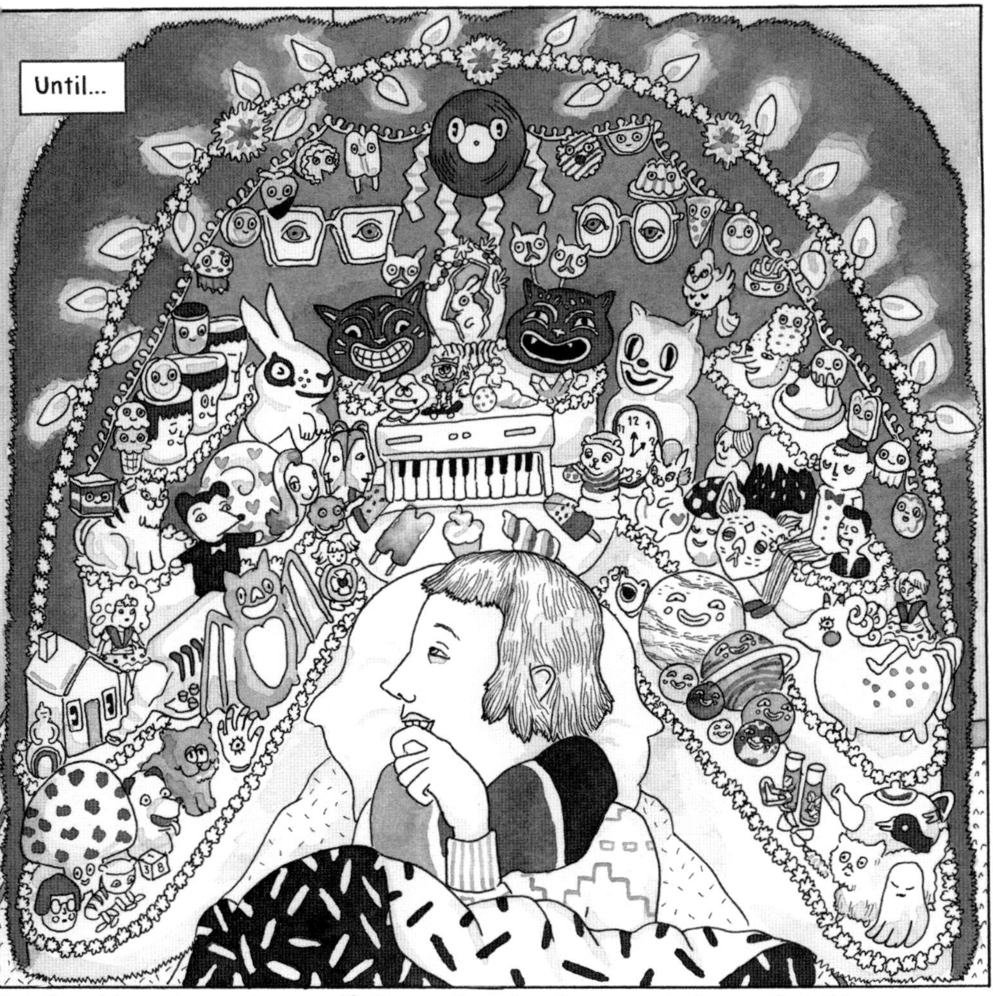
Until...

But then I have to say to myself, Tessa, there's a 50 percent chance that this arrangement will actually cheer you up.

And there's a 50 percent chance that, like Jennie's gold chair and the living room and every other part of confinement, those knick knacks will become a nightmare too.

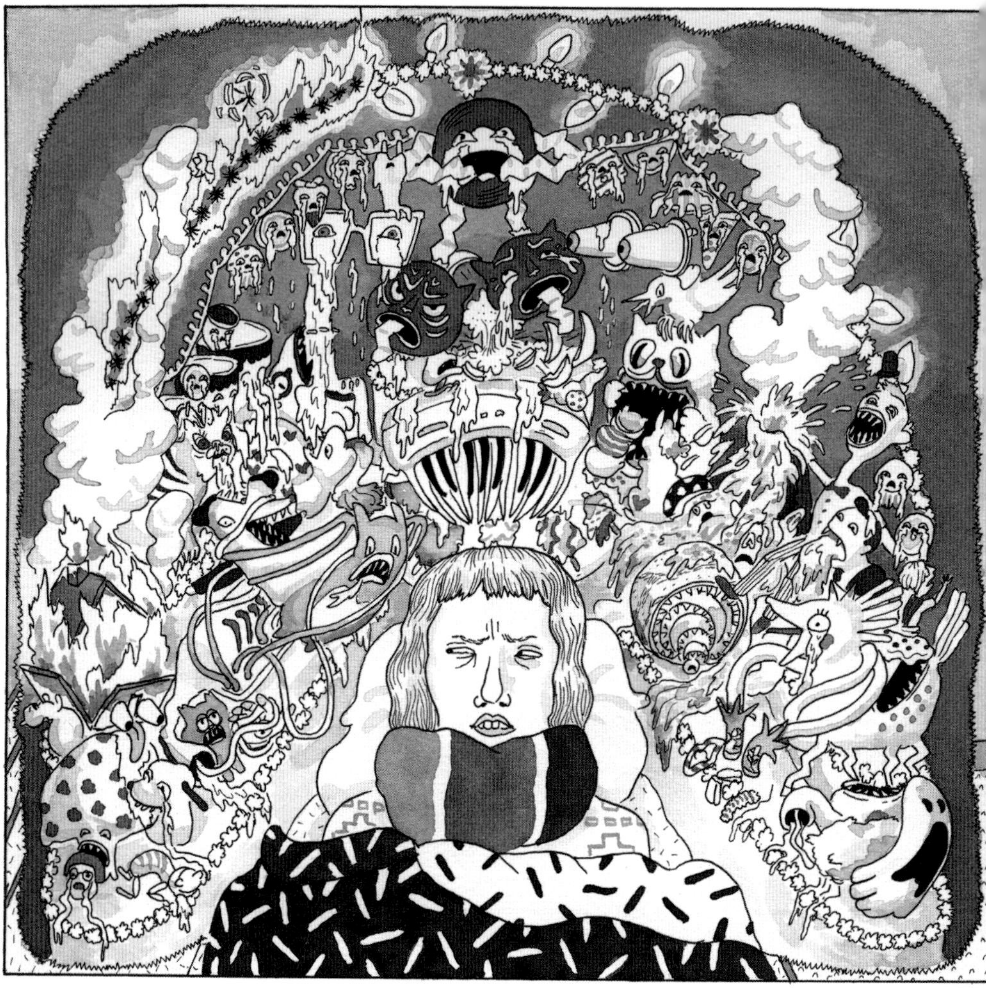

Also, those knick knacks would get really dusty.

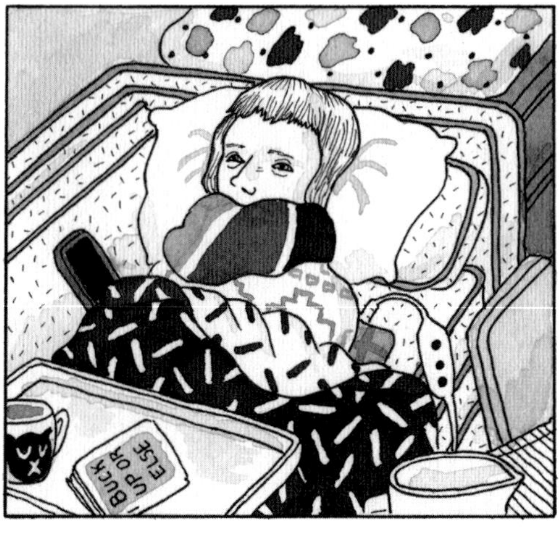
BUCK UP OR ELSE

And you'd elbow them over whenever you napped or ate soup.

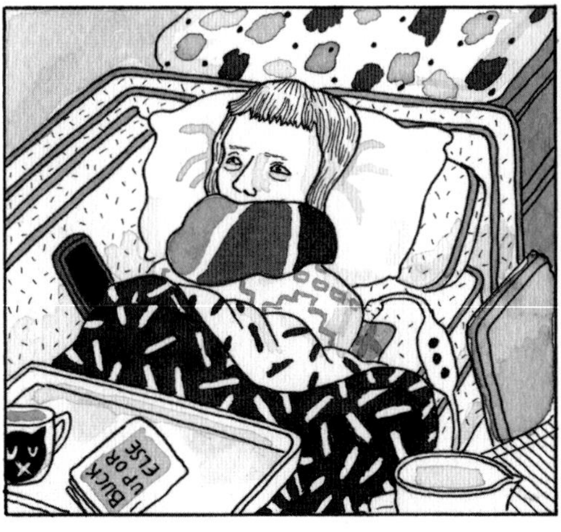
BUCK UP OR ELSE

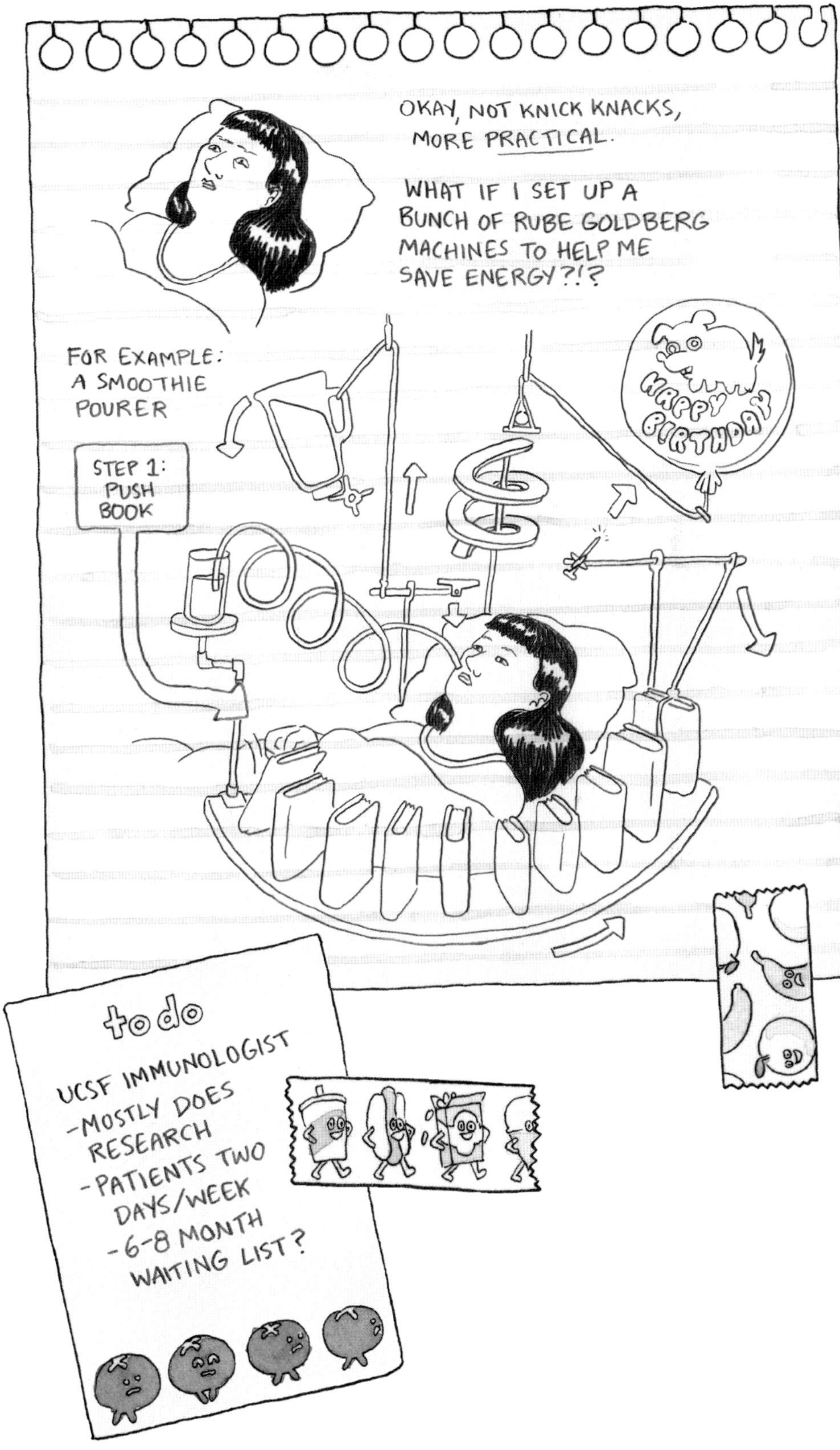
OKAY, NOT KNICK KNACKS, MORE PRACTICAL.
WHAT IF I SET UP A BUNCH OF RUBE GOLDBERG MACHINES TO HELP ME SAVE ENERGY?!?
FOR EXAMPLE: A SMOOTHIE POURER
STEP 1: PUSH BOOK
HAPPY BIRTHDAY
to do
UCSF IMMUNOLOGIST
-MOSTLY DOES RESEARCH
-PATIENTS TWO DAYS/WEEK
-6-8 MONTH WAITING LIST?

HAUNTED HOUSE

Here's a new development in how I'm coping with the illness these days. I now have this fantasy where I haunt the living like a ghost.

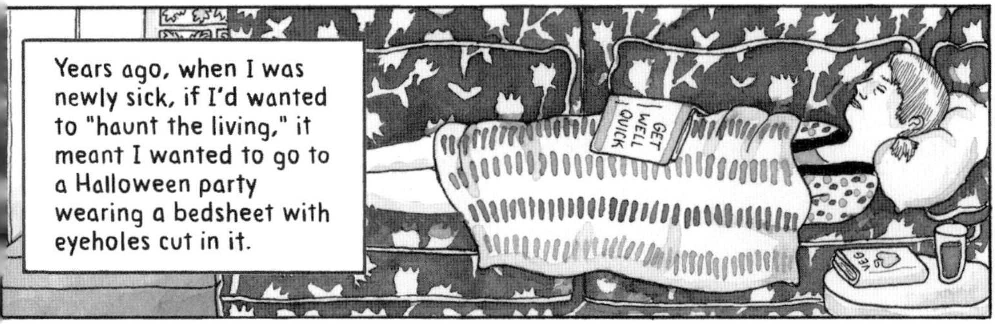
Years ago, when I was newly sick, if I'd wanted to "haunt the living," it meant I wanted to go to a Halloween party wearing a bedsheet with eyeholes cut in it.
GET WELL QUICK
VEG

But these days I want to do serious, scary-movie haunting. The kind of creaking-stairs-and-flickering-lights haunting carried out by ghosts so tormented that their only ambition is to inflict paranormal nightmares on any nearby warm bodies.

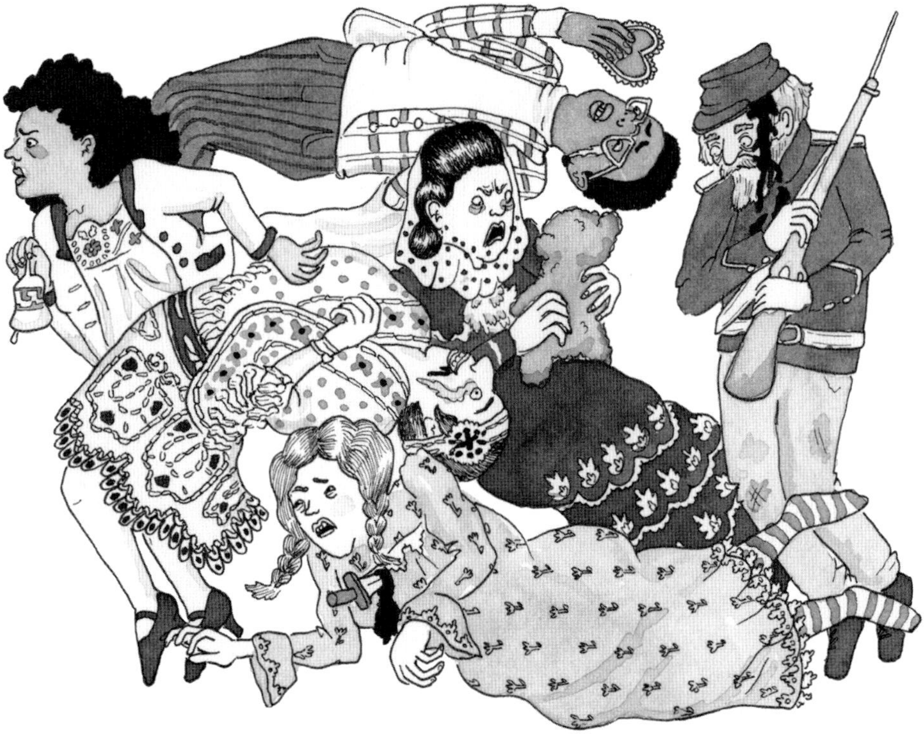

I went through two key steps to develop this fantasy.

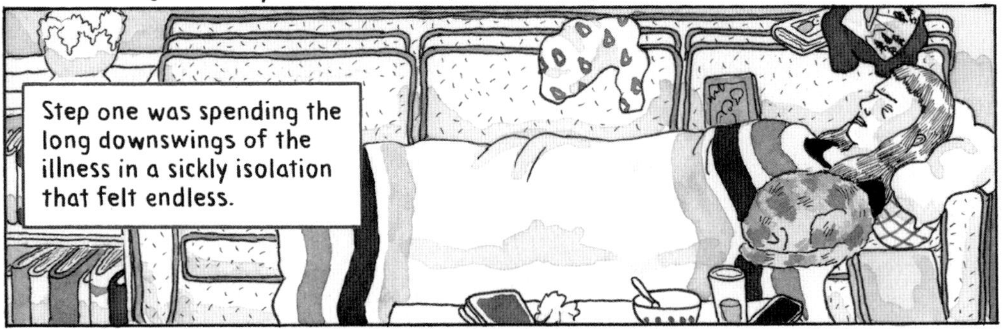
Step one was spending the long downswings of the illness in a sickly isolation that felt endless.

And step two was living under cheery college girls who were always having potlucks.

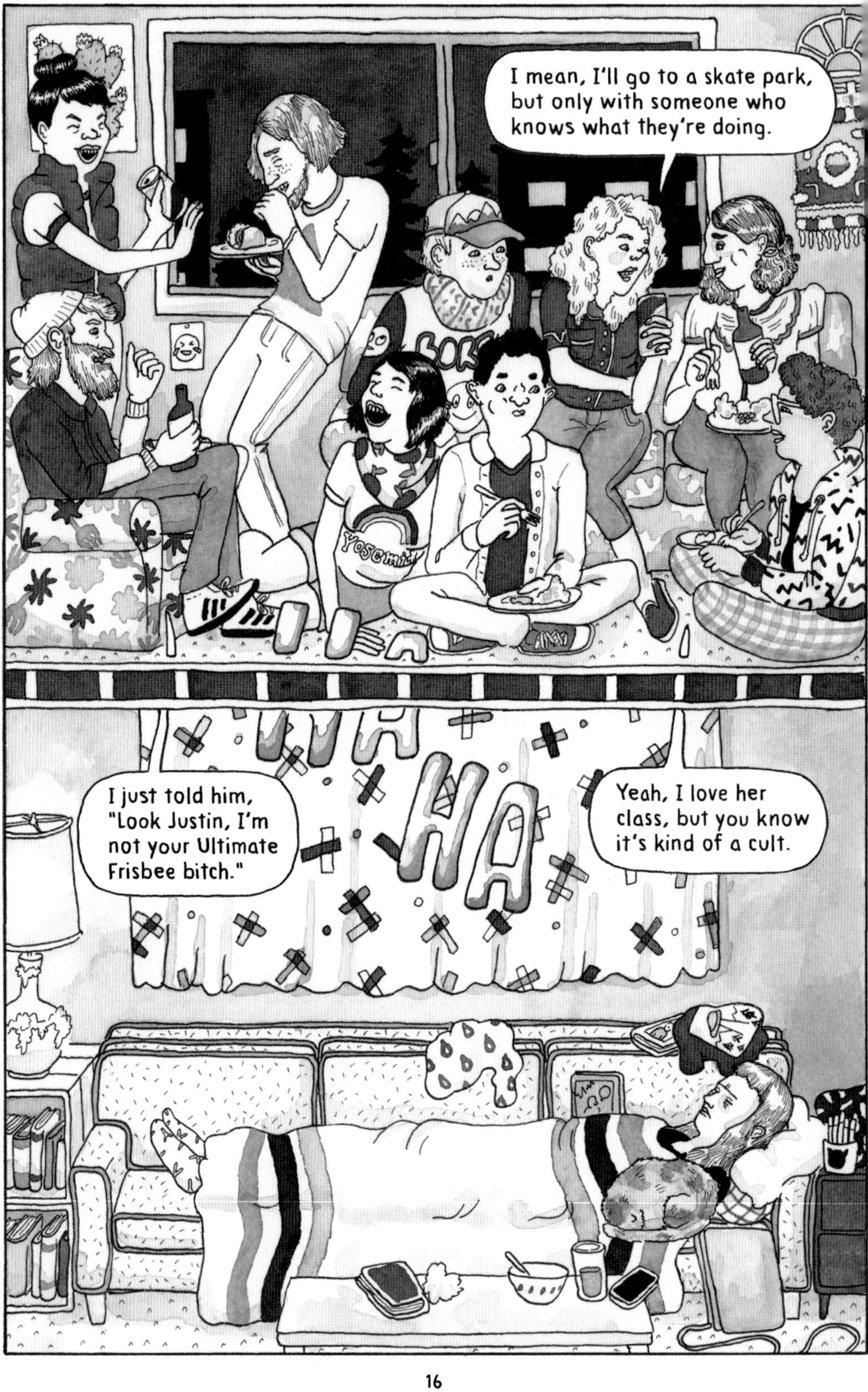
I mean, I'll go to a skate park, but only with someone who knows what they're doing.
BORG
YOSEMITE
I just told him, "Look Justin, I'm not your Ultimate Frisbee bitch."
HA
HA
Yeah, I love her class, but you know it's kind of a cult.

he college girls also had a
ot of "study groups."

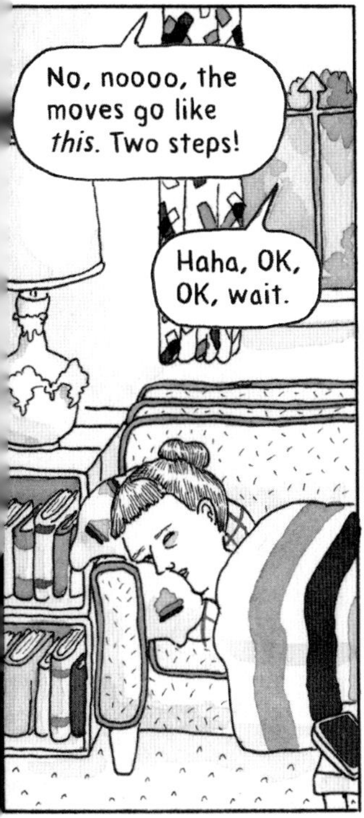

No, noooo, the moves go like *this*. Two steps!
Haha, OK, OK, wait.

And a lot of sex sketched out with bed springs.

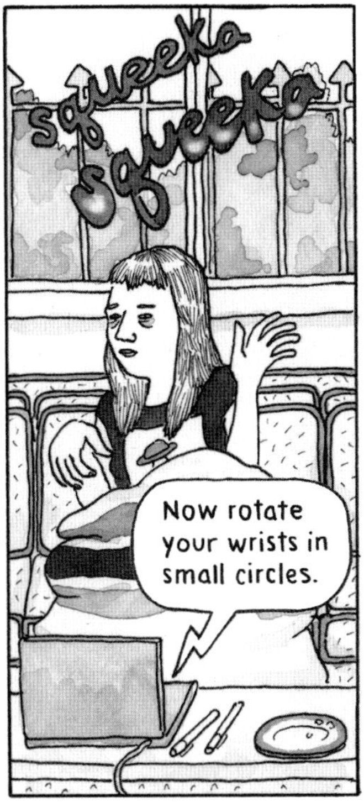

squeeka
squeeka
Now rotate your wrists in small circles.

They were always getting picked up for surfing, dropp-ed off from surfing, picked up for parties, and so on.

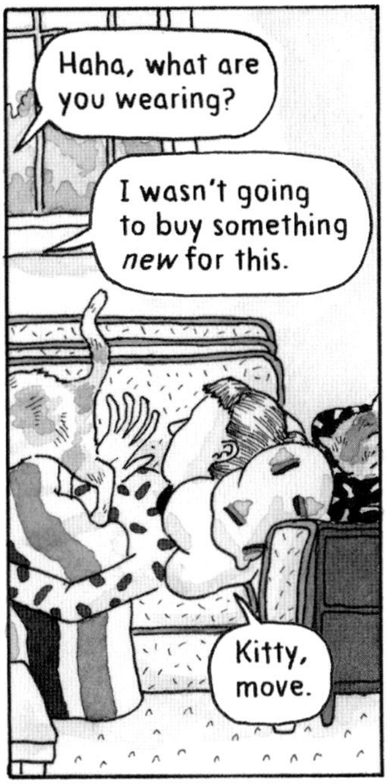

Haha, what are you wearing?
I wasn't going to buy something *new* for this.
Kitty, move.

It was only a matter of time before I realized I needed to shut out their noise.

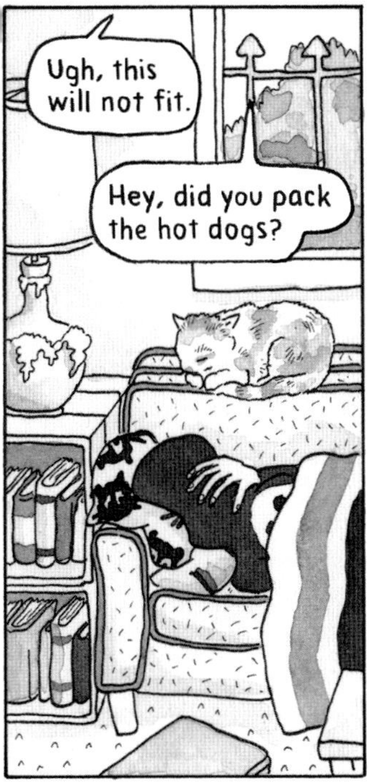

Ugh, this will not fit.
Hey, did you pack the hot dogs?

It was nothing personal. This was how I dealt with any reminders that, in the outside world, people were living not-sick lives.

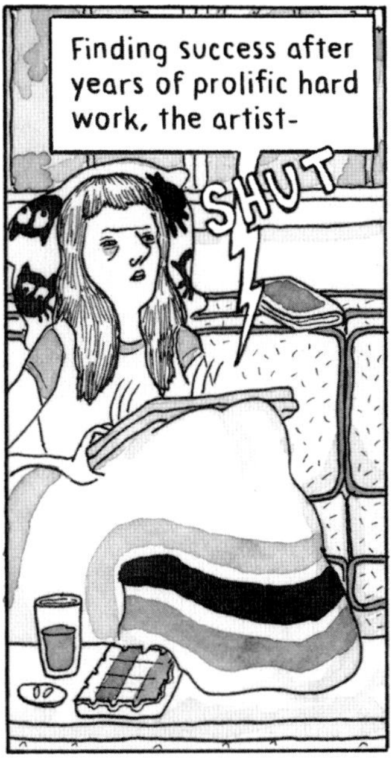

Finding success after years of prolific hard work, the artist-
SHUT

Where things were mostly going according to plan and the future looked promising.

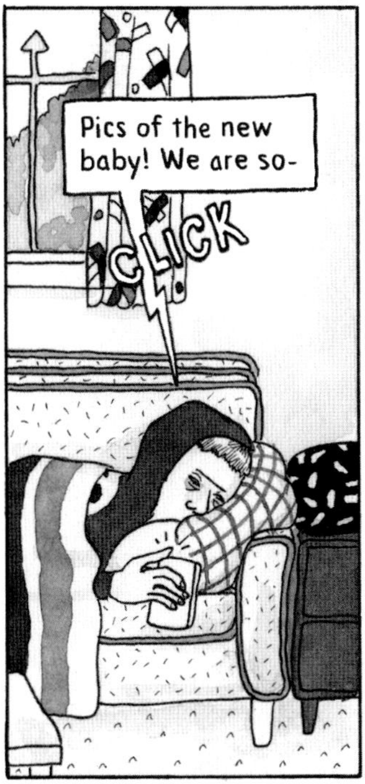

Pics of the new baby! We are so-
CLICK

So I started blasting "rain downpour" on my sleep sounds app.

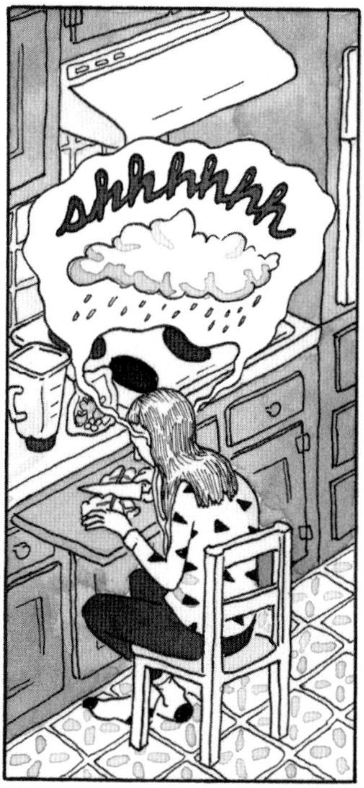
shhhhhh

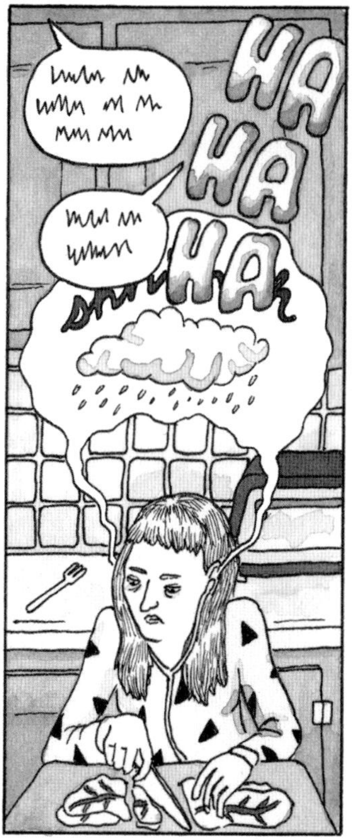
HA
HA
HA

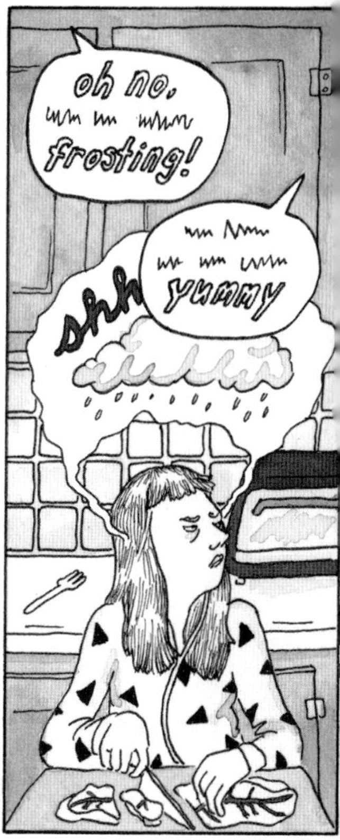
oh no, frosting!
yummy

Then I tried wearing those swimmer's earplugs under industrial safety earmuffs.

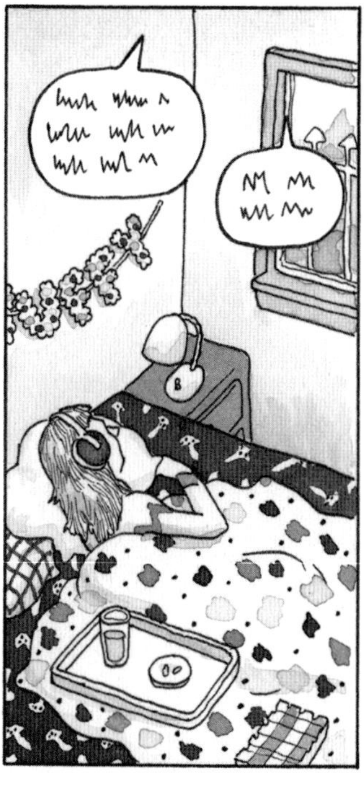

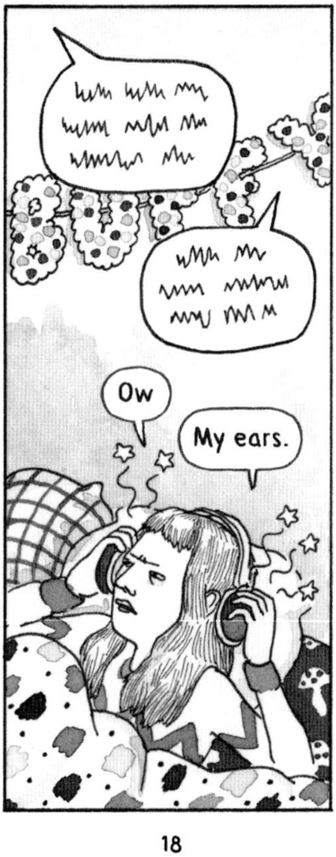
Ow
My ears.

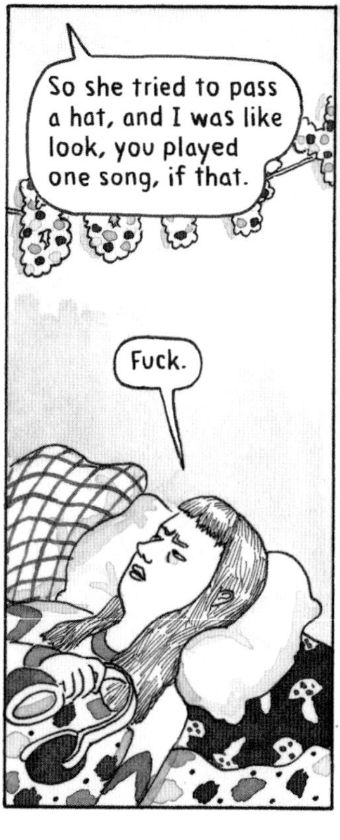
So she tried to pass a hat, and I was like look, you played one song, if that.
Fuck.

Over the next few months, I tried to just be a tolerant, mature adult.

Yeah, Yosemite was amazing.

AHHHH!

MUSHROOMS

But one day I was watching a horror movie, which lord knows I wasn't supposed to do, because it's too "stimulating" to be restful.

Oh yeah?

Yeah.

AHHHH!

Melody?

The movie was about a supernatural house that eats happy schoolgirls alive.

So beautiful.

And I saw a coyote!

Oh cool.

AHHHH!

That's Melody!

I realized I identified with the house.

Oh, and I had the I Ching.

The piano room!

Let's go!

And that I'd like nothing more than to turn the apartment upstairs into a haunted house myself.

Just to read in the tent every morning.

The piano bit me!

The piano?

19

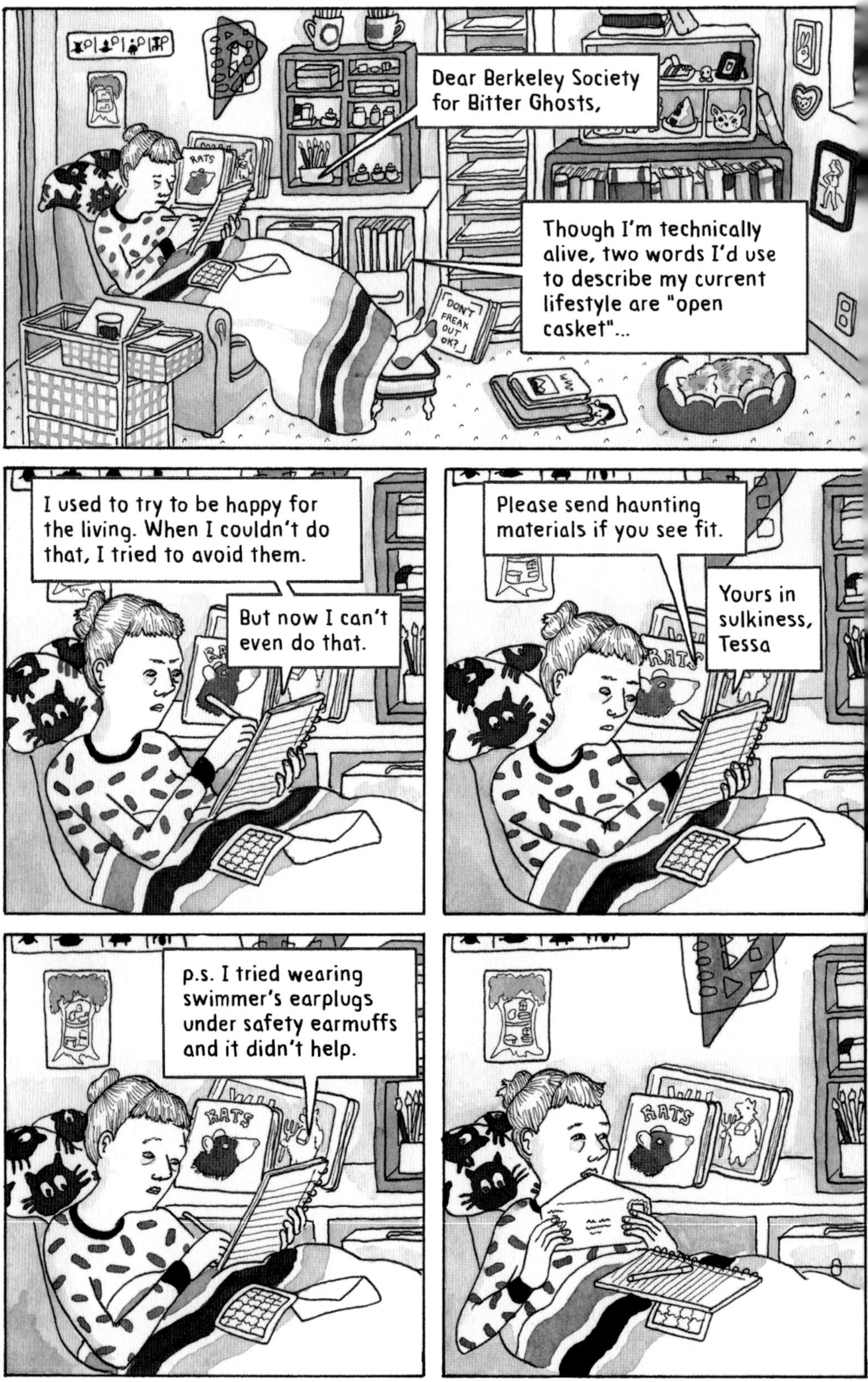
Dear Berkeley Society for Bitter Ghosts,
RATS
Though I'm technically alive, two words I'd use to describe my current lifestyle are "open casket"...
DON'T FREAK OUT OK?
I used to try to be happy for the living. When I couldn't do that, I tried to avoid them.
But now I can't even do that.
Please send haunting materials if you see fit.
Yours in sulkiness, Tessa
p.s. I tried wearing swimmer's earplugs under safety earmuffs and it didn't help.
RATS
RATS

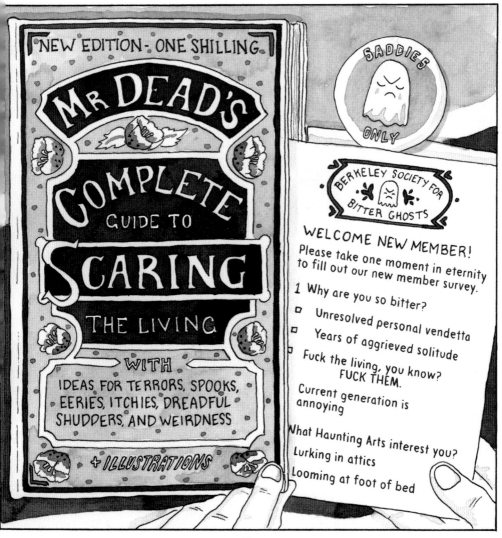

NEW EDITION · ONE SHILLING

MR DEAD'S
COMPLETE
GUIDE TO
SCARING
THE LIVING

WITH
IDEAS FOR TERRORS, SPOOKS,
EERIES, ITCHIES, DREADFUL
SHUDDERS, AND WEIRDNESS

+ ILLUSTRATIONS

SADDIES ONLY

BERKELEY SOCIETY FOR BITTER GHOSTS

WELCOME NEW MEMBER!
Please take one moment in eternity
to fill out our new member survey.

1 Why are you so bitter?

☐   Unresolved personal vendetta

☐   Years of aggrieved solitude

☐ Fuck the living, you know?
      FUCK THEM.

   Current generation is
   annoying

What Haunting Arts interest you?

Lurking in attics

Looming at foot of bed

Welcome, dear spirit!

After death, when we have been sadly exiled from our old lives, many of us come to feel like the living are just rubbing it all in our faces.

Luckily, in the afterlife, we can use the Haunting Arts to repay the living for our torment.

Read on to learn the skills you need to master these arts! Highlights of the next 99 chapters include...

The freakiest footsteps for midnight haunting!

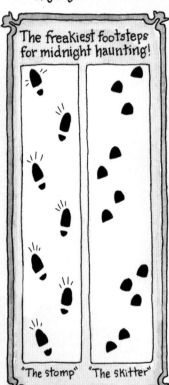

"The stomp"   "The skitter"

Multi-sensory harassment to frighten the dickens out of ding bats!

aural

visual

Gasp

whisper

field of vision

tactile

Sinister postures for shadowy appearances!

Pouncing   Dragging

Making the most of ominous weather!

Fog   Storm   Foggy storm

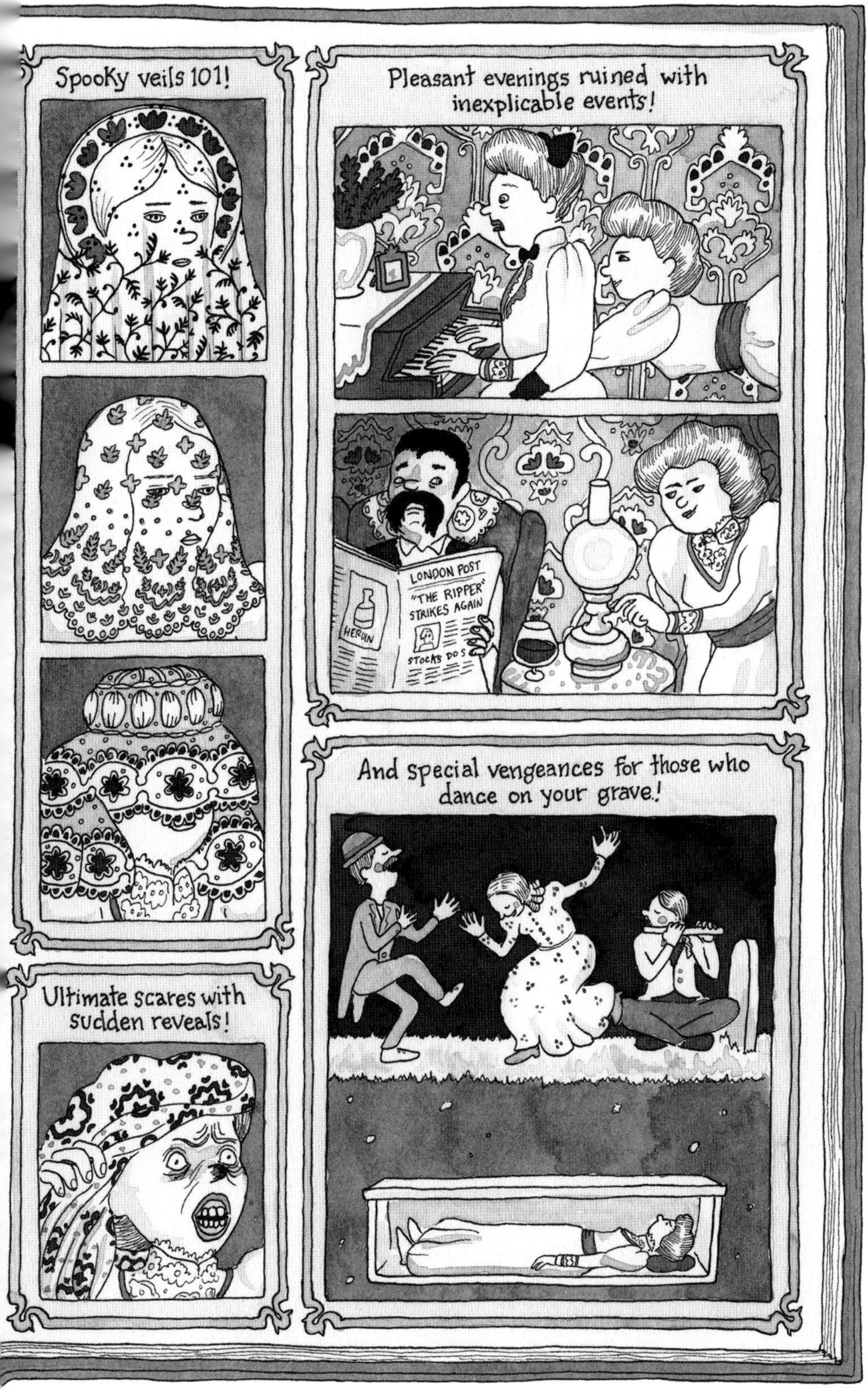
Spooky veils 101!
Pleasant evenings ruined with inexplicable events!
LONDON POST
"THE RIPPER" STRIKES AGAIN
Ultimate scares with sudden reveals!
And special vengeances for those who dance on your grave!

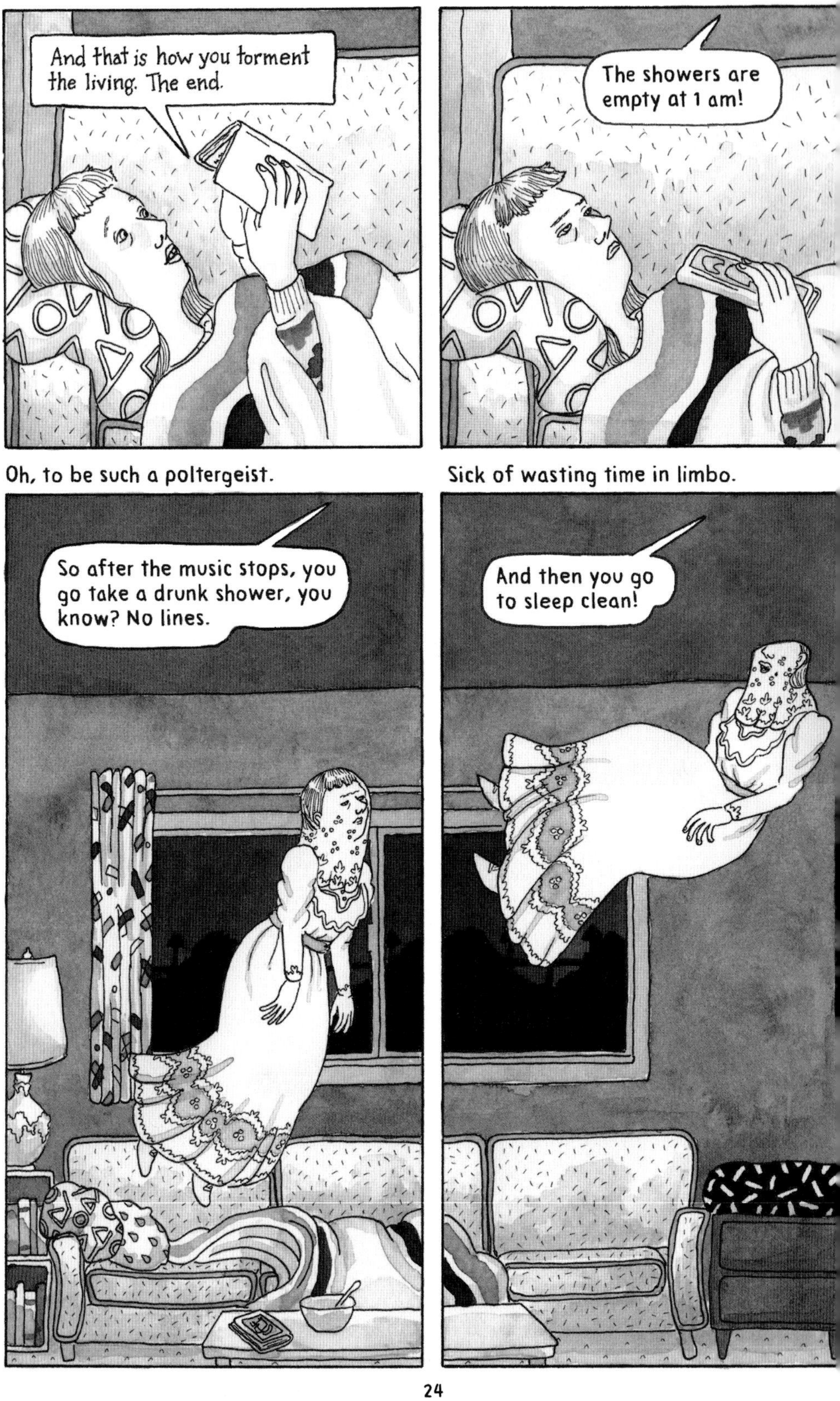
And that is how you torment the living. The end.
The showers are empty at 1 am!
Oh, to be such a poltergeist.
Sick of wasting time in limbo.
So after the music stops, you go take a drunk shower, you know? No lines.
And then you go to sleep clean!

pass a sentence on the living.

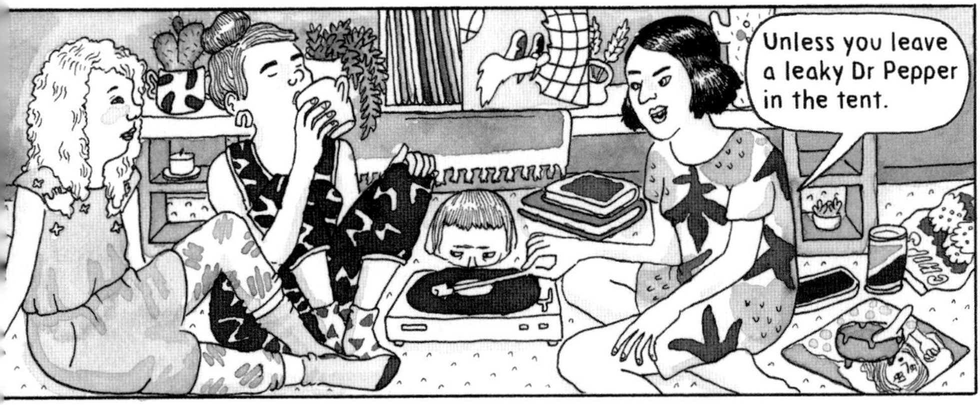
Unless you leave a leaky Dr Pepper in the tent.

st for being happy and loud.

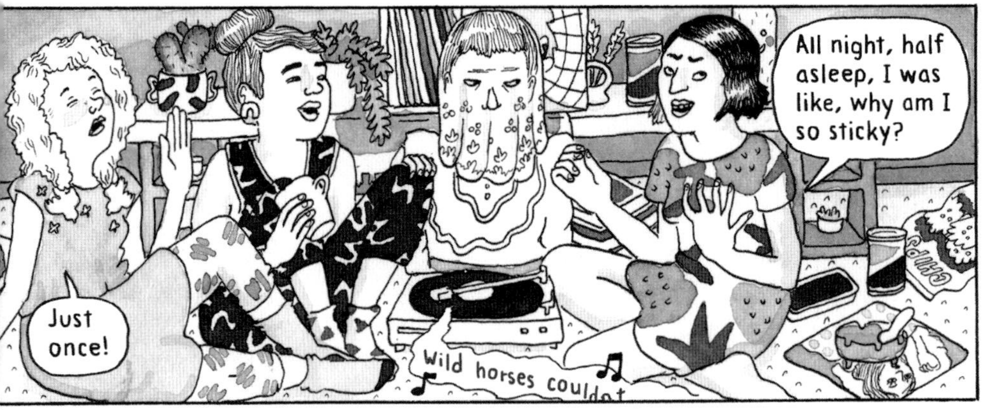
All night, half asleep, I was like, why am I so sticky?
Just once!
Wild horses could

nd then dish out bewildering punishments.

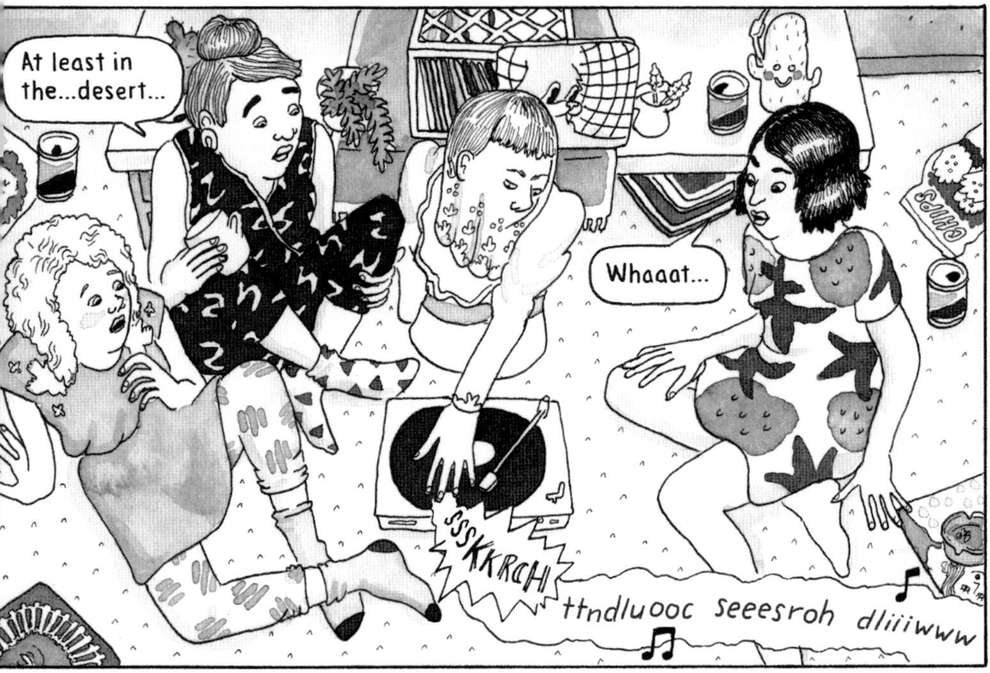
At least in the...desert...
Whaaat...
SSSKKRCH
ttndluooc seeesroh dliiiwww

An invisible force of pettiness.

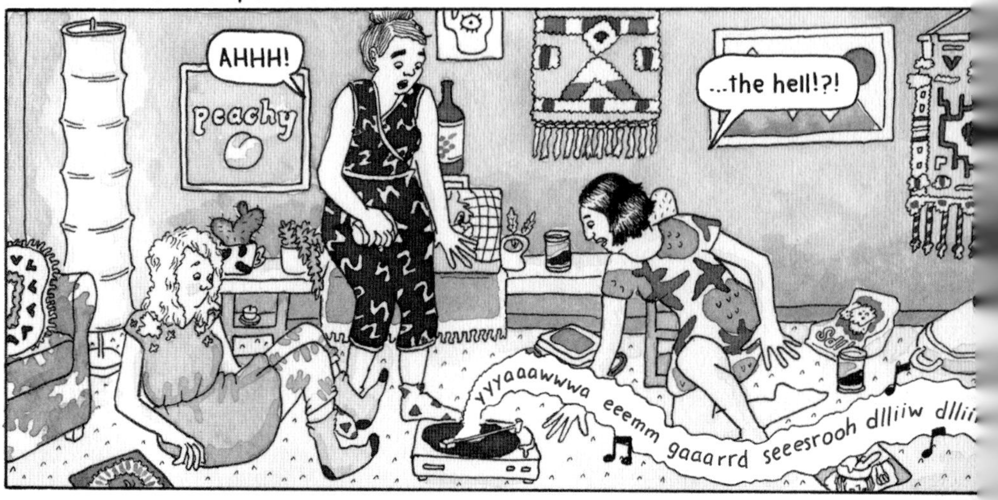
AHHH!
peachy
...the hell!?!
yyyaaawwwa eeemm gaaarrd seeesrooh dlliiw

Going full floating candlesticks and misplaced rage.

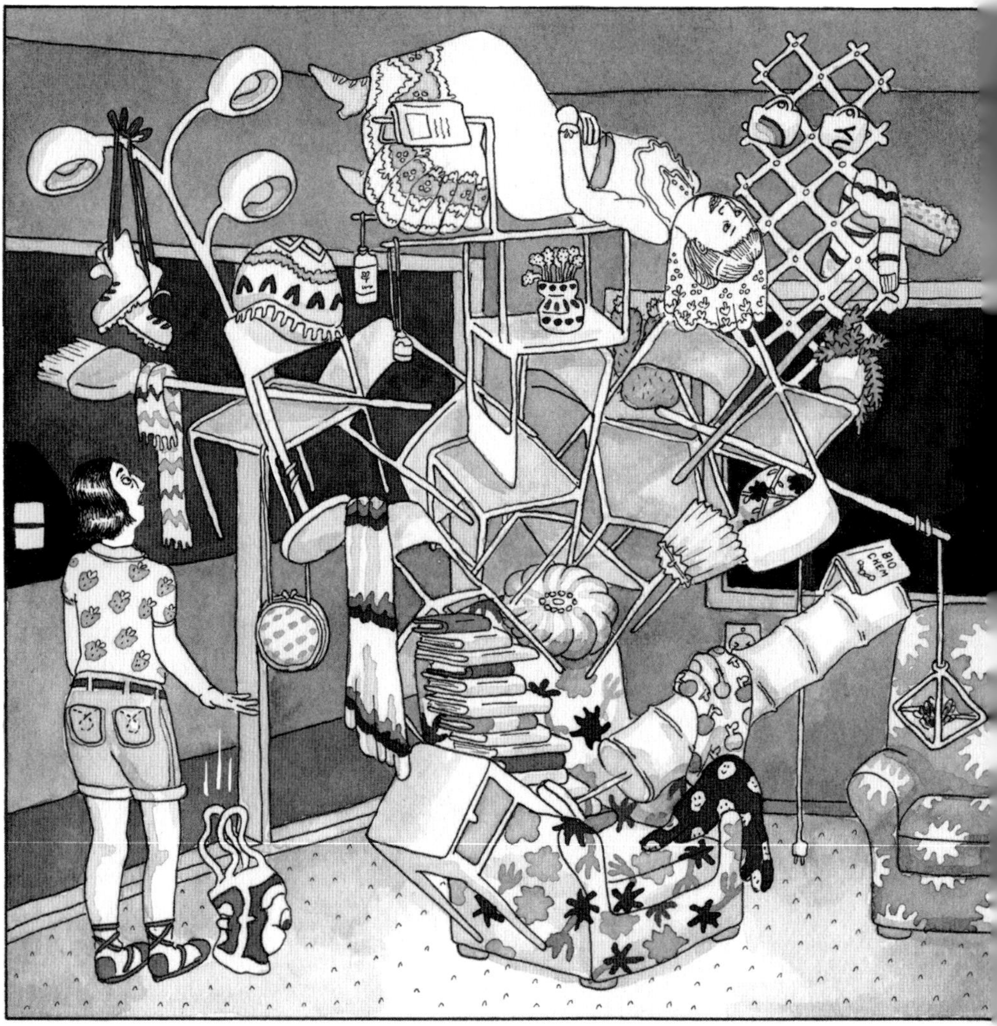
BIO CHEM

t worried about whether it's decent to harass people just for living not-sick lives.

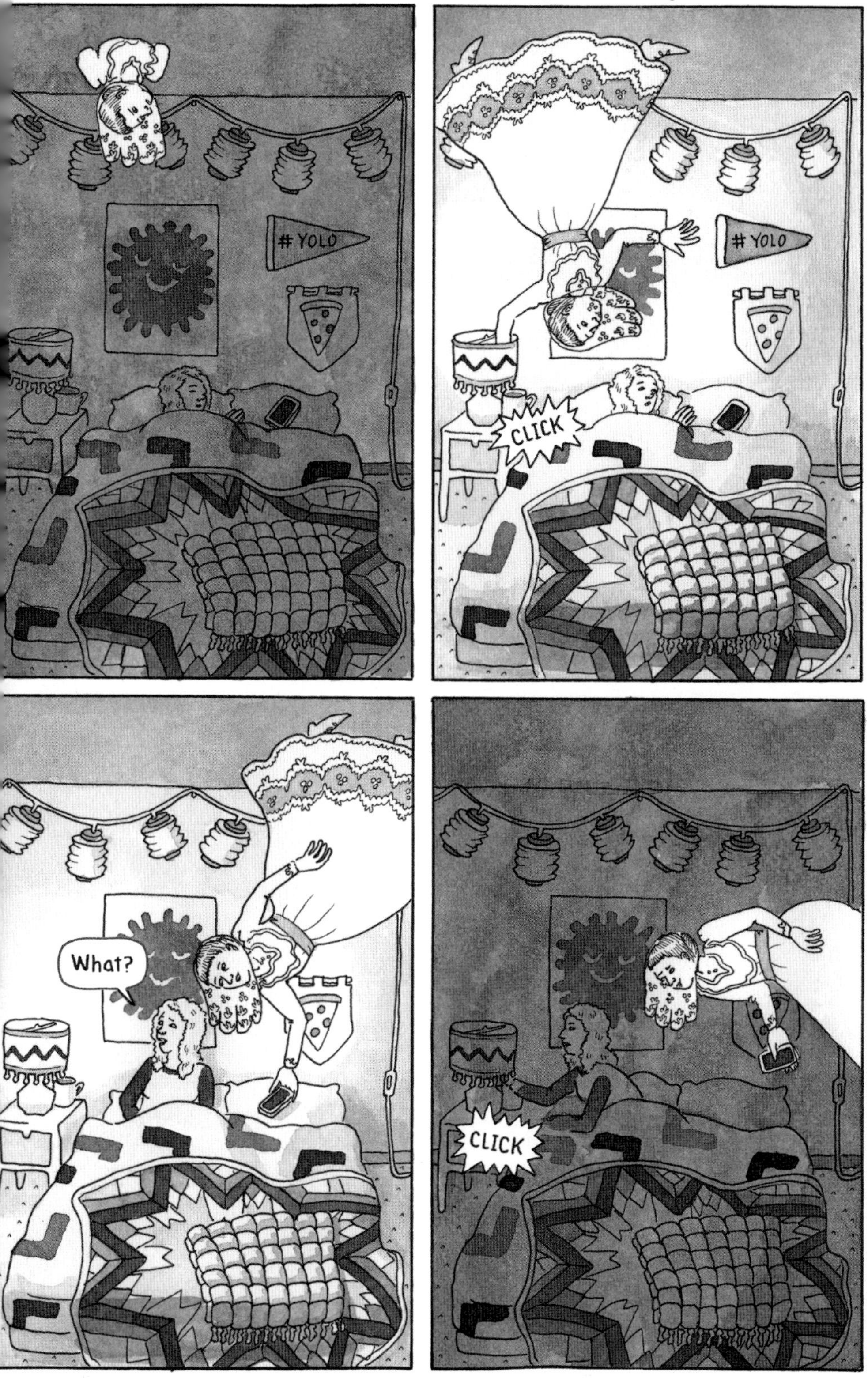
#YOLO
#YOLO
CLICK
What?
CLICK

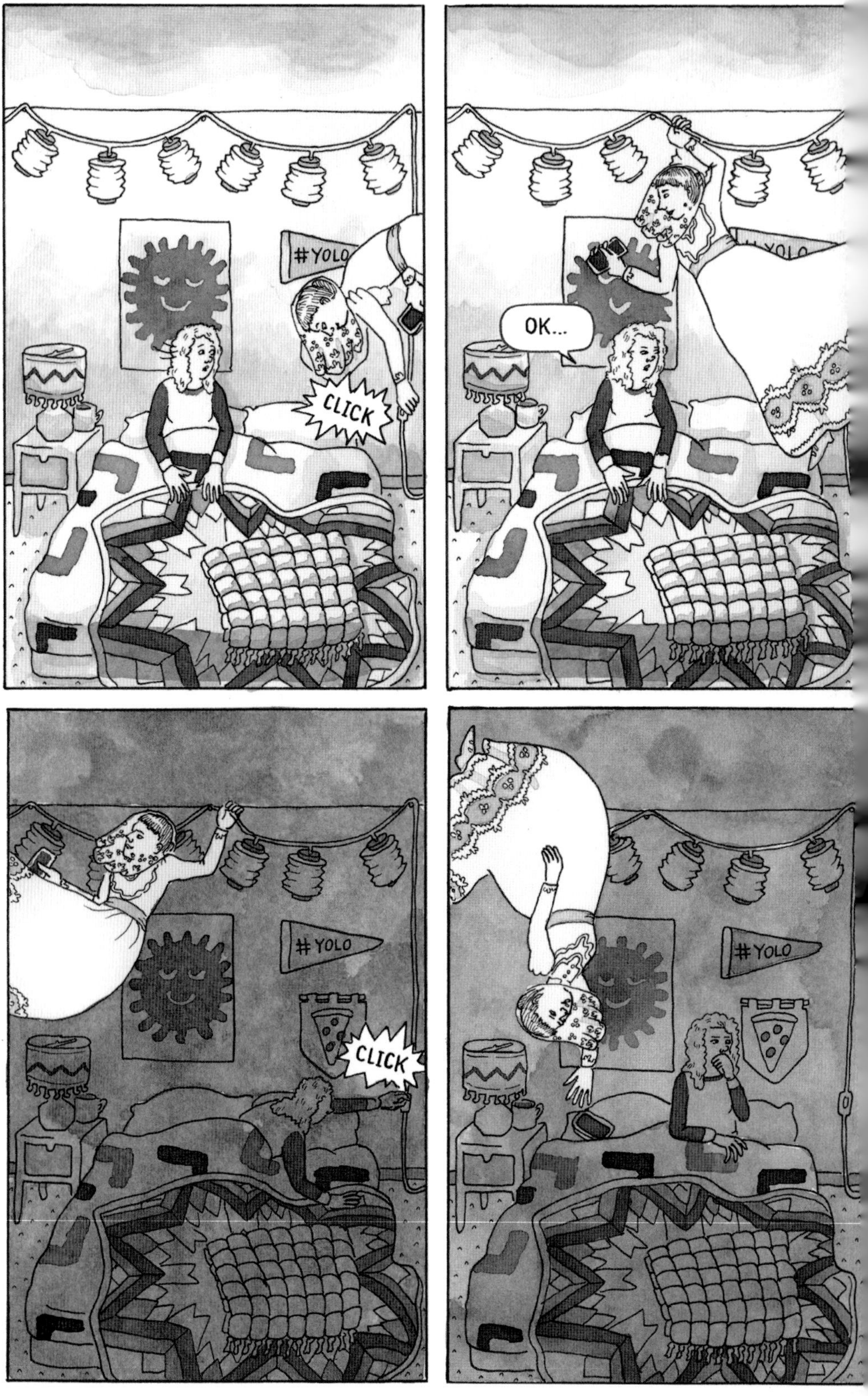
#YOLO
CLICK
OK...
#YOLO
CLICK
#YOLO

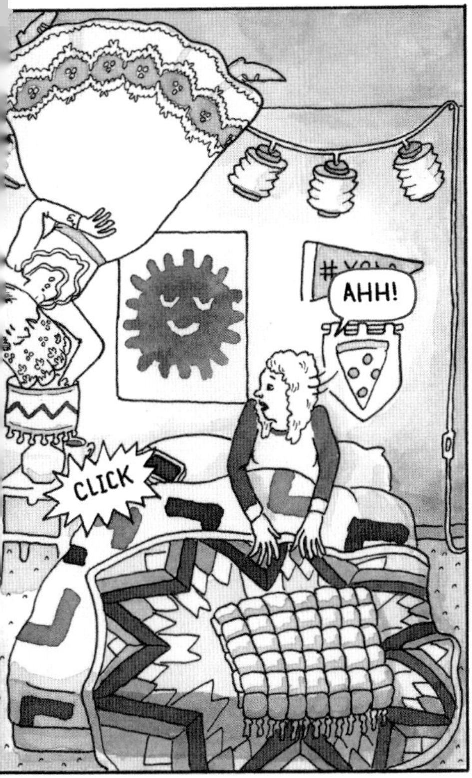
AHH!
CLICK
Ghosts aren't very concerned with decency.

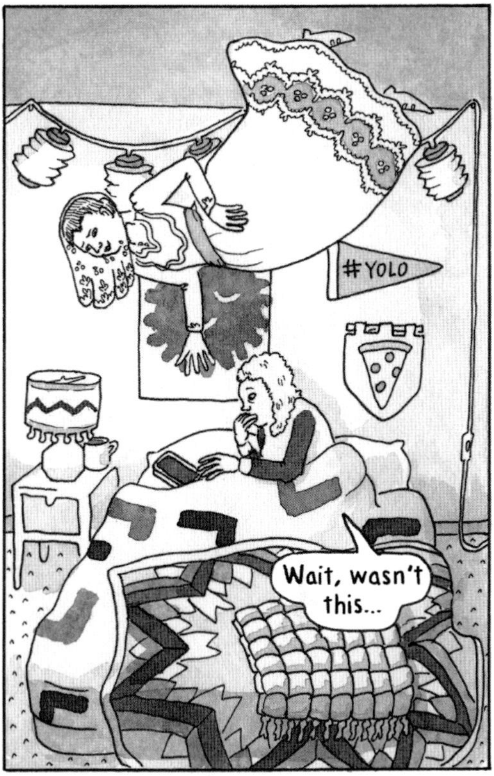
#YOLO
Wait, wasn't this...
Or trying to gracefully accept their fates.

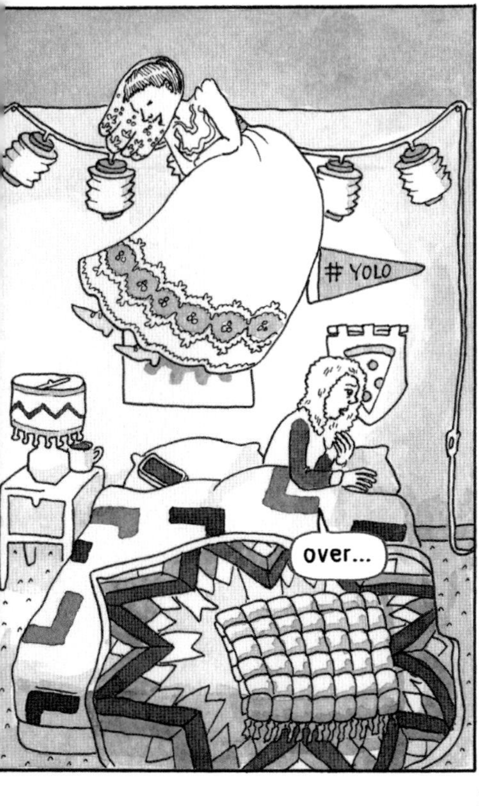
#YOLO
over...

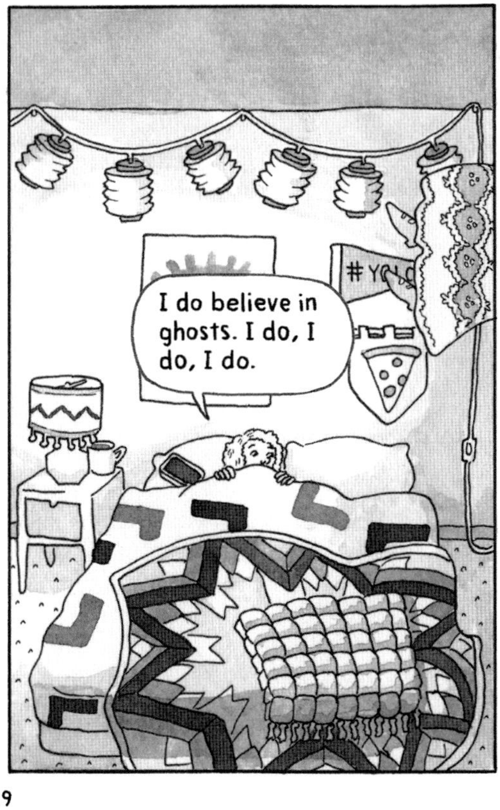
I do believe in ghosts. I do, I do, I do.

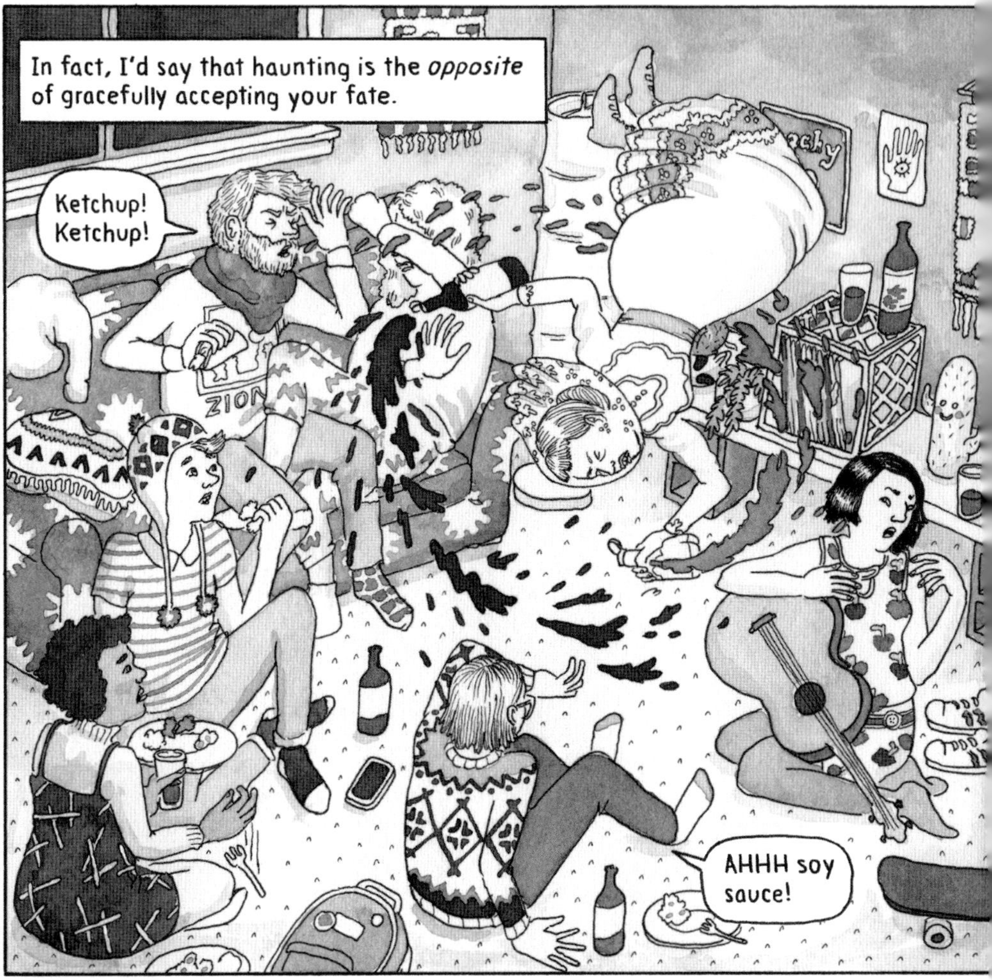
In fact, I'd say that haunting is the *opposite* of gracefully accepting your fate.
Ketchup! Ketchup!
AHHH soy sauce!

It is turning your misfortune into a house that eats happy people alive.

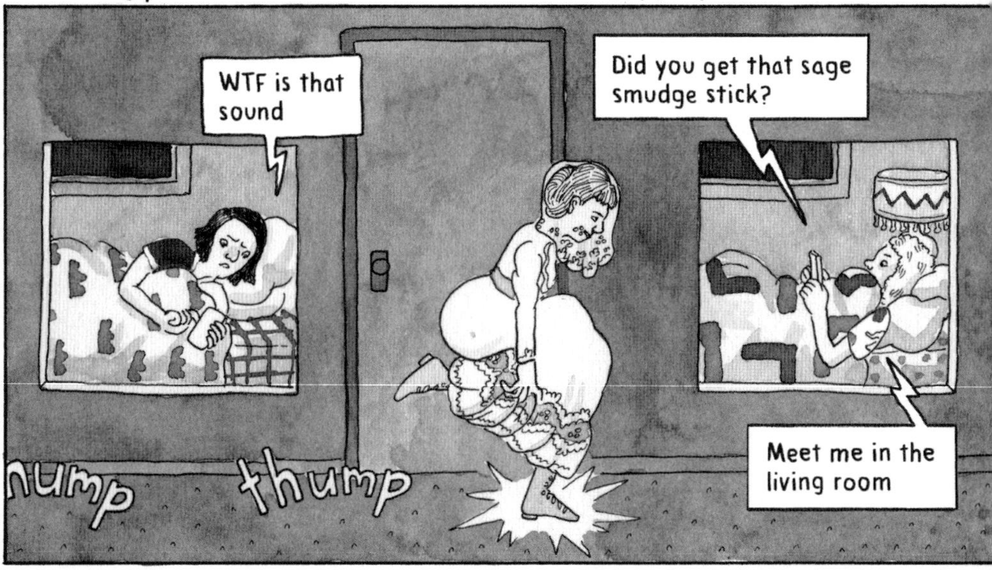
WTF is that sound
Did you get that sage smudge stick?
Meet me in the living room
thump

can't accept my bad luck, and I can't accept the good luck of others.

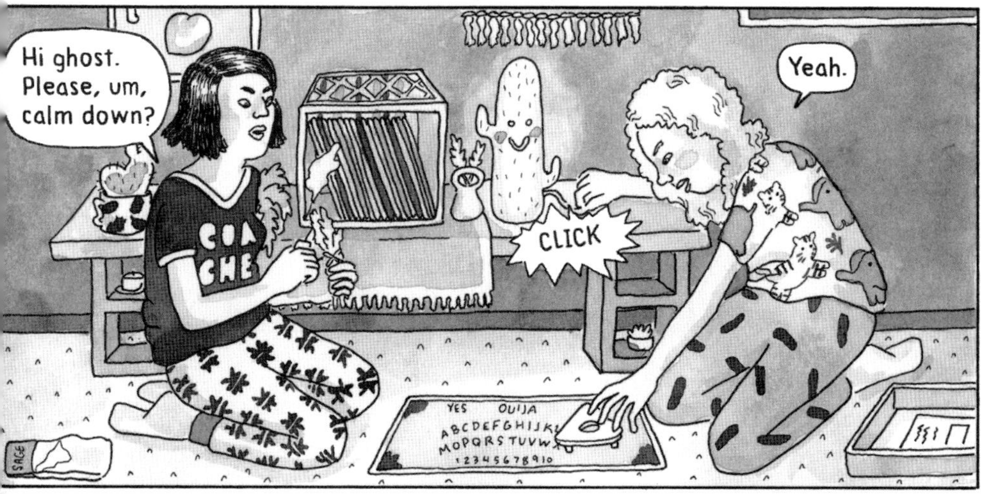

Hi ghost. Please, um, calm down?
Yeah.
CLICK

ntil I can, I'll never move on.

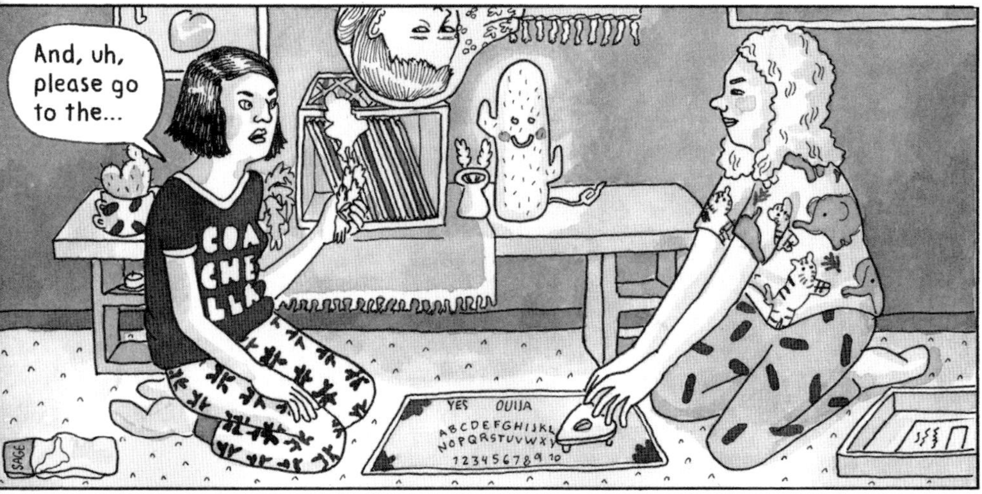

And, uh, please go to the...

And sometimes I fear I'll be stuck here forever.

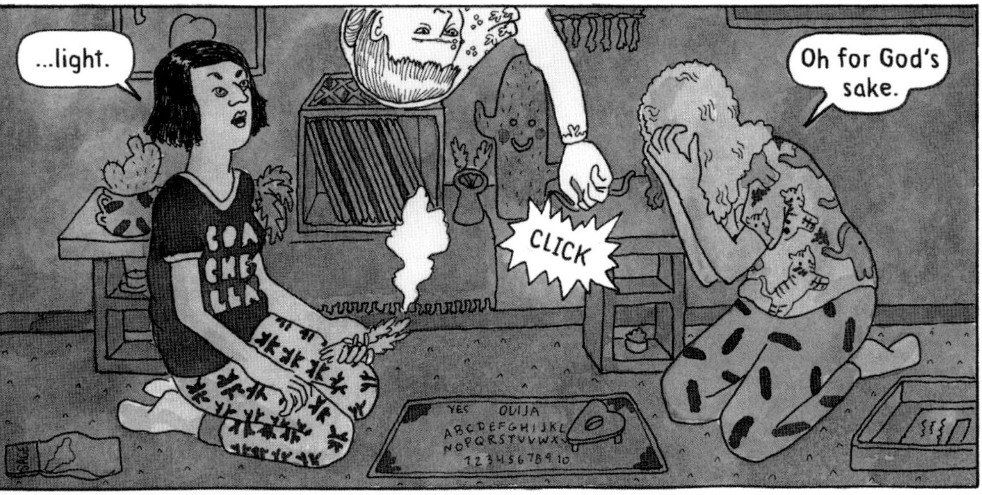

...light.
Oh for God's sake.
CLICK

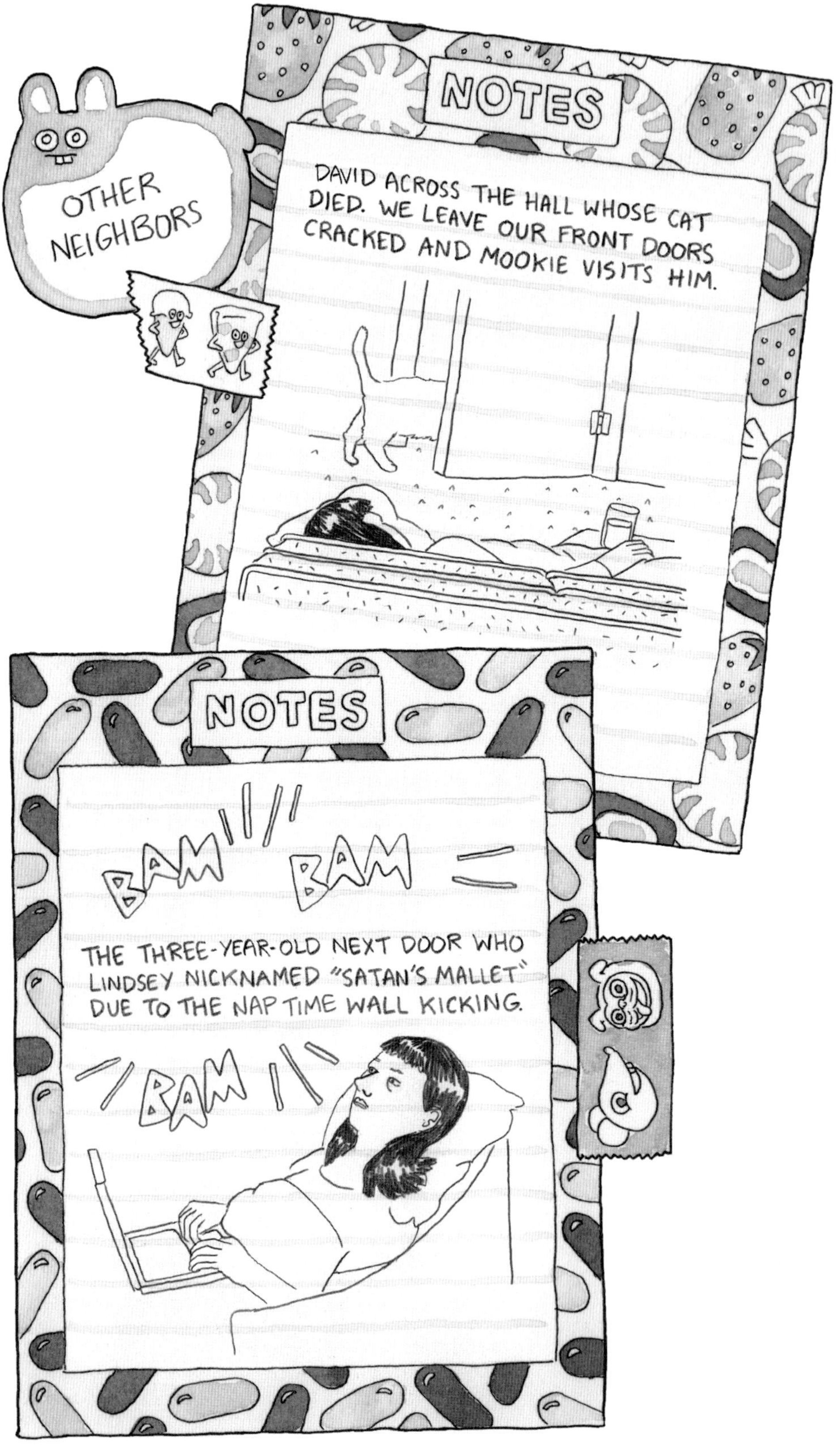
OTHER NEIGHBORS
NOTES
DAVID ACROSS THE HALL WHOSE CAT DIED. WE LEAVE OUR FRONT DOORS CRACKED AND MOOKIE VISITS HIM.
NOTES
BAM BAM
THE THREE-YEAR-OLD NEXT DOOR WHO LINDSEY NICKNAMED "SATAN'S MALLET" DUE TO THE NAP TIME WALL KICKING.
BAM

BED MOBILES

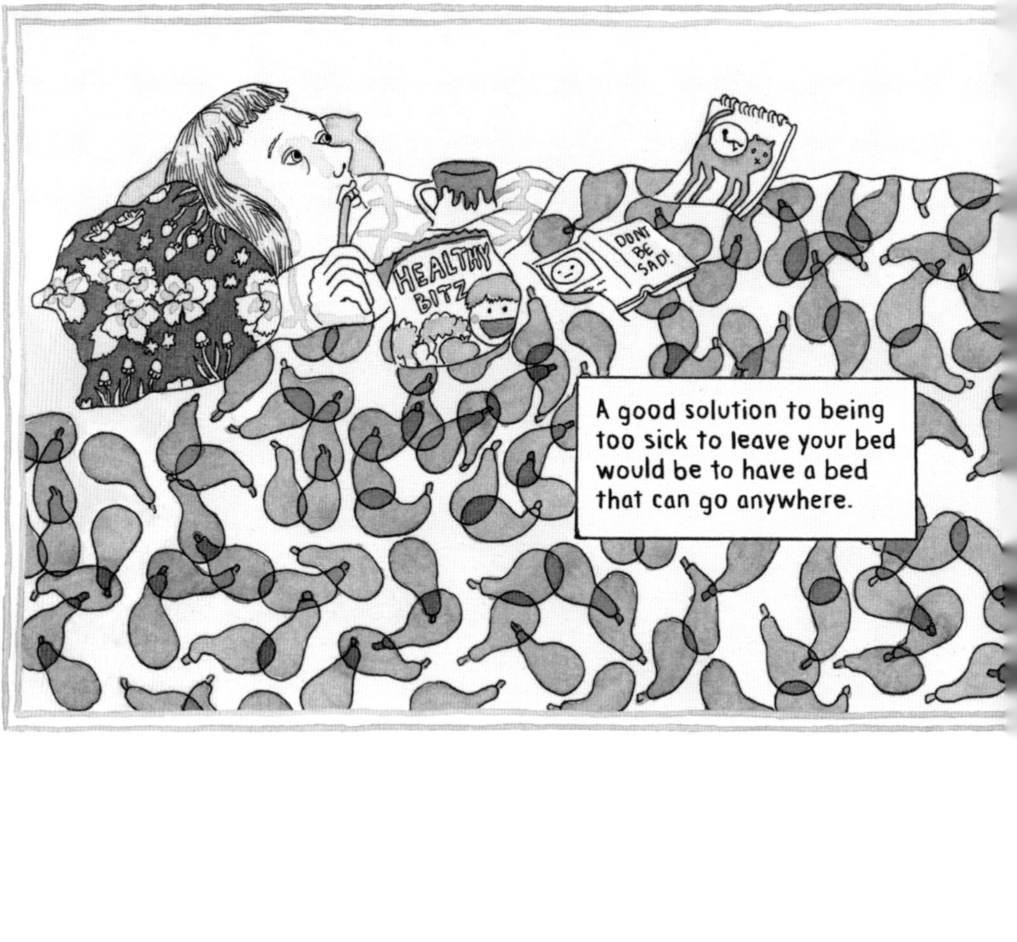
HEALTHY BITZ
DON'T BE SAD!
A good solution to being too sick to leave your bed would be to have a bed that can go anywhere.

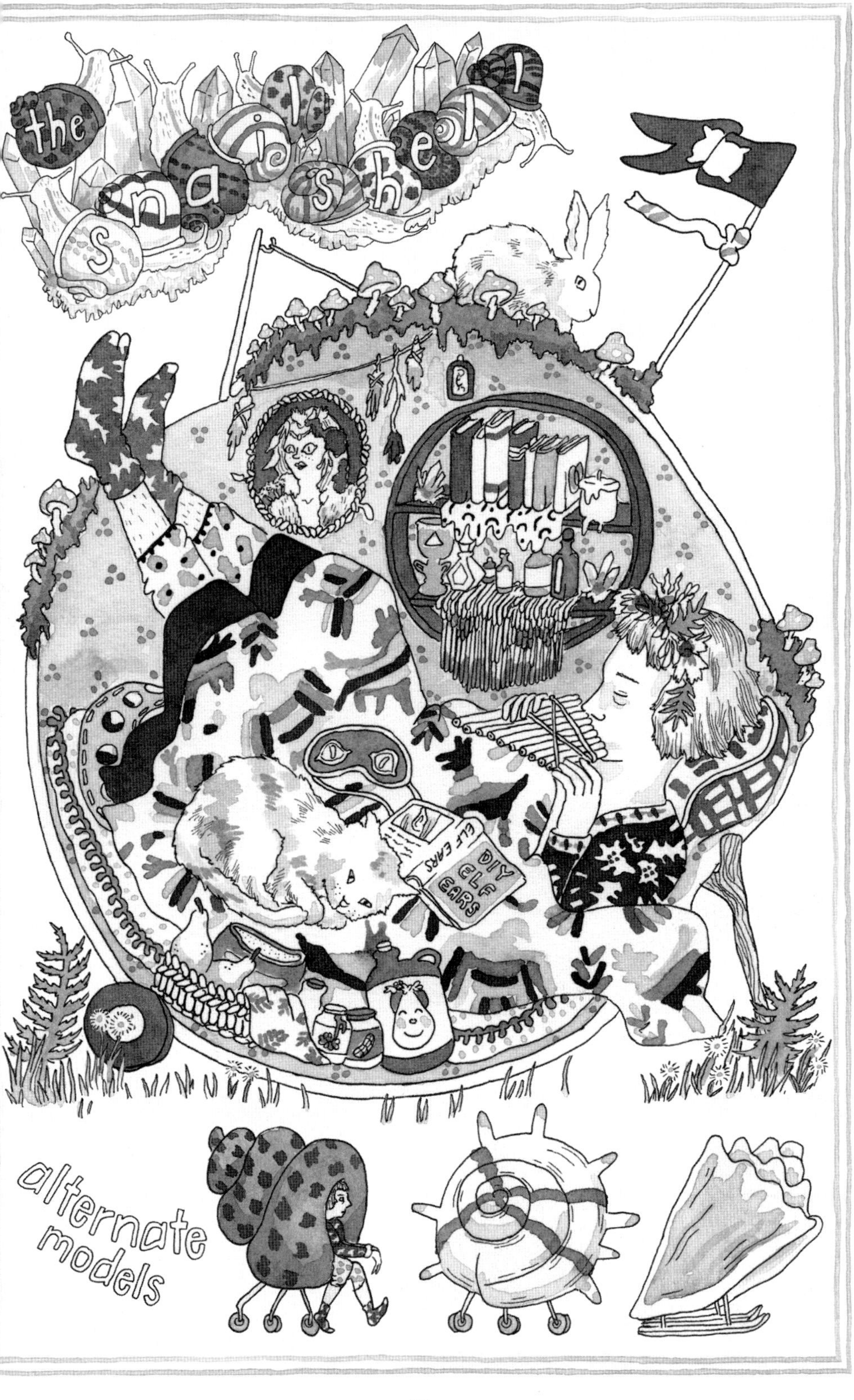
the snail shell
DIY ELF EARS
ELF EARS
alternate models

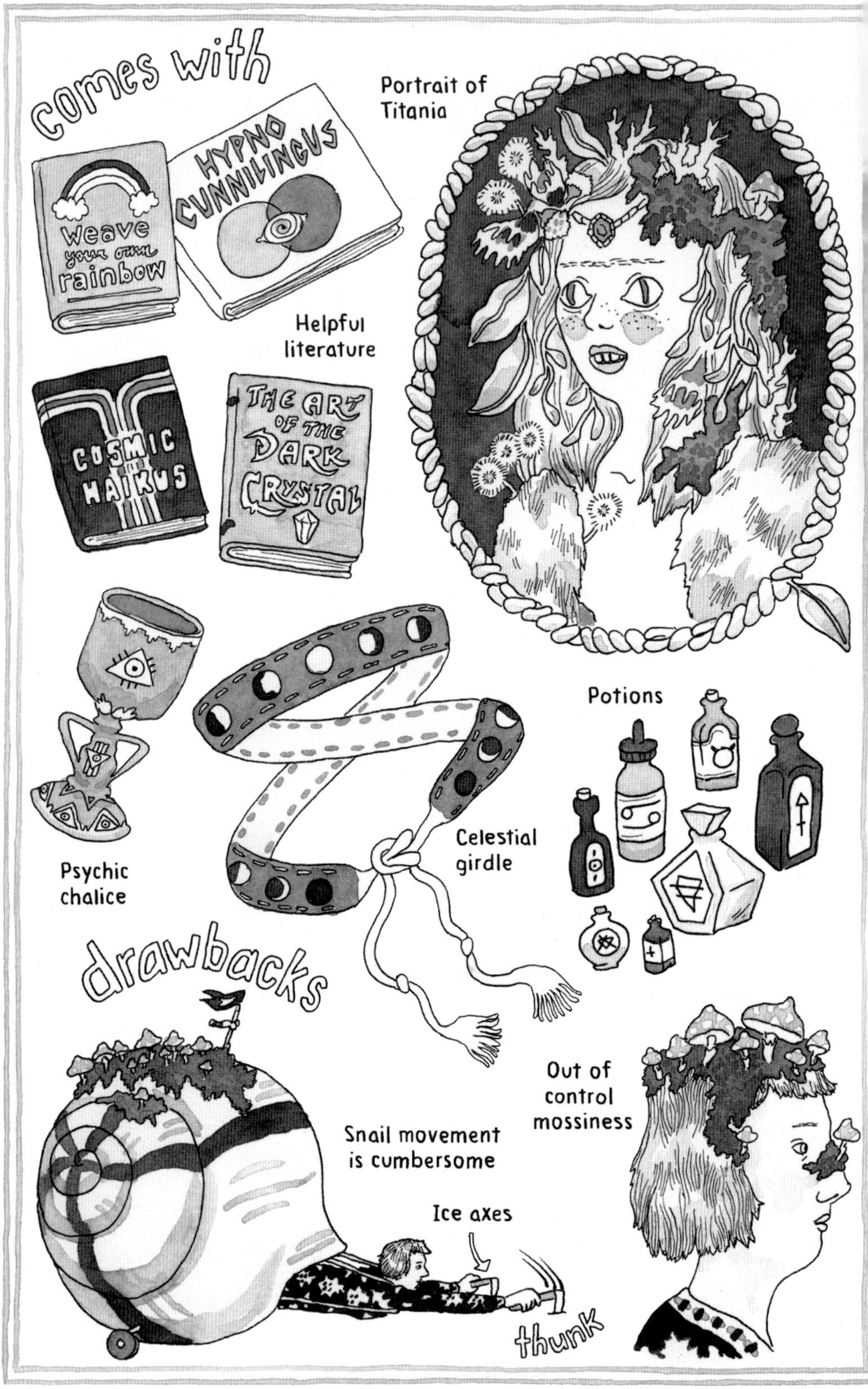
comes with
Weave your own rainbow
HYPNO CUNNILINGUS
Portrait of Titania
Helpful literature
COSMIC HAIKUS
THE ART OF THE DARK CRYSTAL
Psychic chalice
Celestial girdle
Potions
drawbacks
Out of control mossiness
Snail movement is cumbersome
Ice axes
thunk

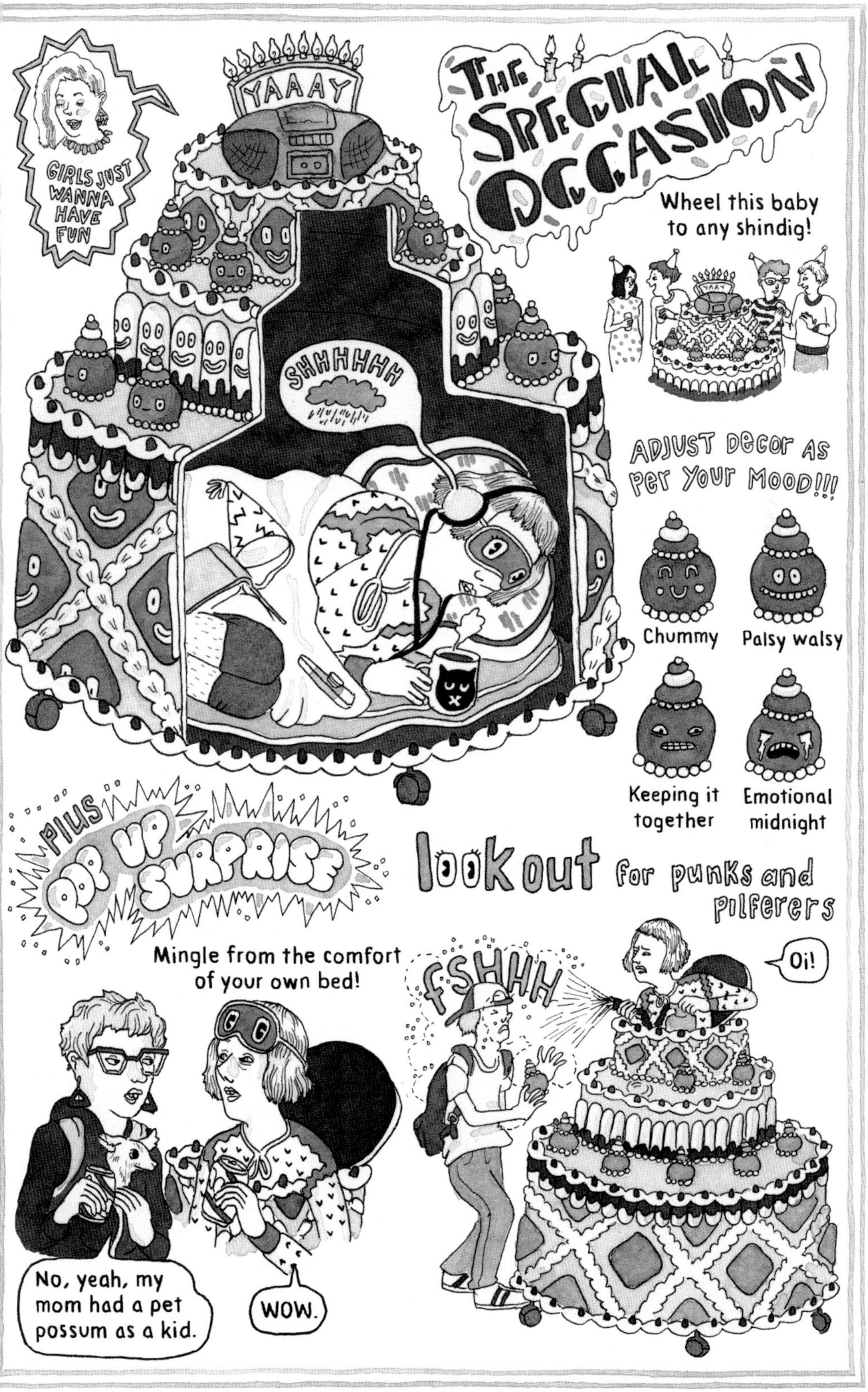

GIRLS JUST WANNA HAVE FUN
YAAAY
THE SPECIAL OCCASION
Wheel this baby to any shindig!
SHHHHHH
ADJUST DECOR AS PER YOUR MOOD!!!
Chummy
Palsy walsy
Keeping it together
Emotional midnight
PLUS POP UP SURPRISE
Mingle from the comfort of your own bed!
No, yeah, my mom had a pet possum as a kid.
WOW.
lookout for punks and pilferers
FSHHH
Oi!

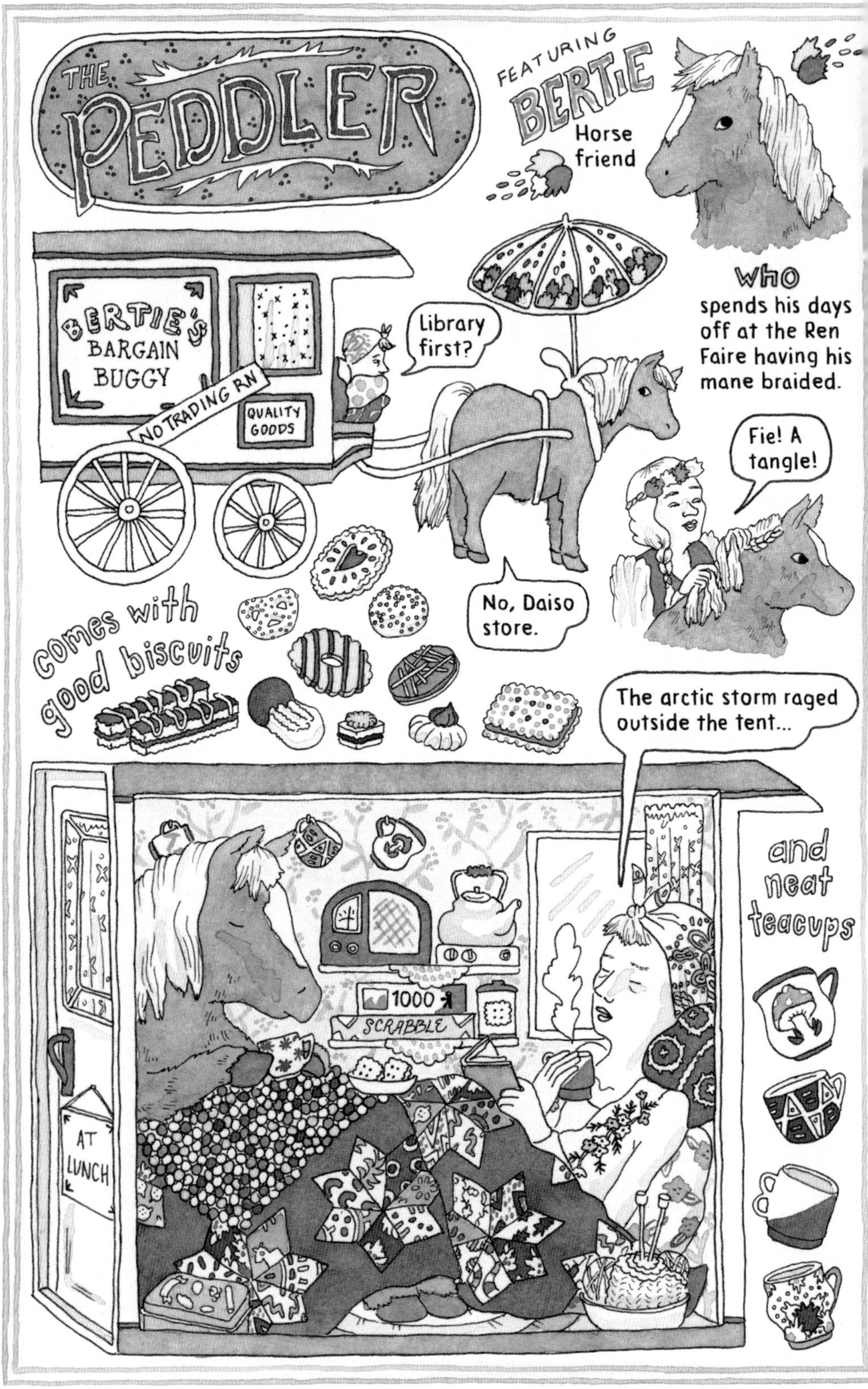
THE PEDDLER
FEATURING BERTIE
Horse friend
BERTIE'S BARGAIN BUGGY
NO TRADING RN
QUALITY GOODS
Library first?
No, Daiso store.
who spends his days off at the Ren Faire having his mane braided.
Fie! A tangle!
comes with good biscuits
The arctic storm raged outside the tent...
1000
SCRABBLE
AT LUNCH
and neat teacups

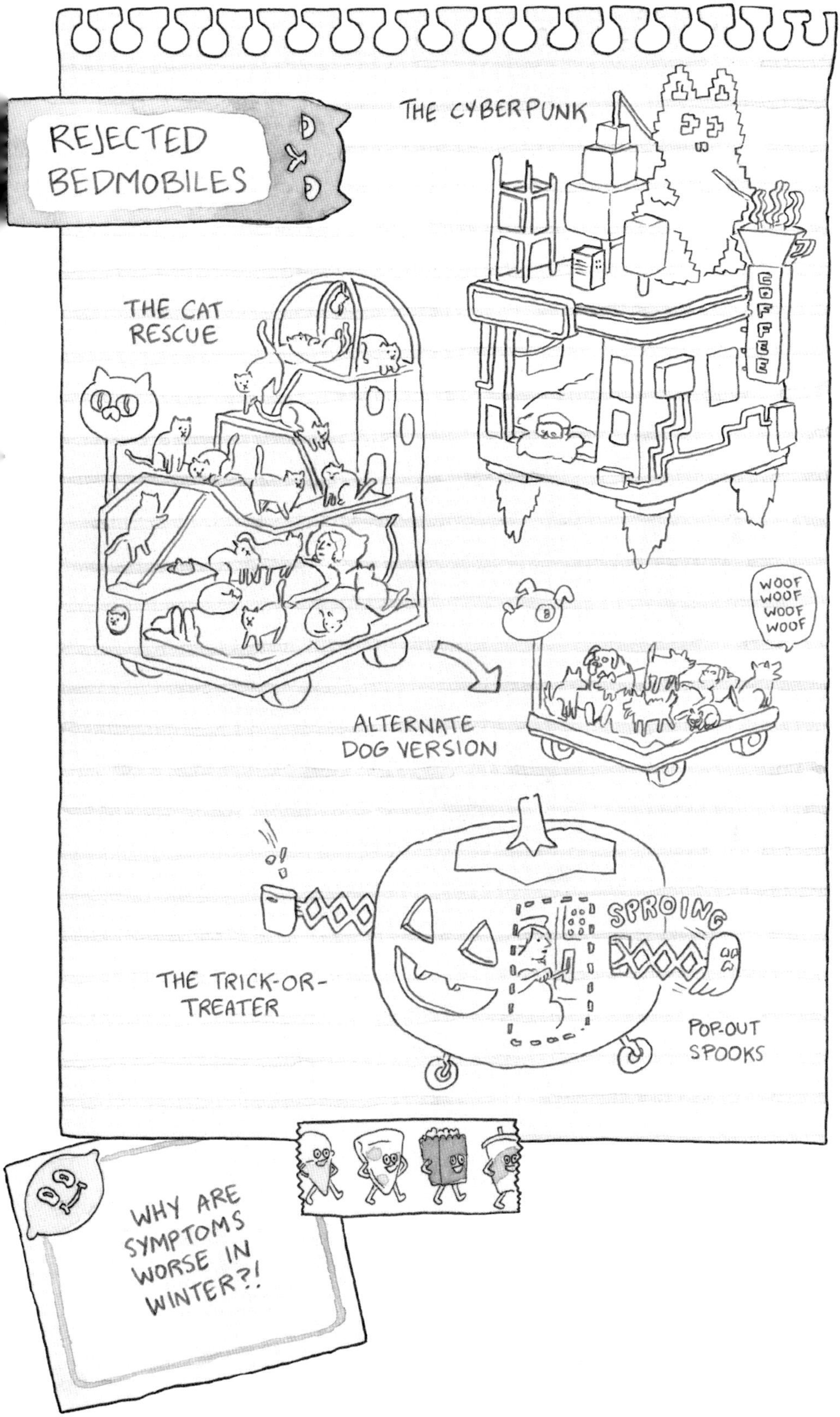

REJECTED BEDMOBILES
THE CYBERPUNK
COFFEE
THE CAT RESCUE
ALTERNATE DOG VERSION
WOOF WOOF WOOF WOOF
SPROING
THE TRICK-OR-TREATER
POP-OUT SPOOKS
WHY ARE SYMPTOMS WORSE IN WINTER?!

Gratitude

One afternoon in March, I was trying to feel grateful instead of trapped.

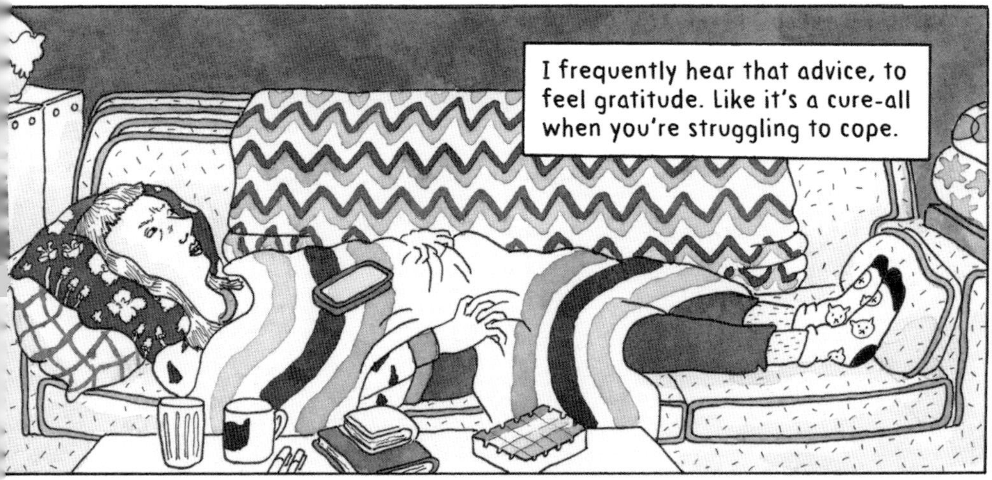
I frequently hear that advice, to feel gratitude. Like it's a cure-all when you're struggling to cope.

I understand why. Feeling gratitude focuses you on what's beloved the same way that feeling fear focuses you on the weird noise coming from your basement.

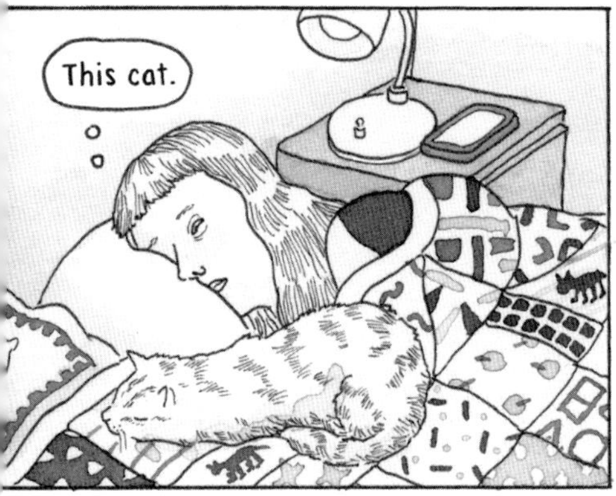
This cat.

The stuffy room, the symptoms, the little miseries, become unimportant.

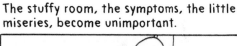

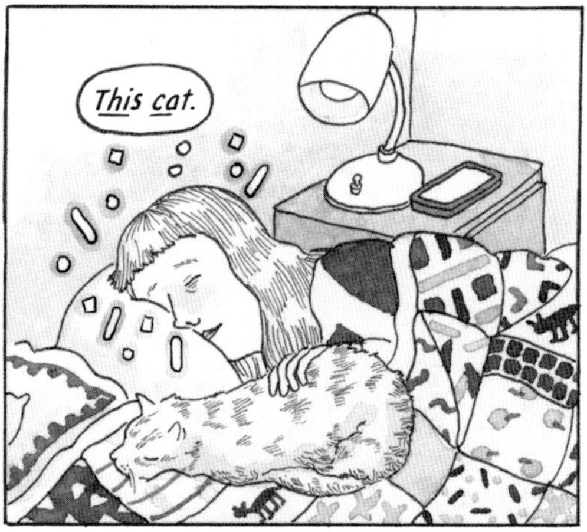
This cat.

But I hadn't learned the trick of summoning gratitude on command.

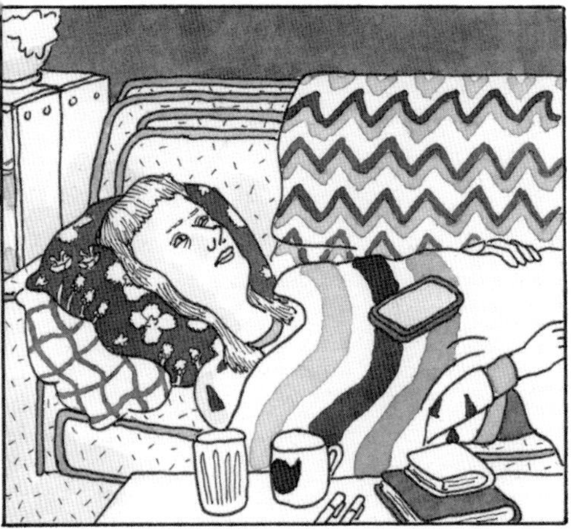

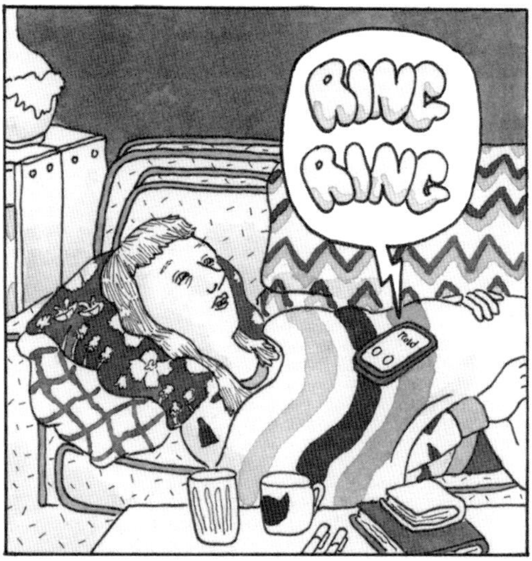
RING
RING

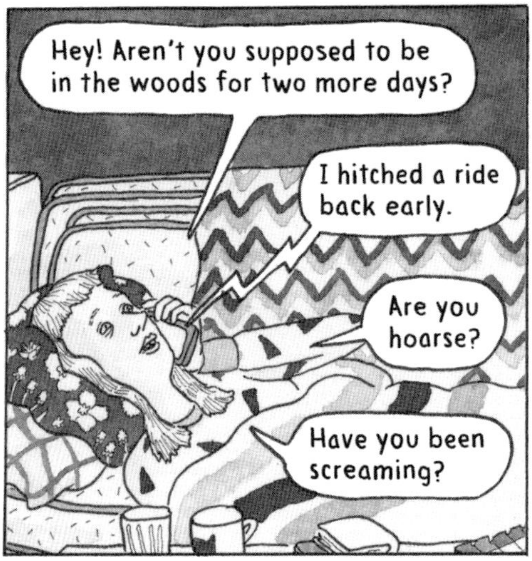
Hey! Aren't you supposed to be in the woods for two more days?
I hitched a ride back early.
Are you hoarse?
Have you been screaming?

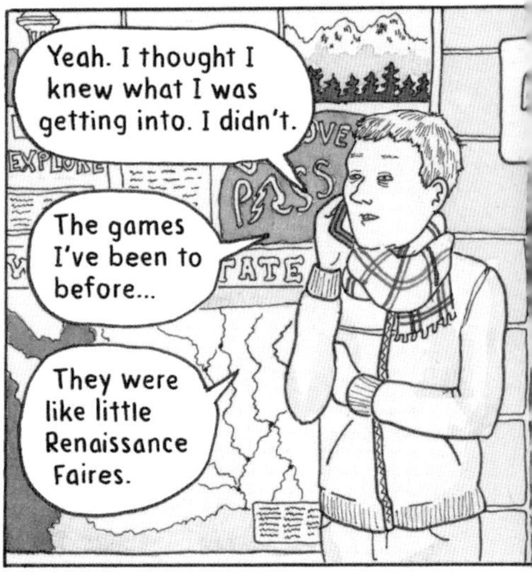
Yeah. I thought I knew what I was getting into. I didn't.
The games I've been to before...
They were like little Renaissance Faires.

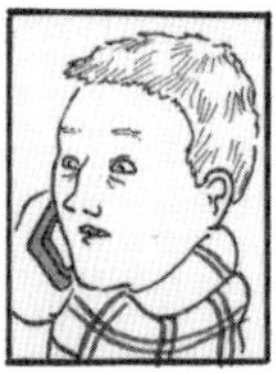

But the setting for this game was "apocalypse." There were 300 people in the woods, very committed to role-playing a horrifying apocalypse. Then a rainstorm started.

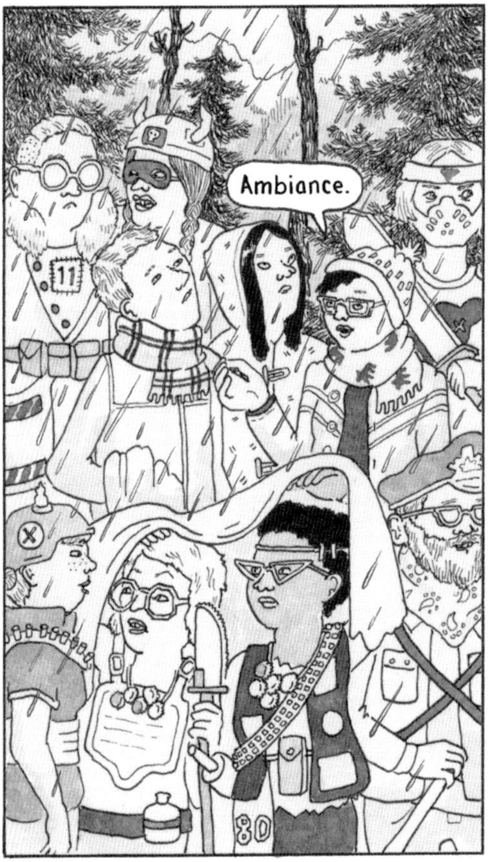
Ambiance.

Groups of "monsters" and "bandits" roame the woods, picking off weak players.

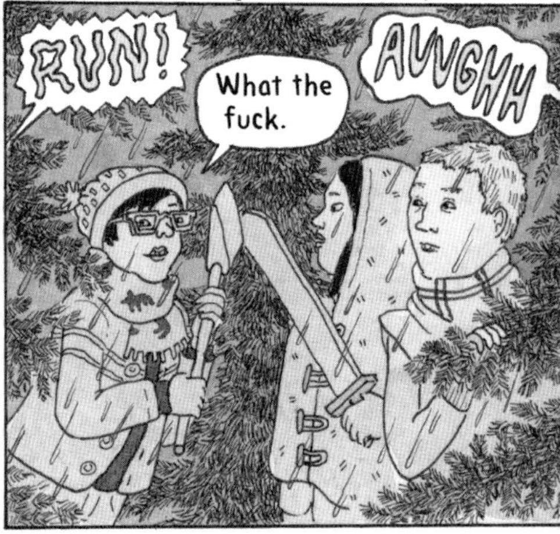
RUN!
What the fuck.
AWGHH

As new, low-level players, it turned out we were also weak. We couldn't fight anyone -we could only run and hide.

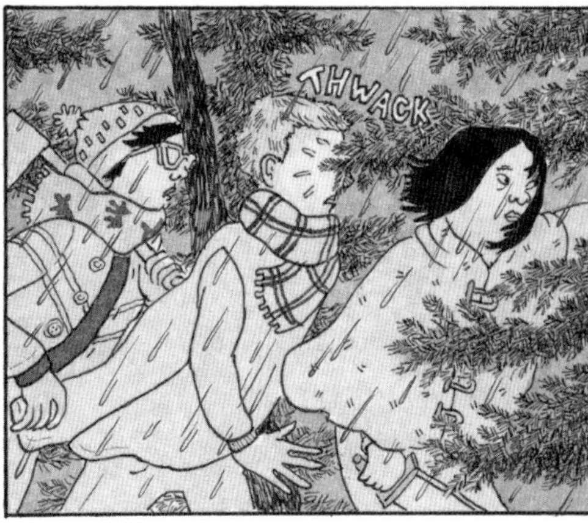
THWACK

didn't eat or drink for the first nine ours because we were just running.

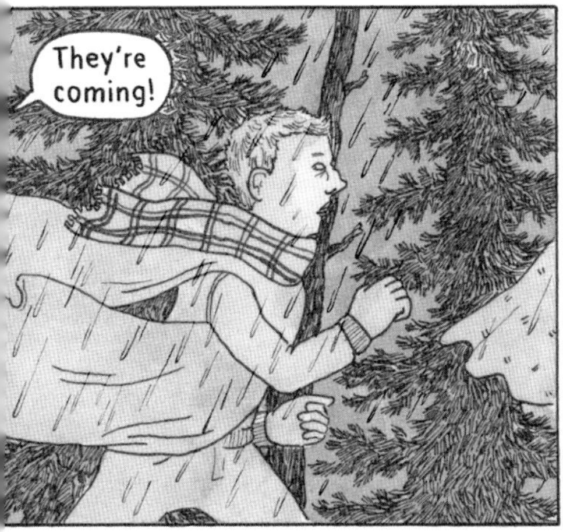
They're coming!

I was so thirsty I licked rain off my poncho.

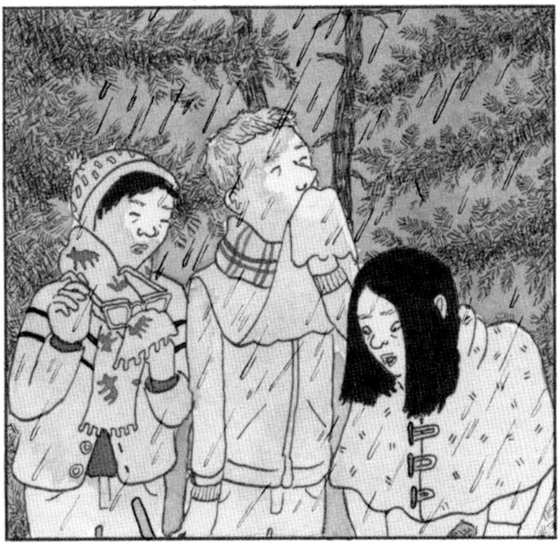

Then, at 2 am, I had "monster squad duty." The game organizers put us in monster costumes and sent us out to terrorize other players for hours.

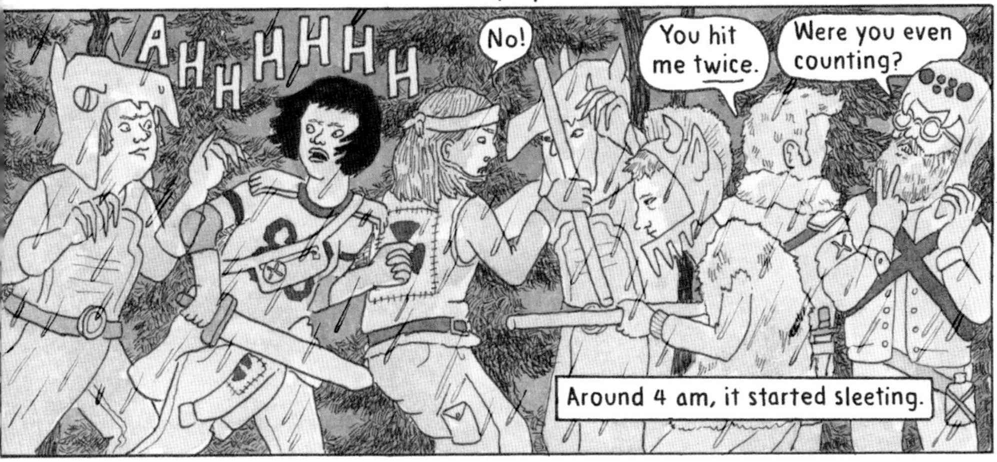
AHHHHHHH
No!
You hit me twice.
Were you even counting?
Around 4 am, it started sleeting.

I tried to sleep at dawn, but our cabin had no walls and monsters kept attacking.

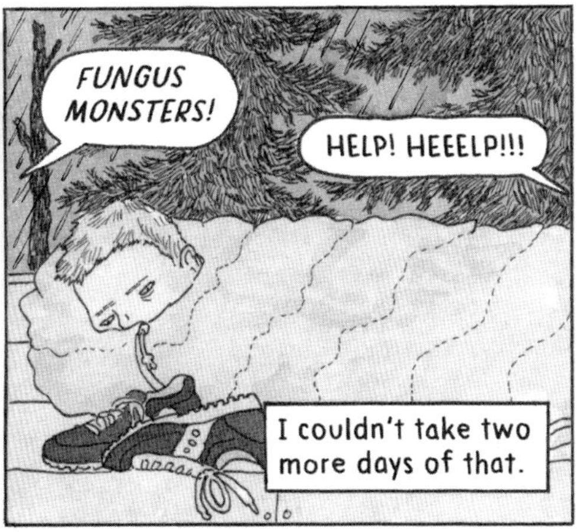
FUNGUS MONSTERS!
HELP! HEEELP!!!
I couldn't take two more days of that.

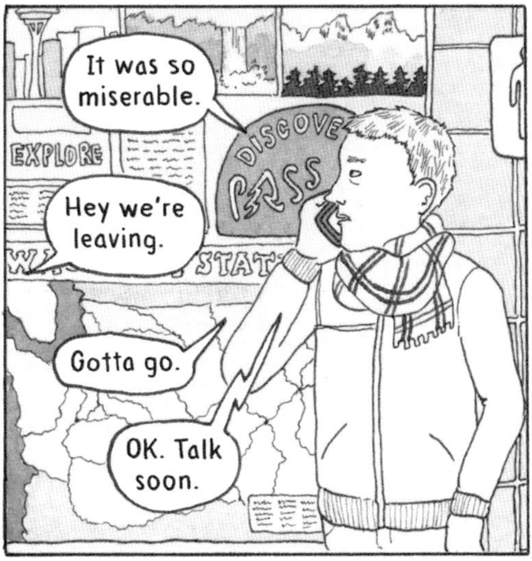
EXPLORE
DISCOVER
PASS
It was so miserable.
Hey we're leaving.
Gotta go.
OK. Talk soon.

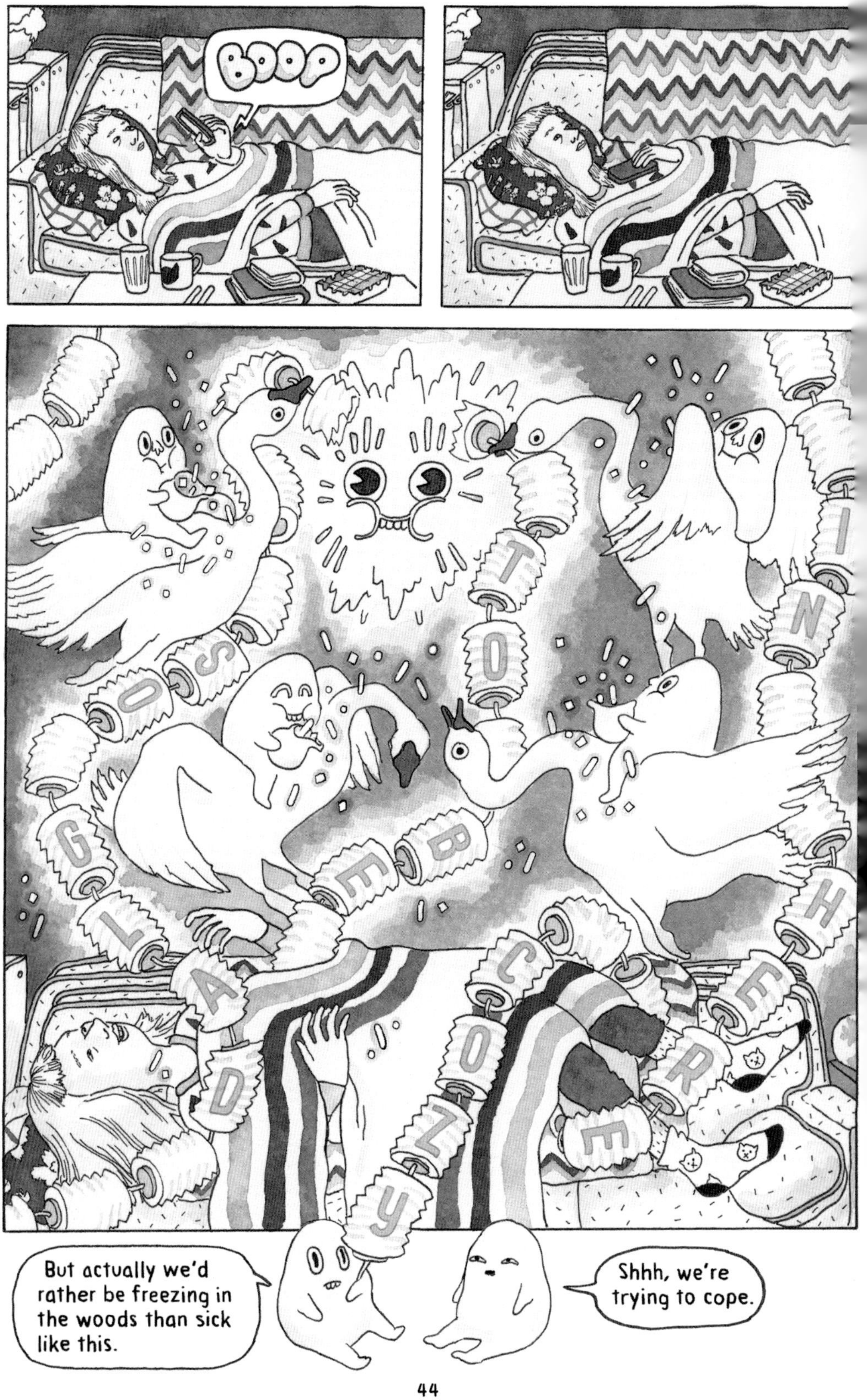

BOOP
SO GLAD TO BE COZY IN HERE
But actually we'd rather be freezing in the woods than sick like this.
Shhh, we're trying to cope.

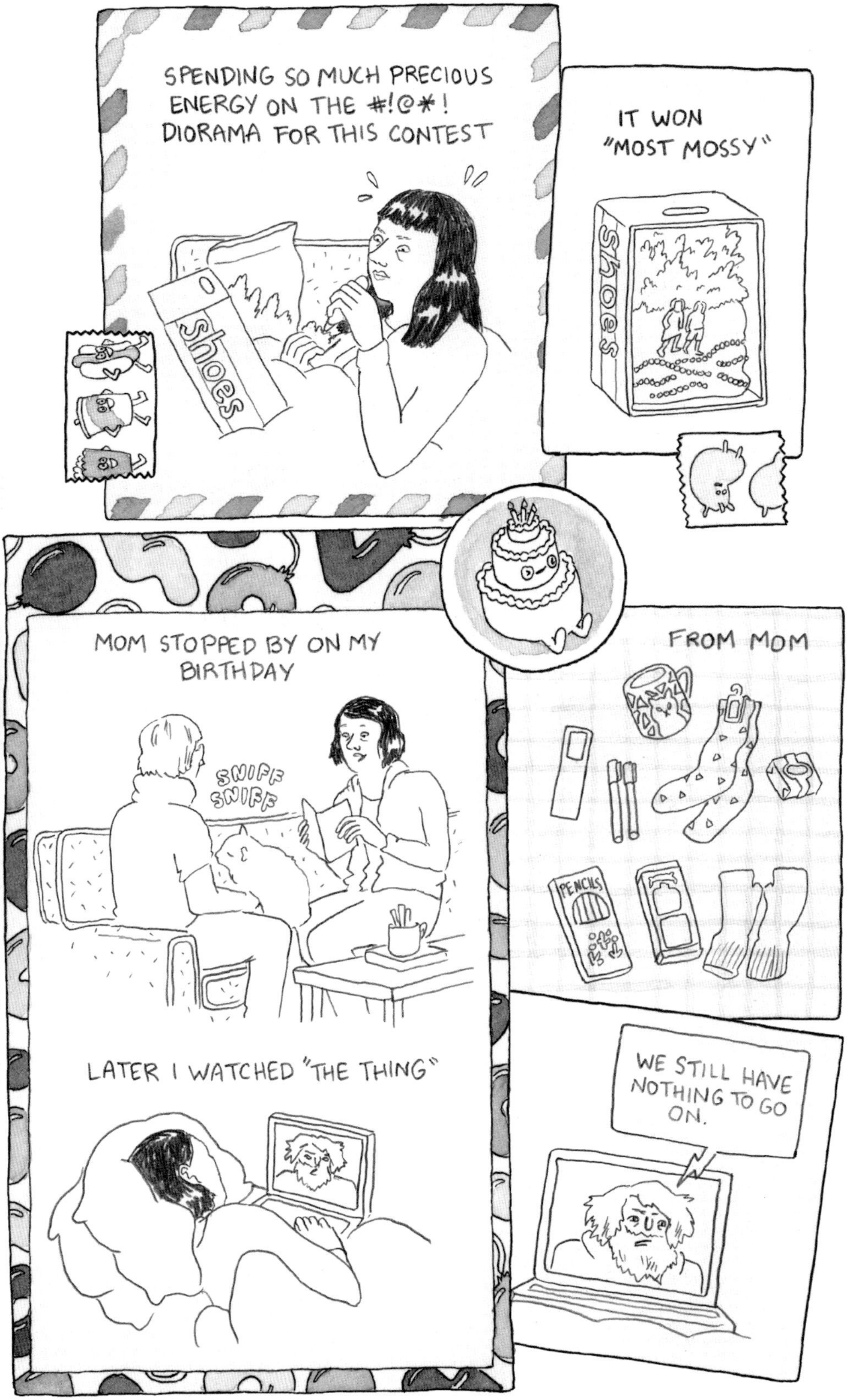
SPENDING SO MUCH PRECIOUS ENERGY ON THE #!@*! DIORAMA FOR THIS CONTEST
shoes
IT WON "MOST MOSSY"
shoes
MOM STOPPED BY ON MY BIRTHDAY
SNIFF SNIFF
FROM MOM
PENCILS
LATER I WATCHED "THE THING"
WE STILL HAVE NOTHING TO GO ON.

The Tower

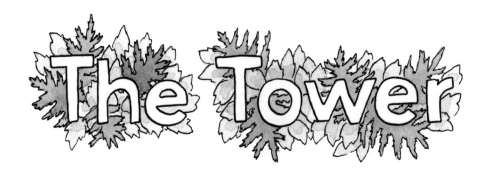

HOUSEBOUND DREAM HOUSES INCORPORATED

APPLICATION

"Making really really cool houses since 1962 using magic or something don't worry about it."

NAME

TESSA "TURN UP THAT AUDIOBOOK" BRUNTON

PLEASE DESCRIBE YOUR HOUSEBOUND LIFESTYLE

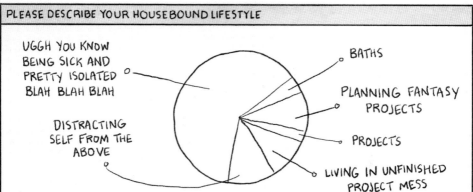

UGGH YOU KNOW BEING SICK AND PRETTY ISOLATED BLAH BLAH BLAH

DISTRACTING SELF FROM THE ABOVE

BATHS

PLANNING FANTASY PROJECTS

PROJECTS

LIVING IN UNFINISHED PROJECT MESS

IDEAL HOME TYPE (CIRCLE ONE)

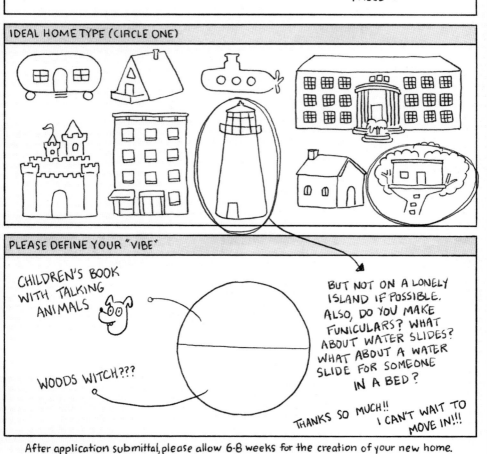

PLEASE DEFINE YOUR "VIBE"

CHILDREN'S BOOK WITH TALKING ANIMALS

WOODS WITCH???

BUT NOT ON A LONELY ISLAND IF POSSIBLE. ALSO, DO YOU MAKE FUNICULARS? WHAT ABOUT WATER SLIDES? WHAT ABOUT A WATER SLIDE FOR SOMEONE IN A BED?

THANKS SO MUCH!! I CAN'T WAIT TO MOVE IN!!!

After application submittal, please allow 6-8 weeks for the creation of your new home.

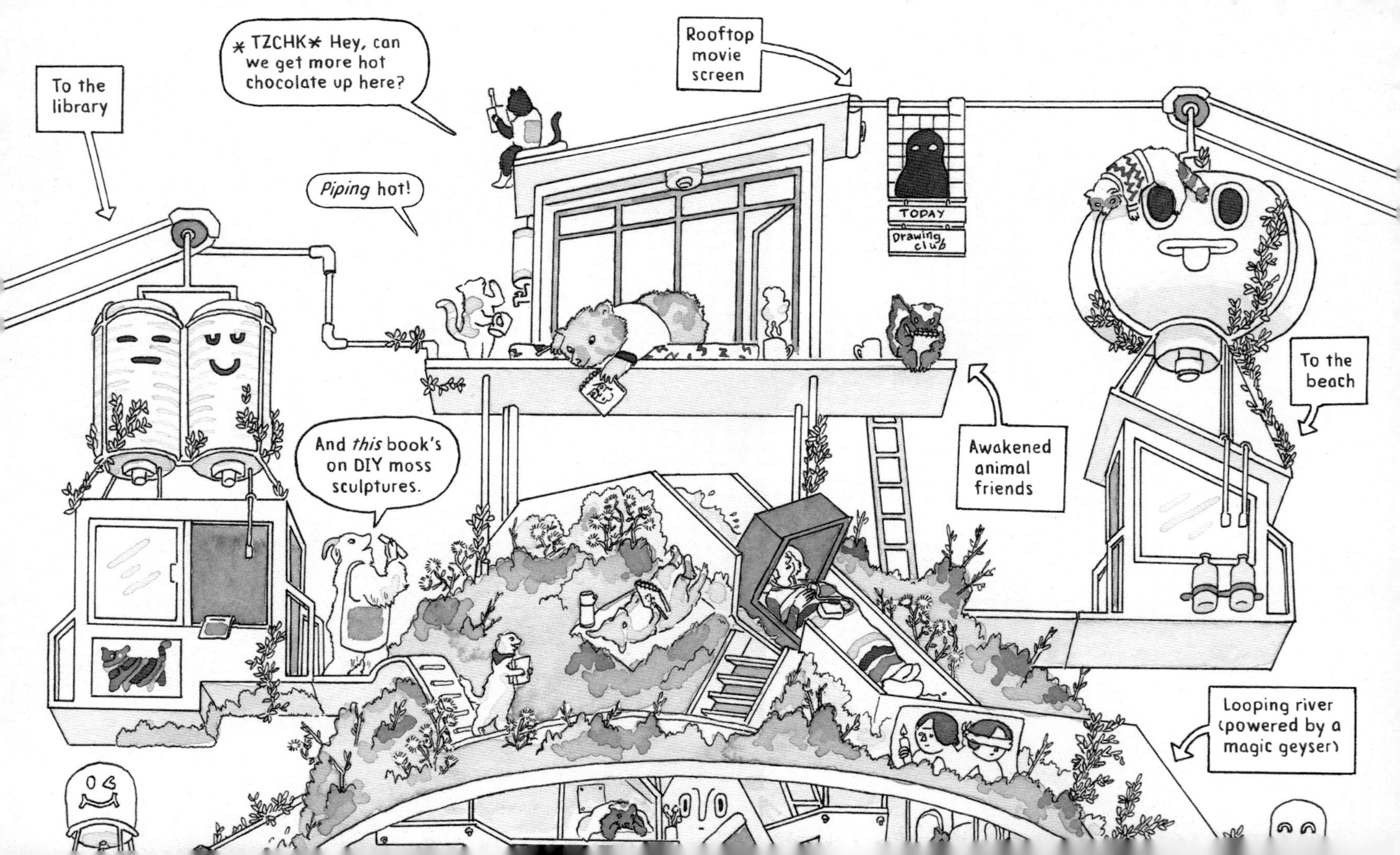
To the library
TZCHK Hey, can we get more hot chocolate up here?
Piping hot!
Rooftop movie screen
TODAY
Drawing club
To the beach
And this book's on DIY moss sculptures.
Awakened animal friends
Looping river (powered by a magic geyser)

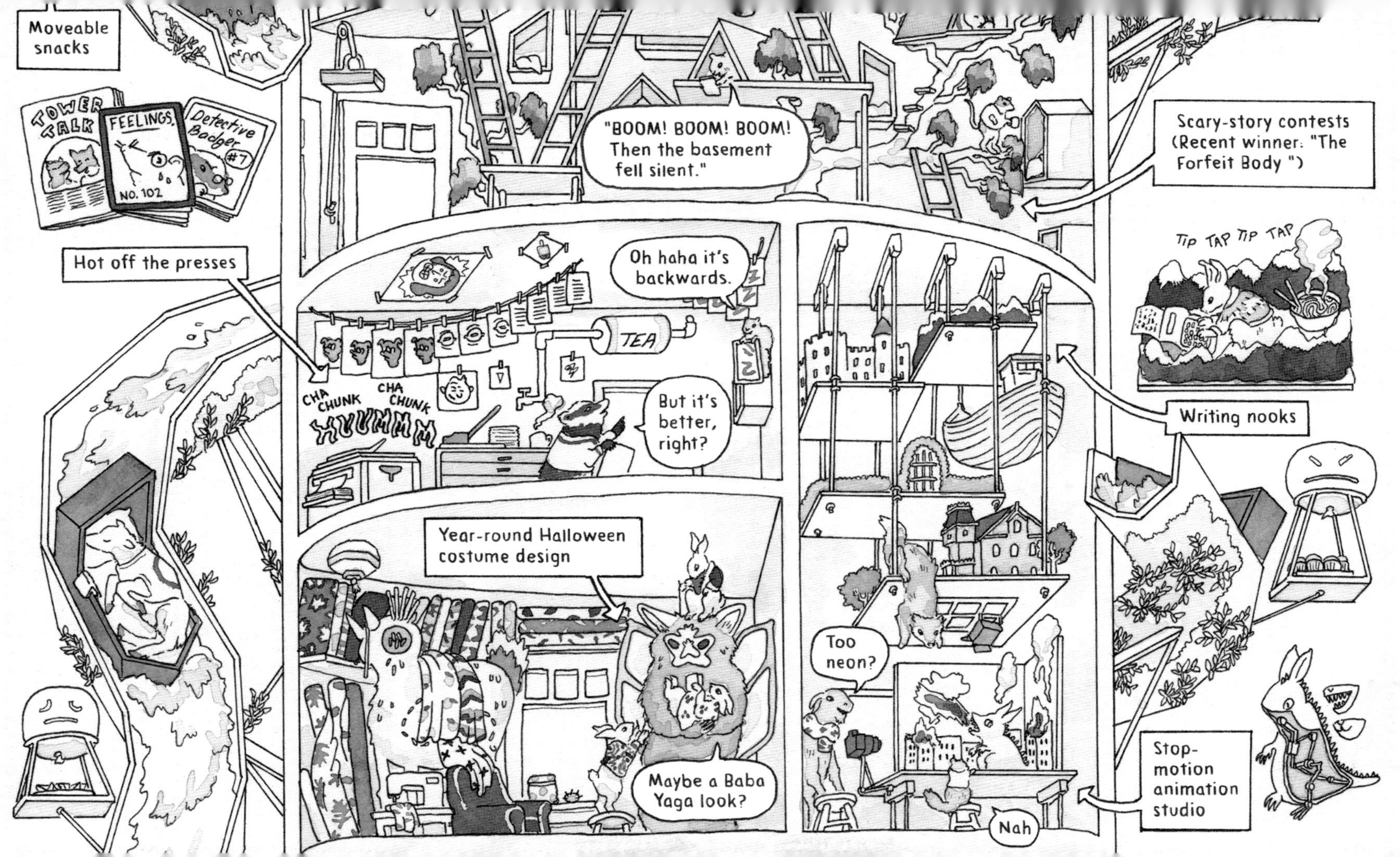
Moveable snacks
TOWER TALK
FEELINGS
NO. 102
Detective Badger #7
Hot off the presses
"BOOM! BOOM! BOOM! Then the basement fell silent."
Scary-story contests (Recent winner: "The Forfeit Body")
Oh haha it's backwards.
TEA
CHA CHUNK
CHA CHUNK
HMMMM
But it's better, right?
TIP TAP TIP TAP
Writing nooks
Year-round Halloween costume design
Maybe a Baba Yaga look?
Too neon?
Nah
Stop-motion animation studio

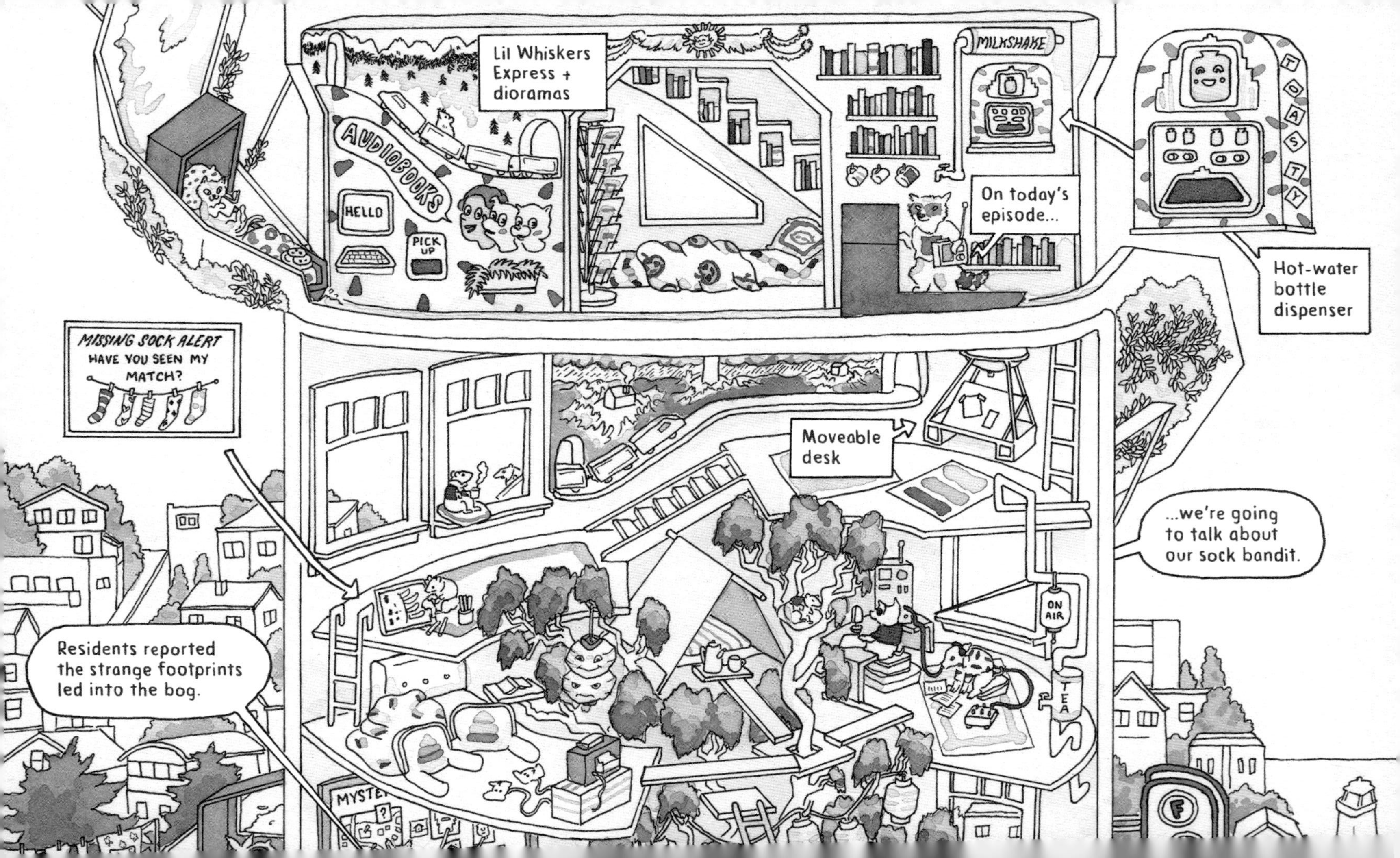
Lil Whiskers Express + dioramas
AUDIOBOOKS
HELLO
PICK UP
MILKSHAKE
On today's episode...
TOASTY
Hot-water bottle dispenser
MISSING SOCK ALERT
HAVE YOU SEEN MY MATCH?
Moveable desk
...we're going to talk about our sock bandit.
ON AIR
TEA
Residents reported the strange footprints led into the bog.

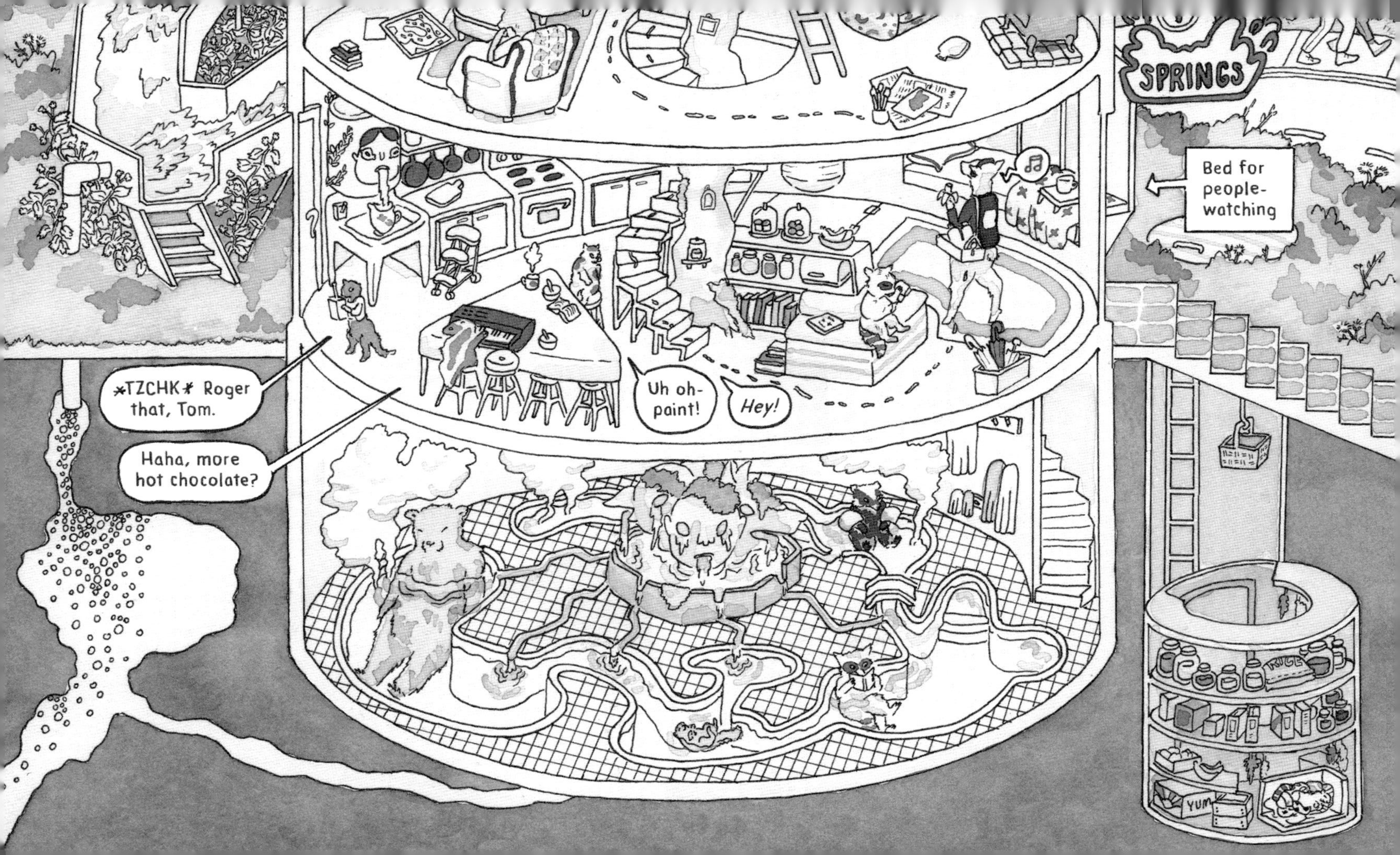
SPRINGS
Bed for people-watching
TZCHK Roger that, Tom.
Haha, more hot chocolate?
Uh oh- paint!
Hey!
YUM

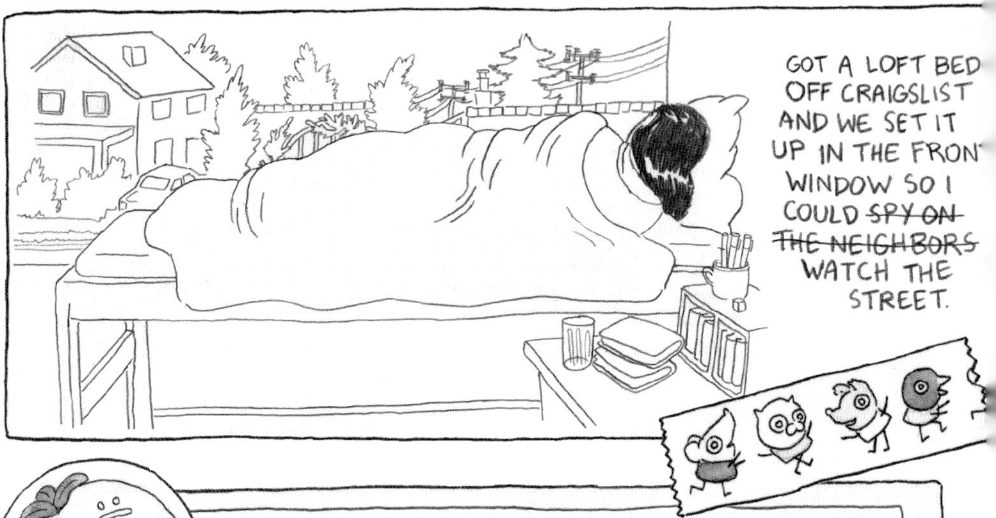
GOT A LOFT BED OFF CRAIGSLIST AND WE SET IT UP IN THE FRONT WINDOW SO I COULD ~~SPY ON THE NEIGHBORS~~ WATCH THE STREET.

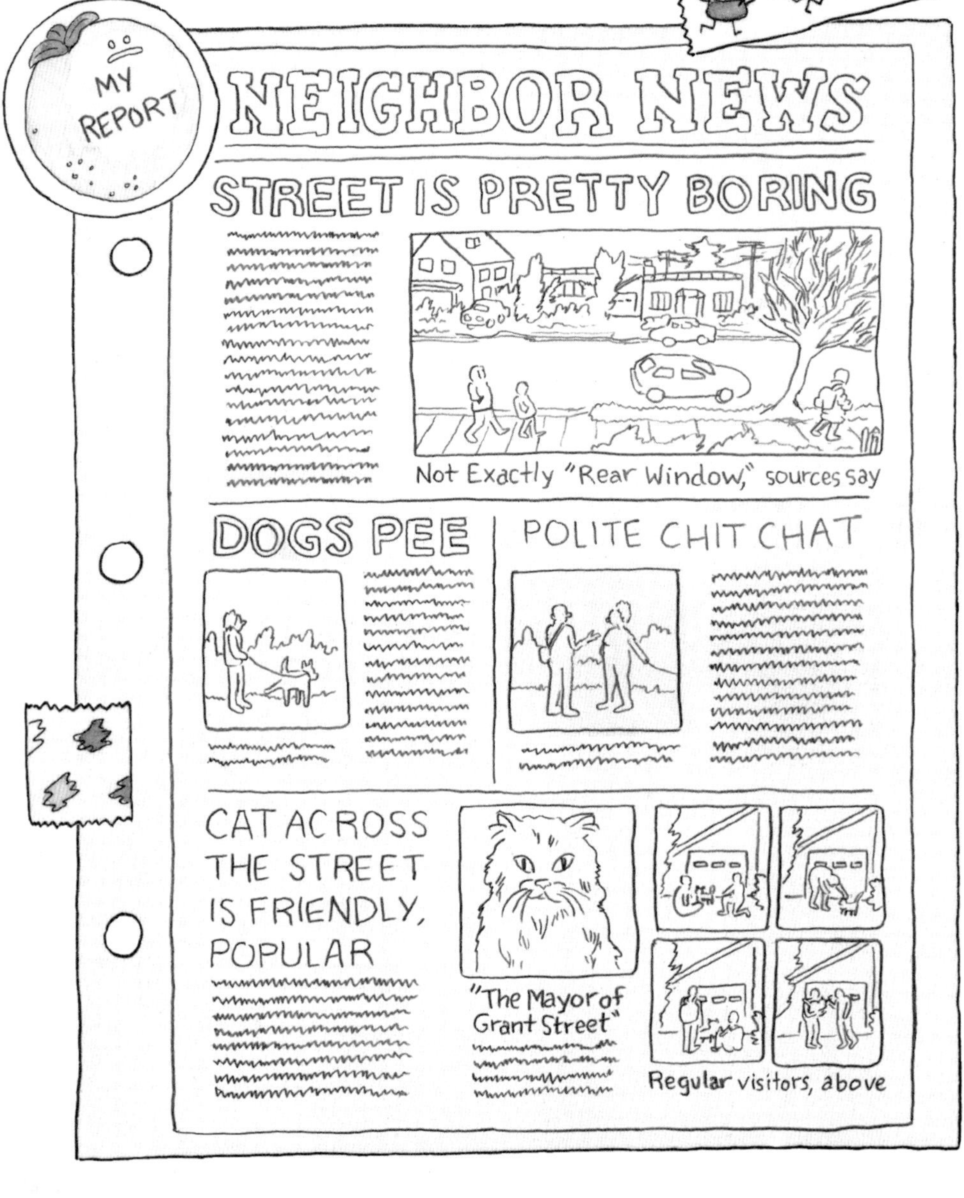
MY REPORT
NEIGHBOR NEWS
STREET IS PRETTY BORING
Not Exactly "Rear Window," sources say
DOGS PEE
POLITE CHIT CHAT
CAT ACROSS THE STREET IS FRIENDLY, POPULAR
"The Mayor of Grant Street"
Regular visitors, above

MISTAKES

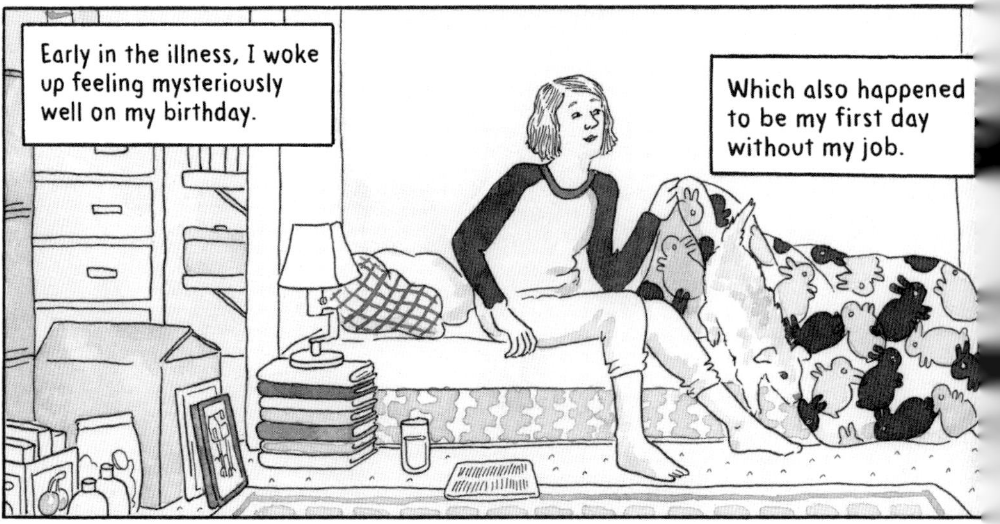
Early in the illness, I woke up feeling mysteriously well on my birthday.
Which also happened to be my first day without my job.

Quitting my job hadn't broken my heart. It was stressful, underpaid nonprofit work, and I'd wanted to leave eventually.

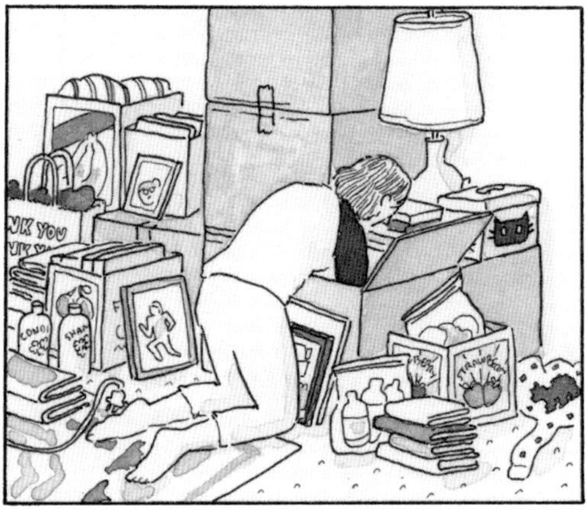

But I'd always thought I'd quit because I was doing something else, like going back to school or moving to a new city.

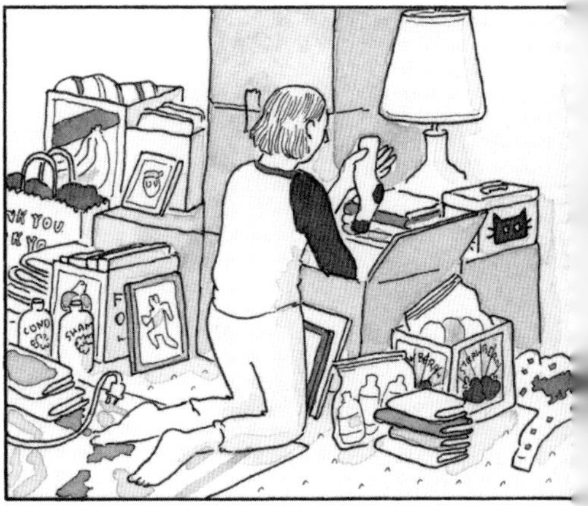

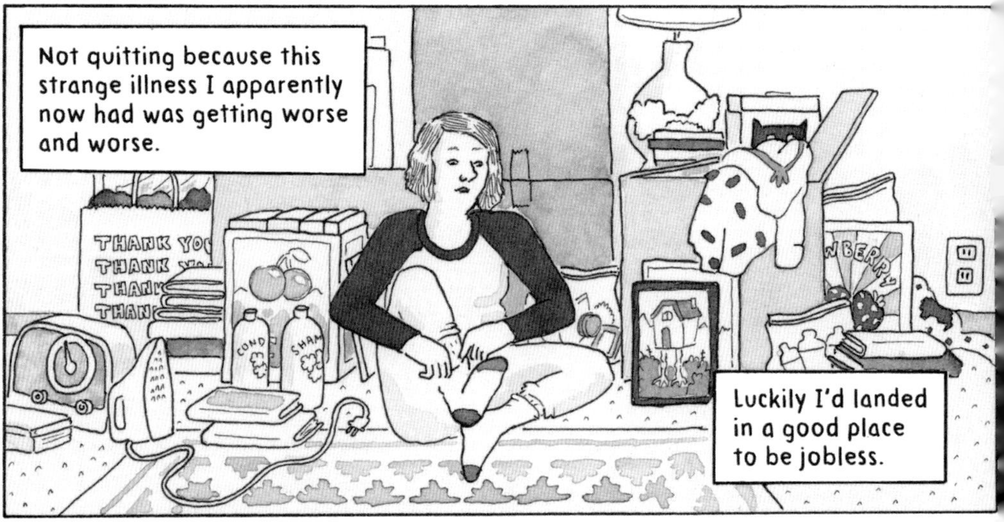
Not quitting because this strange illness I apparently now had was getting worse and worse.
Luckily I'd landed in a good place to be jobless.

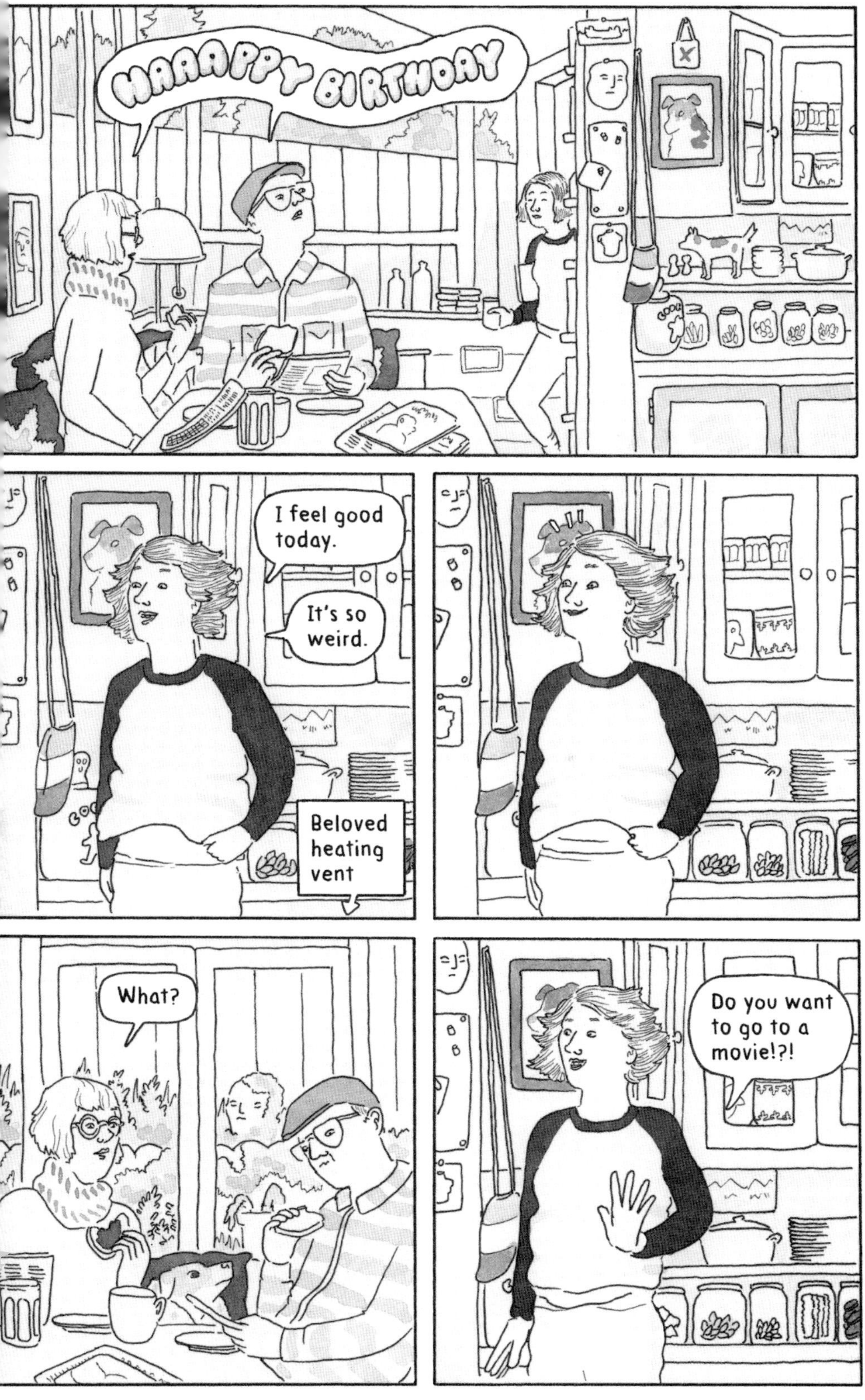
HAAAPPY BIRTHDAY
I feel good today.
It's so weird.
Beloved heating vent
What?
Do you want to go to a movie!?!

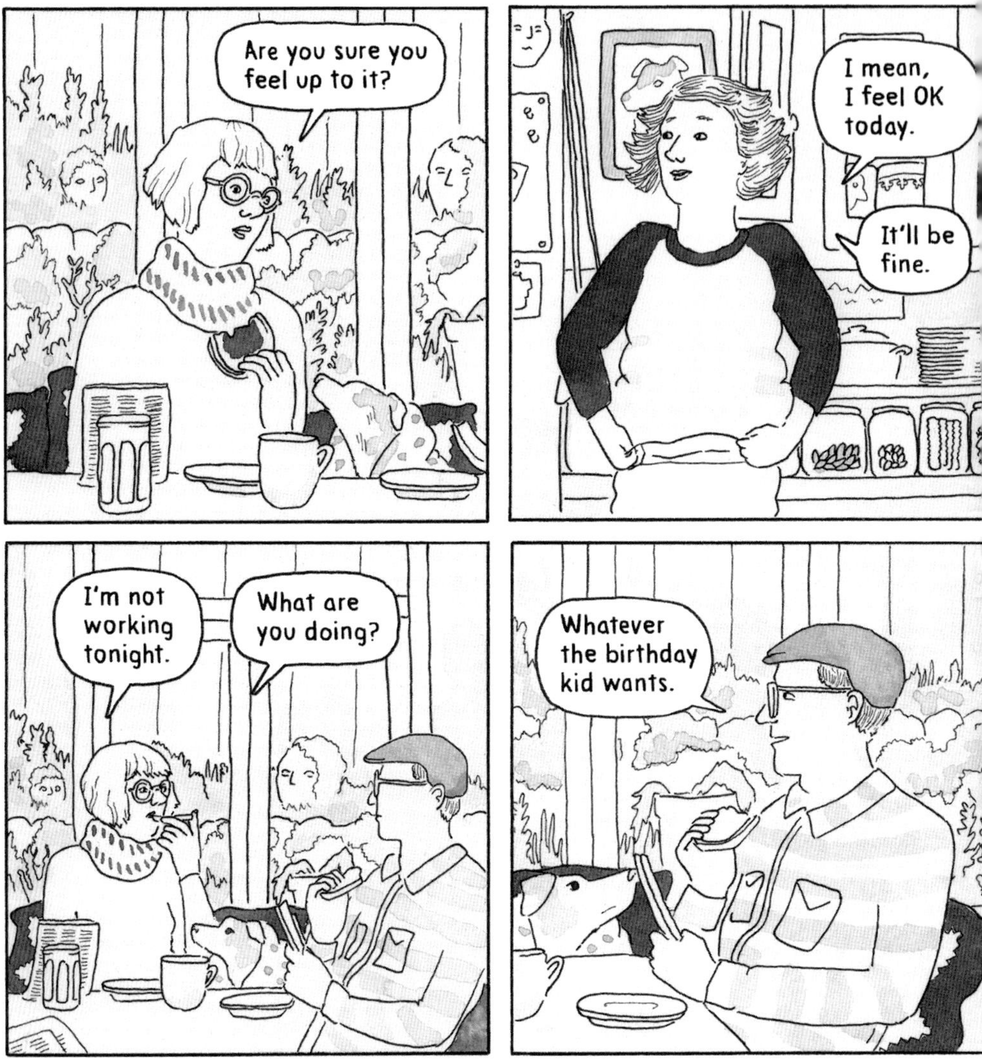
Are you sure you feel up to it?
I mean, I feel OK today.
It'll be fine.
I'm not working tonight.
What are you doing?
Whatever the birthday kid wants.

Even though I'd been barely making it to work for weeks, going to a movie didn't seem reckless.

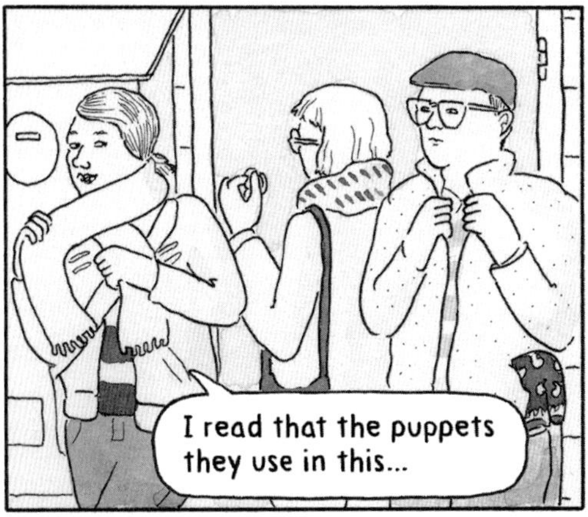
I read that the puppets they use in this...

Feeling well on my birthday just felt like a gift. A happy surprise!

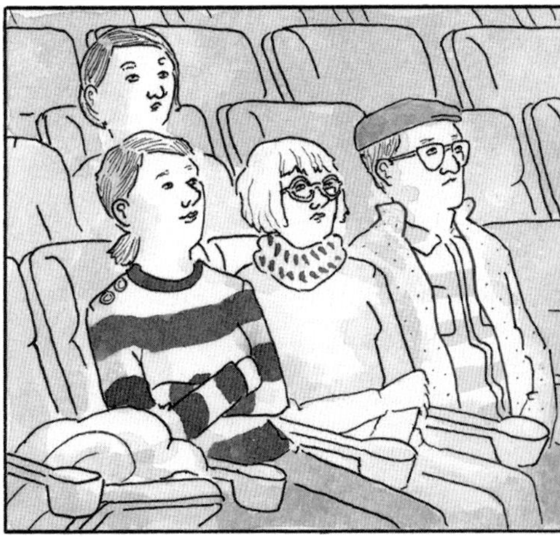

I was unaware I was making a painful mistake.

I mean physically painful.

With no diagnosis, I knew so little about the illness.

Figuring out how it worked involved so much trial and error.

And I was just identifying a crucial feature of the illness: the more you do, the sicker you get, even if you feel well.

Activity, no matter how simple, causes symptoms.

click

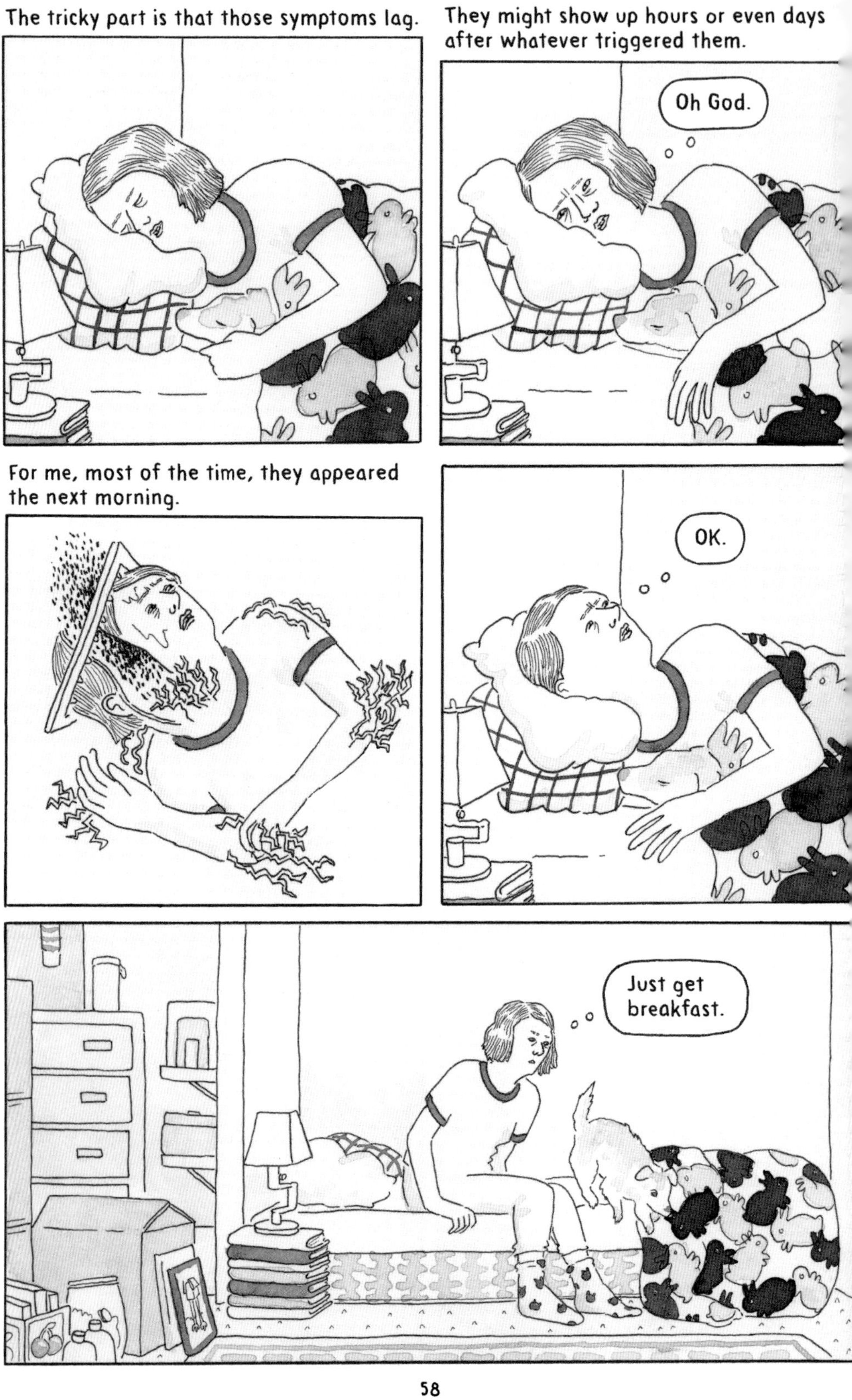
The tricky part is that those symptoms lag.
They might show up hours or even days after whatever triggered them.
Oh God.
For me, most of the time, they appeared the next morning.
OK.
Just get breakfast.

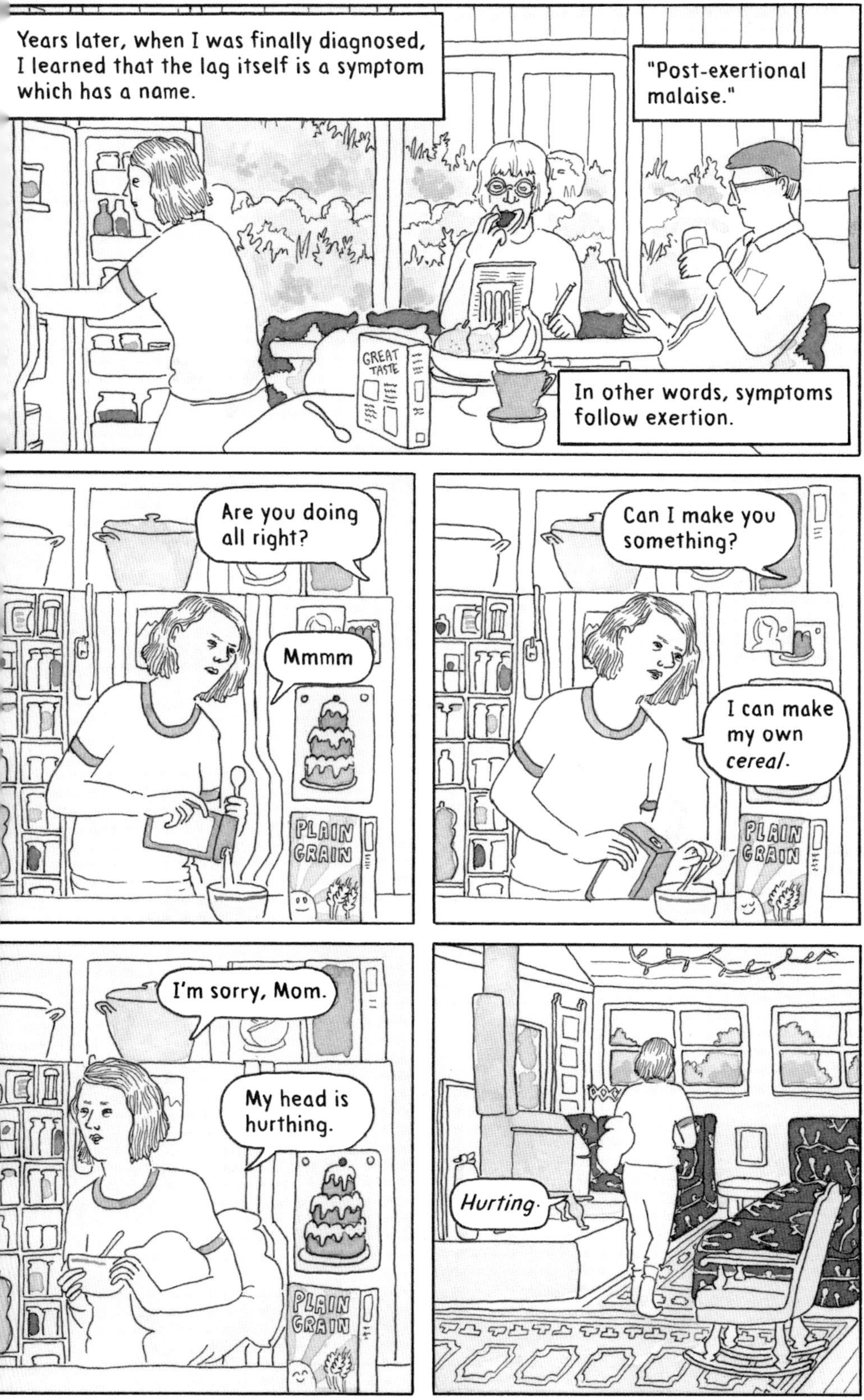
Years later, when I was finally diagnosed, I learned that the lag itself is a symptom which has a name.
"Post-exertional malaise."
GREAT TASTE
In other words, symptoms follow exertion.
Are you doing all right?
Mmmm
PLAIN GRAIN
Can I make you something?
I can make my own *cereal*.
PLAIN GRAIN
I'm sorry, Mom.
My head is hurthing.
PLAIN GRAIN
Hurting.

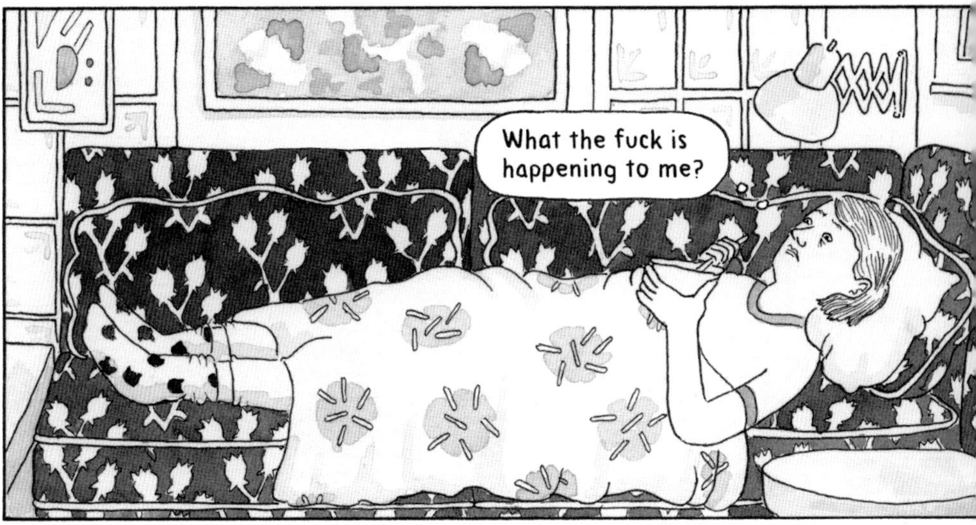
What the fuck is happening to me?

Resting seemed to help me recover.

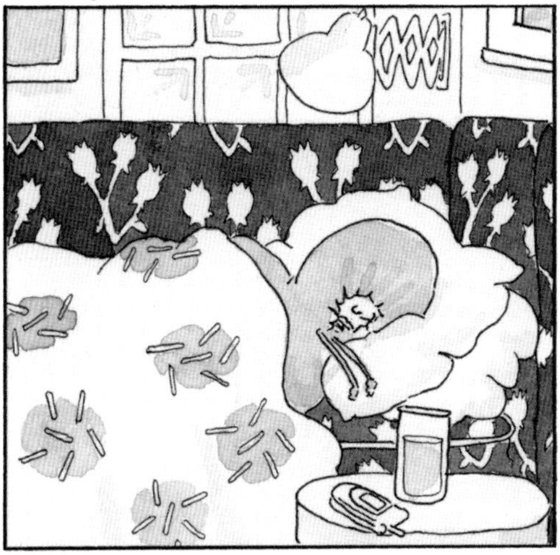

It was weak medicine.

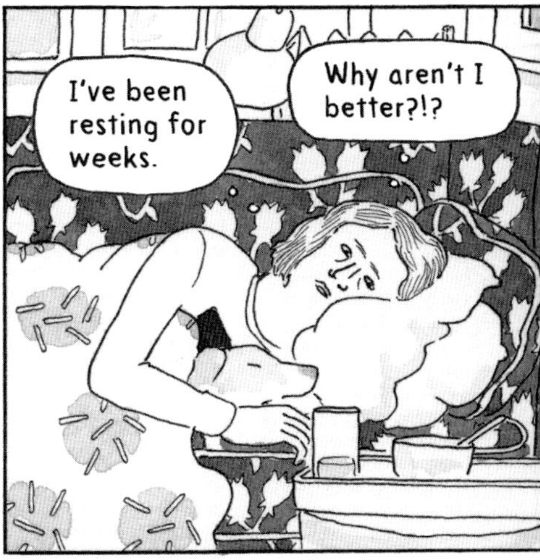
I've been resting for weeks.
Why aren't I better?!?

It was also the only medicine.

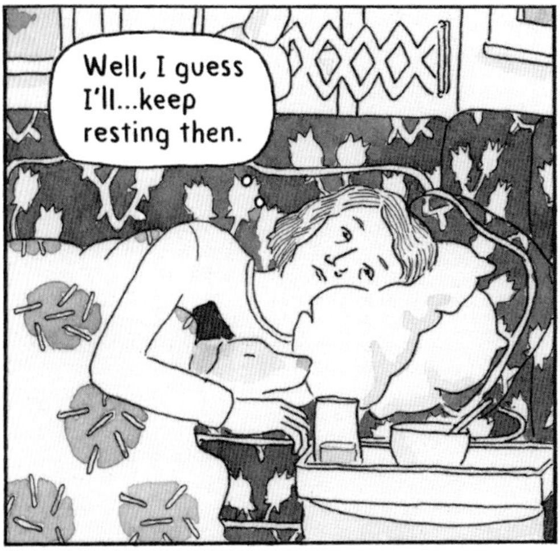
Well, I guess I'll...keep resting then.

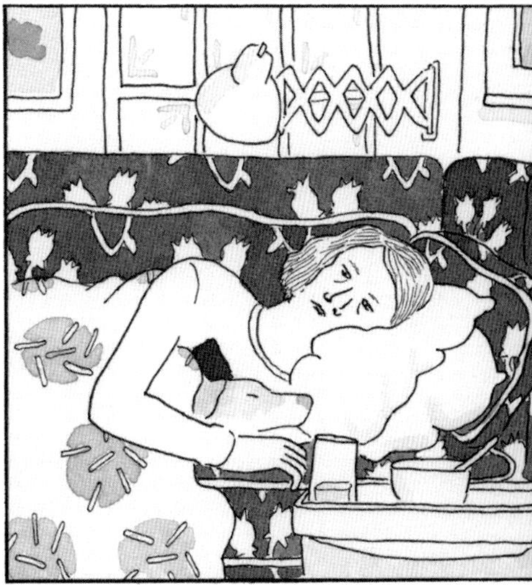

hen I'd finally recover, it would be like aking up on my birthday again. I'd feel ell, or at least well enough.

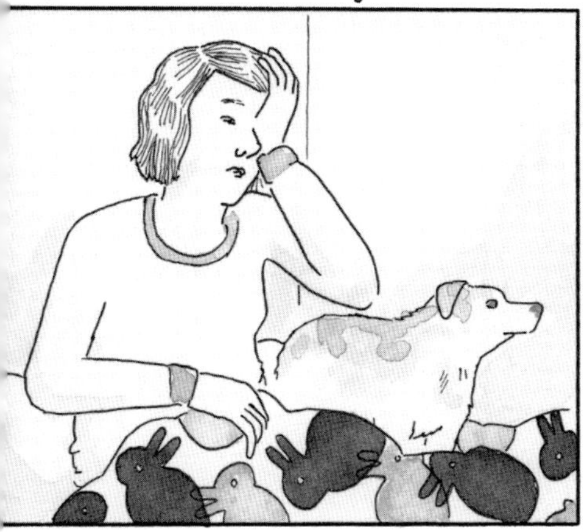

Eventually, I'd understand that the wellness was an illusion. I wasn't actually well.

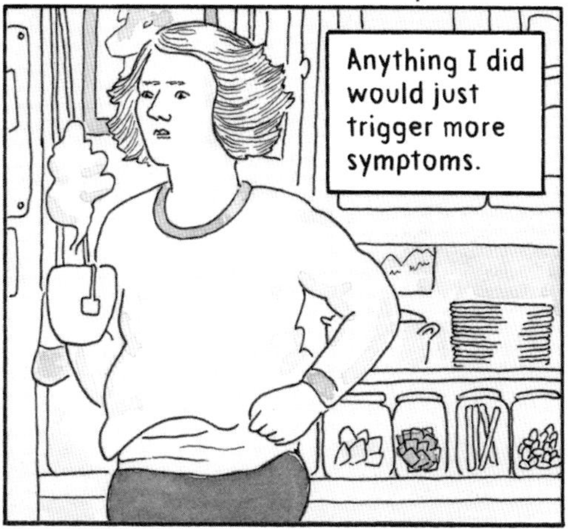
Anything I did would just trigger more symptoms.

wish I could say that as soon as I learned 'his, I tried to accept this new limitation.

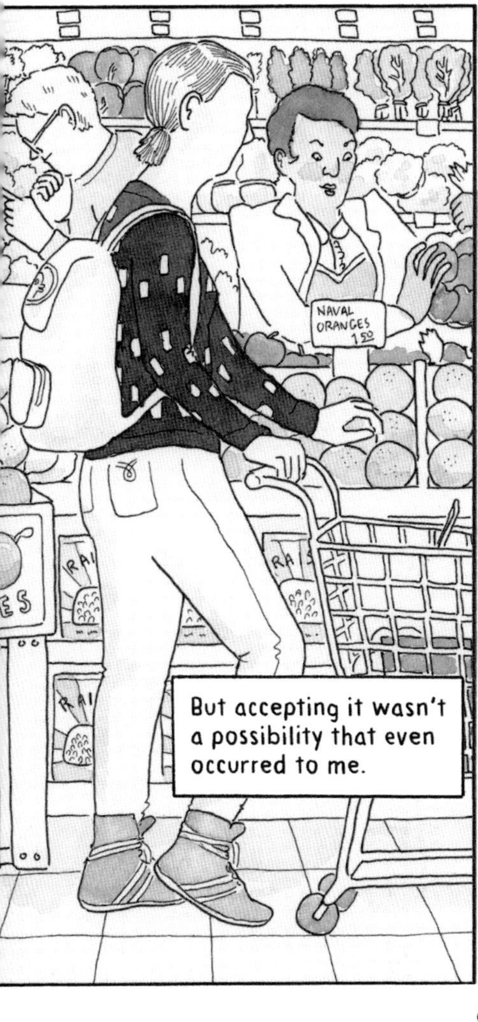
NAVAL ORANGES 1.50
But accepting it wasn't a possibility that even occurred to me.

Instead, I started trying to exploit the lag, maneuvering my life into the windows of "wellness" between my latest recovery and the next round of symptoms.

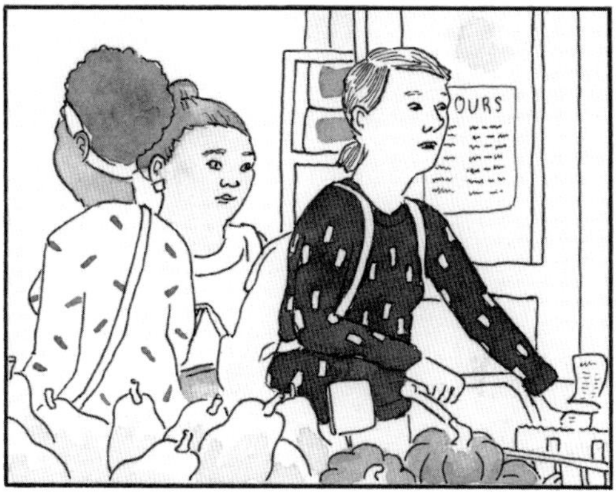
OURS

The basic mechanics of my life began to depend entirely on these little windows.

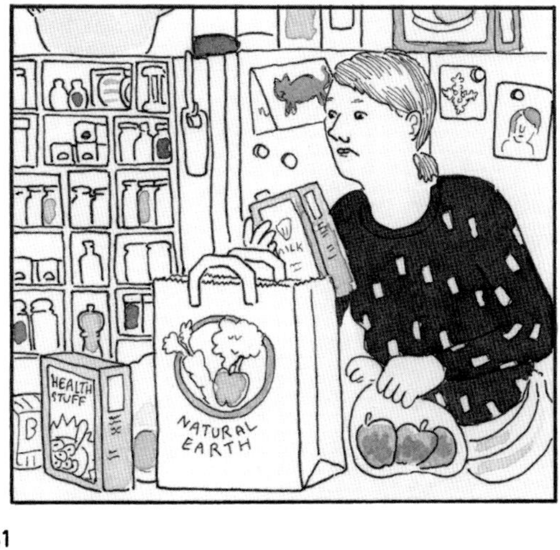
MILK
HEALTH STUFF
NATURAL EARTH

And I relied more and more on my one tool: the small amount of influence that resting gave me over the illness.

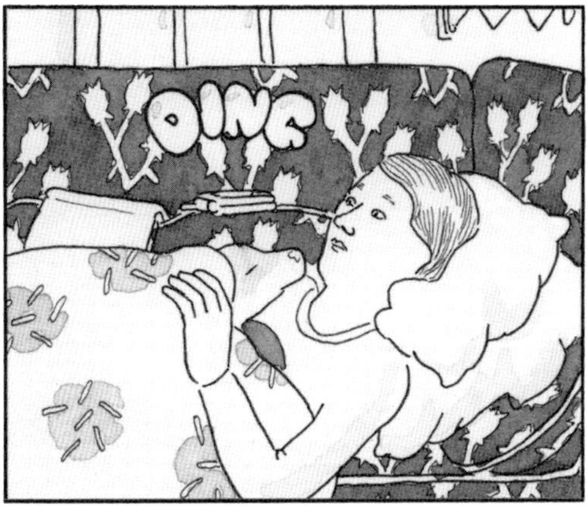
DING

Say I wanted to do something wild, like make a plan.

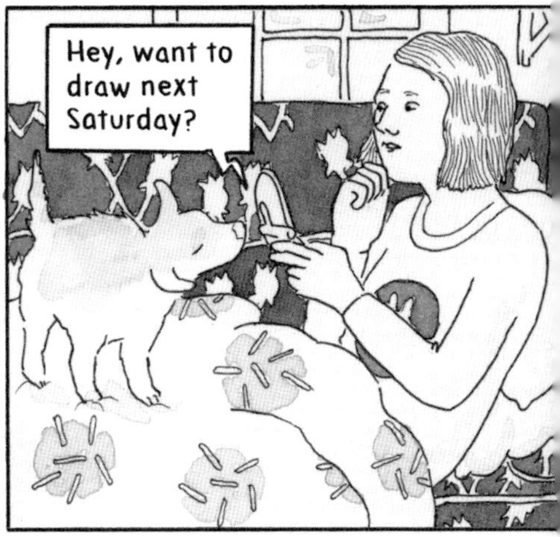
Hey, want to draw next Saturday?

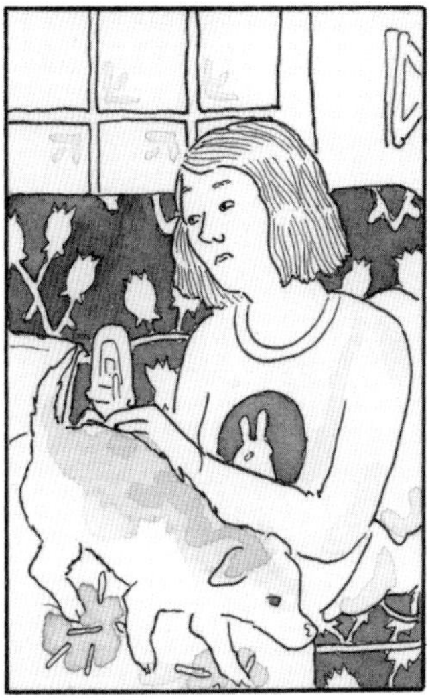

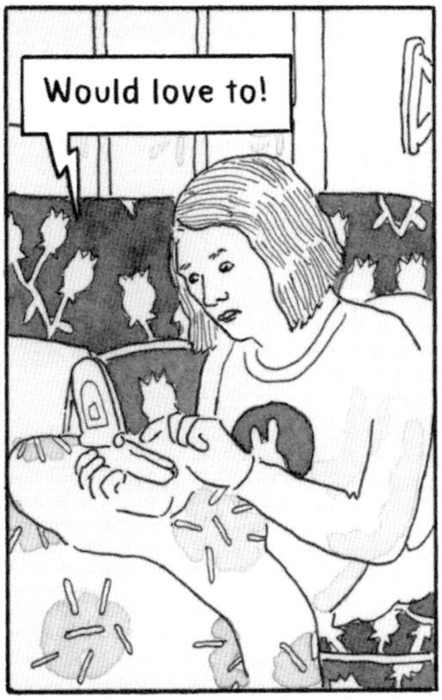
Would love to!

I'd then come up with a resting strategy.

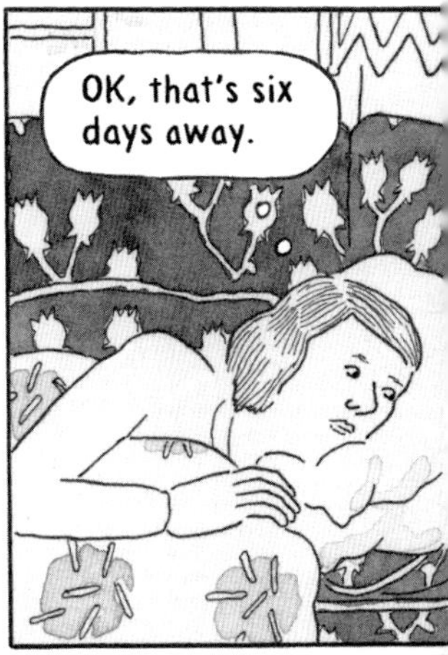
OK, that's six days away.

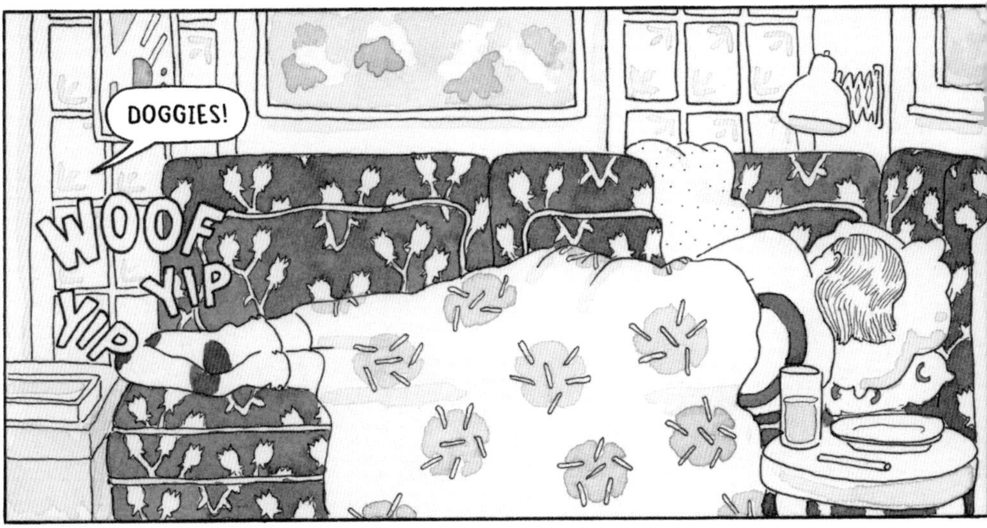
DOGGIES!
WOOF
YIP
YIP

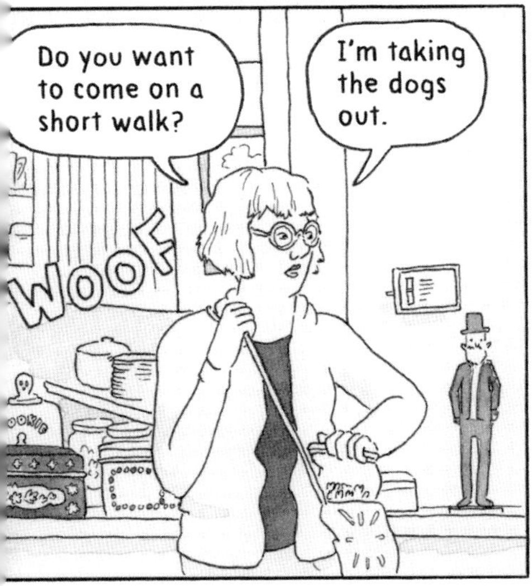
Do you want to come on a short walk?
I'm taking the dogs out.
WOOF

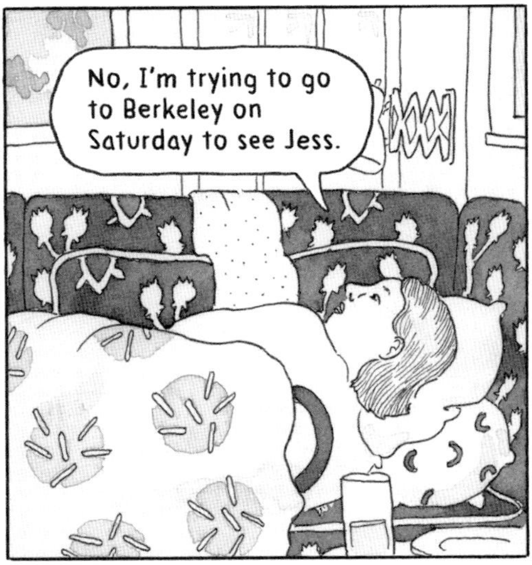
No, I'm trying to go to Berkeley on Saturday to see Jess.

Was I foolish to try this? Who knows.

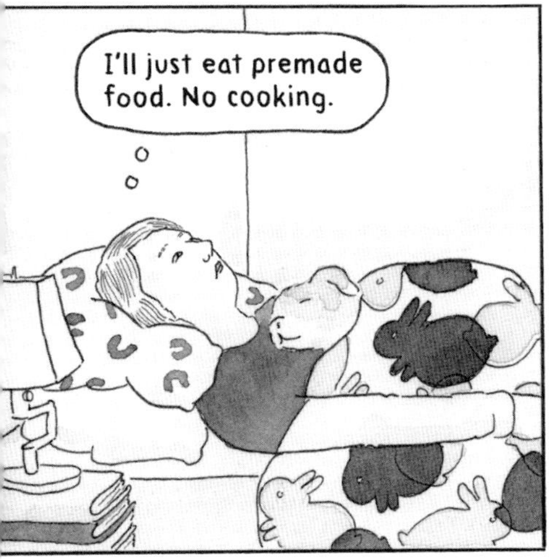
I'll just eat premade food. No cooking.

Not only was estimating my recovery times a joke, but I could never be sure what activity would finally kick off symptoms.

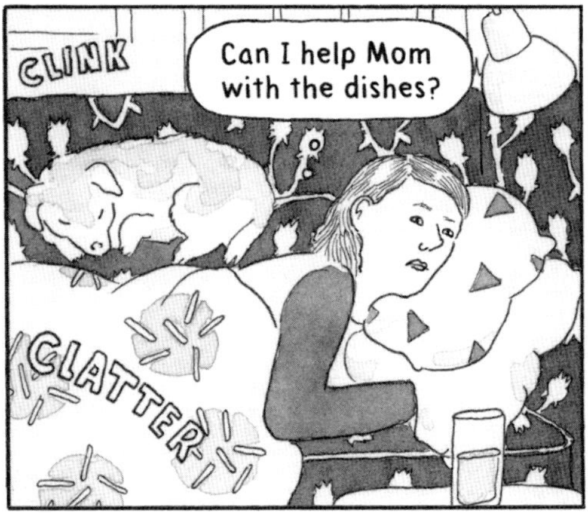
CLINK
Can I help Mom with the dishes?
CLATTER

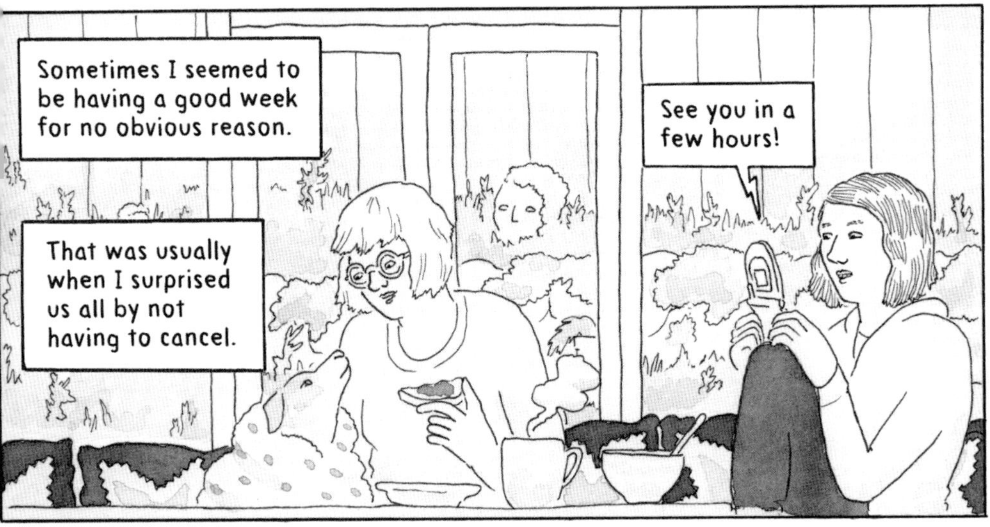
Sometimes I seemed to be having a good week for no obvious reason.
That was usually when I surprised us all by not having to cancel.
See you in a few hours!

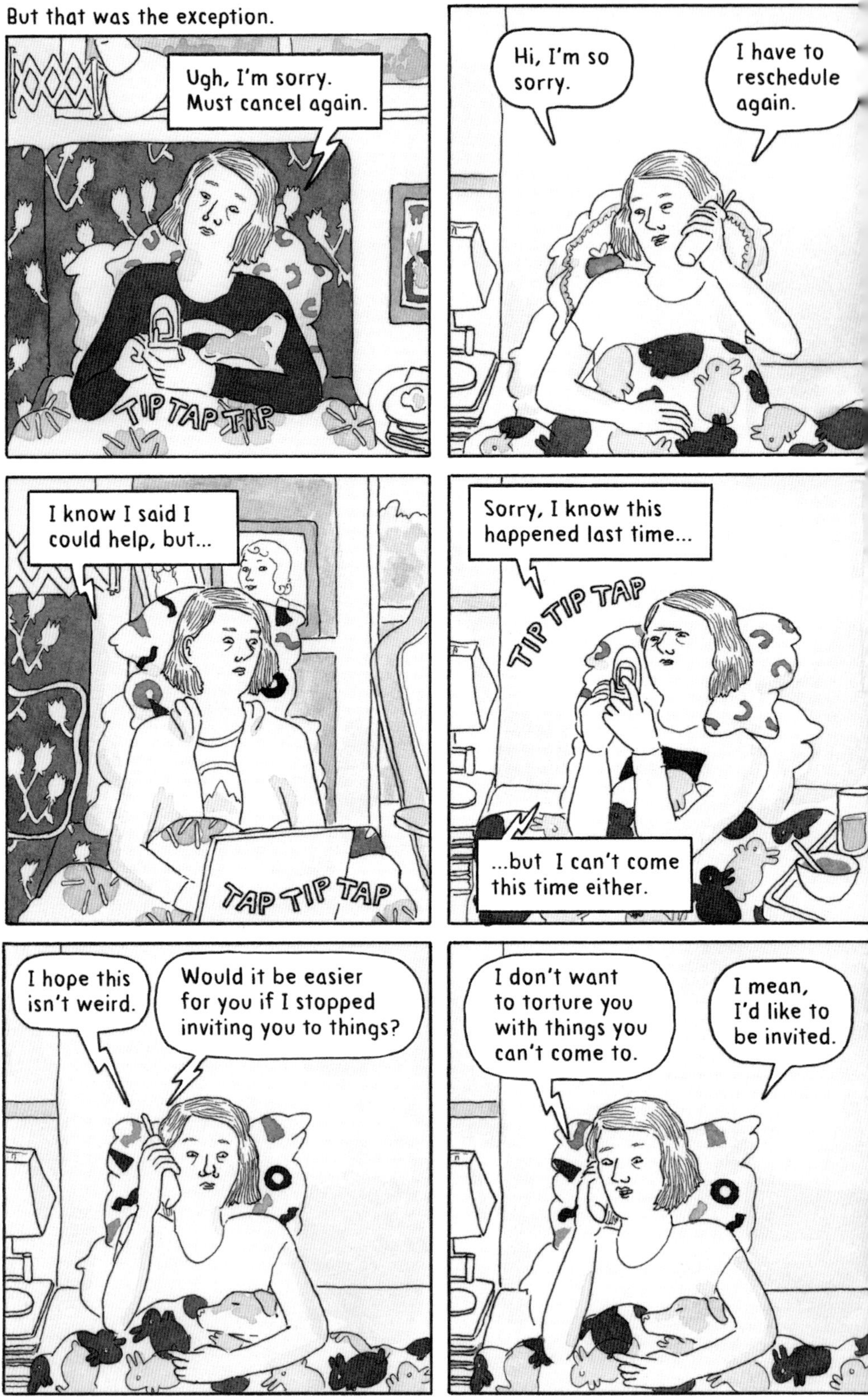
But that was the exception.
Ugh, I'm sorry. Must cancel again.
TIP TAP TIP
Hi, I'm so sorry.
I have to reschedule again.
I know I said I could help, but...
TAP TIP TAP
Sorry, I know this happened last time...
TIP TIP TAP
...but I can't come this time either.
I hope this isn't weird.
Would it be easier for you if I stopped inviting you to things?
I don't want to torture you with things you can't come to.
I mean, I'd like to be invited.

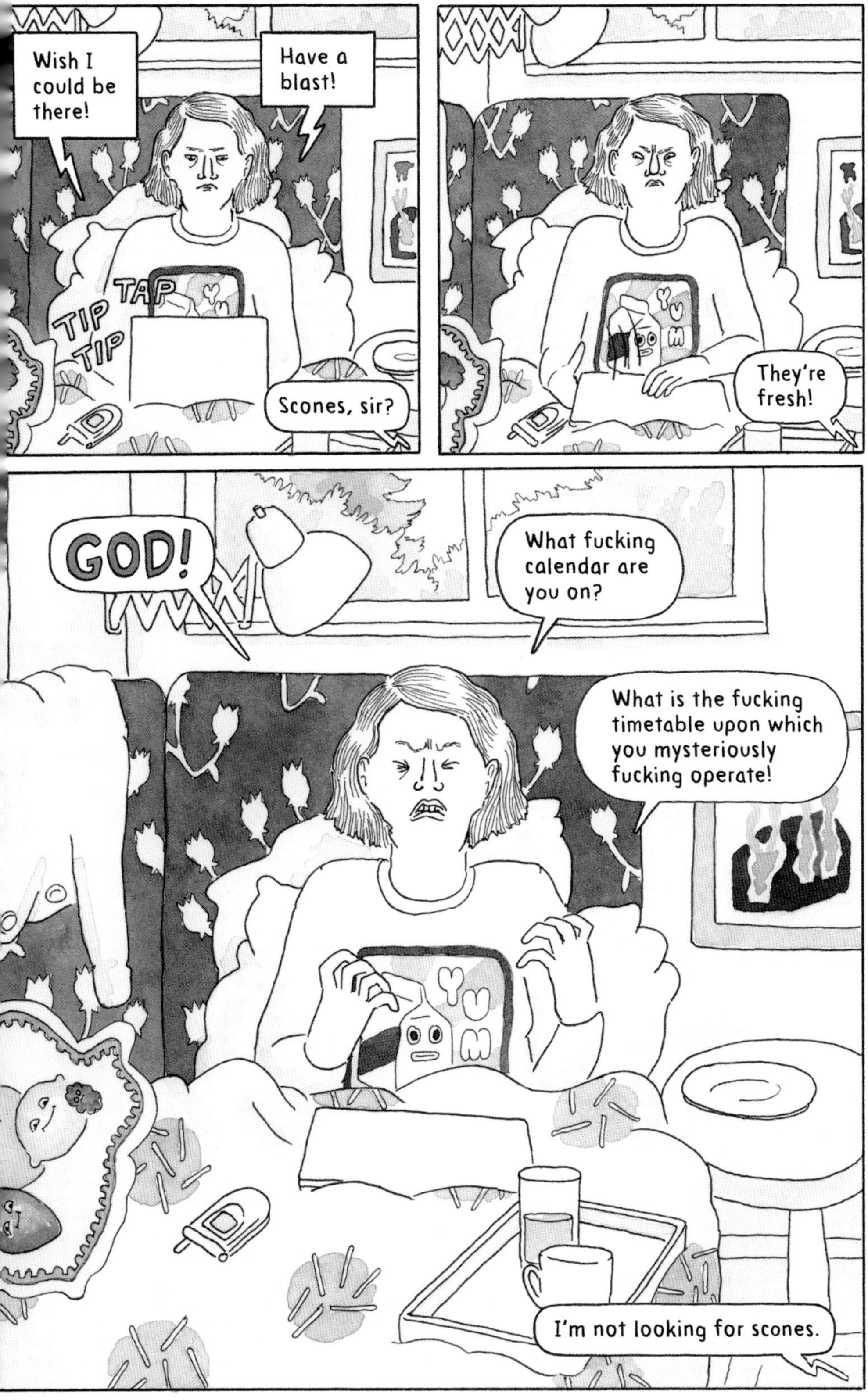
Wish I could be there!
Have a blast!
TIP TAP TIP
Scones, sir?
They're fresh!
GOD!
What fucking calendar are you on?
What is the fucking timetable upon which you mysteriously fucking operate!
I'm not looking for scones.

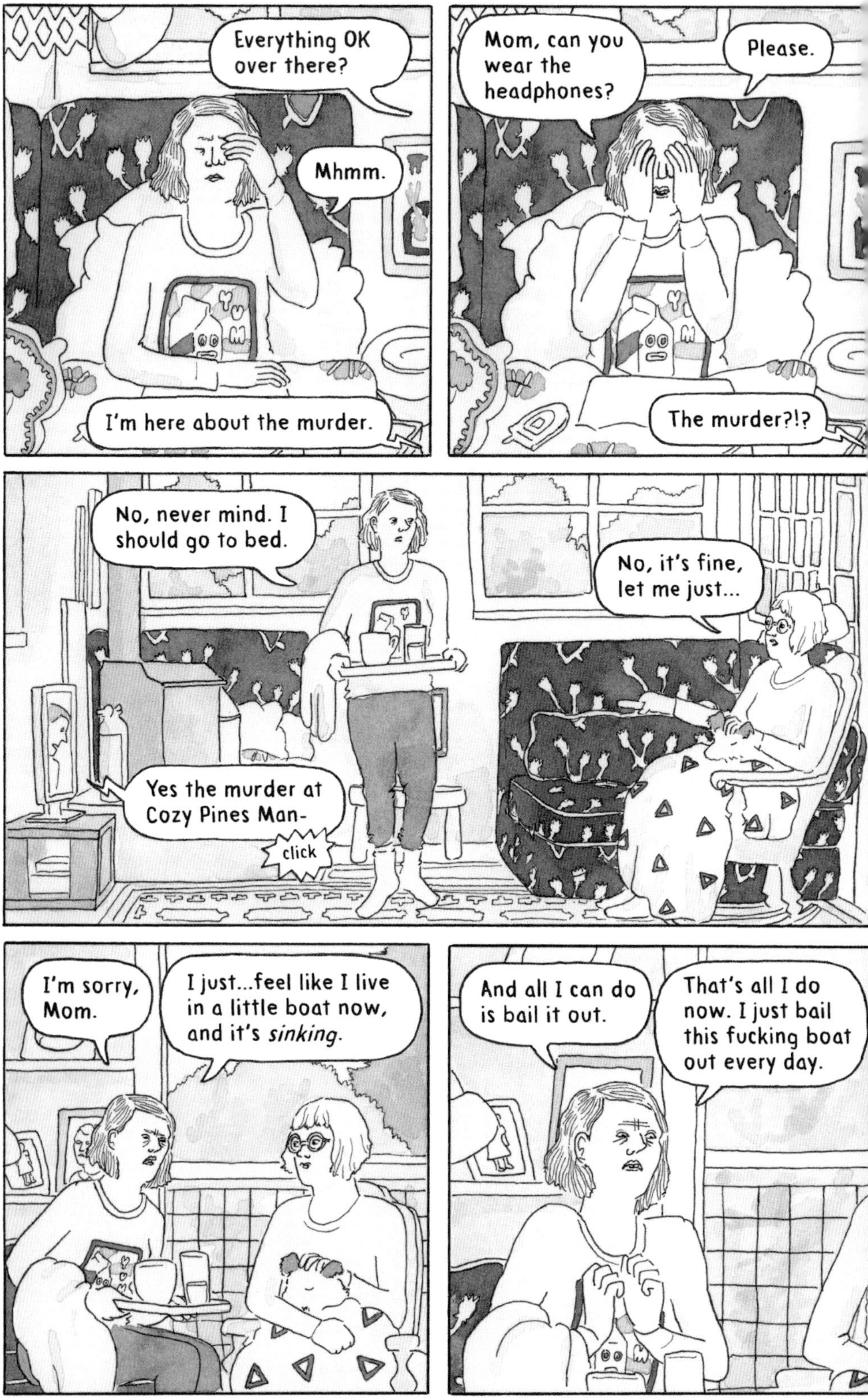

Everything OK over there?
Mhmm.
I'm here about the murder.
Mom, can you wear the headphones?
Please.
The murder?!?
No, never mind. I should go to bed.
No, it's fine, let me just...
Yes the murder at Cozy Pines Man-
click
I'm sorry, Mom.
I just...feel like I live in a little boat now, and it's *sinking*.
And all I can do is bail it out.
That's all I do now. I just bail this fucking boat out every day.

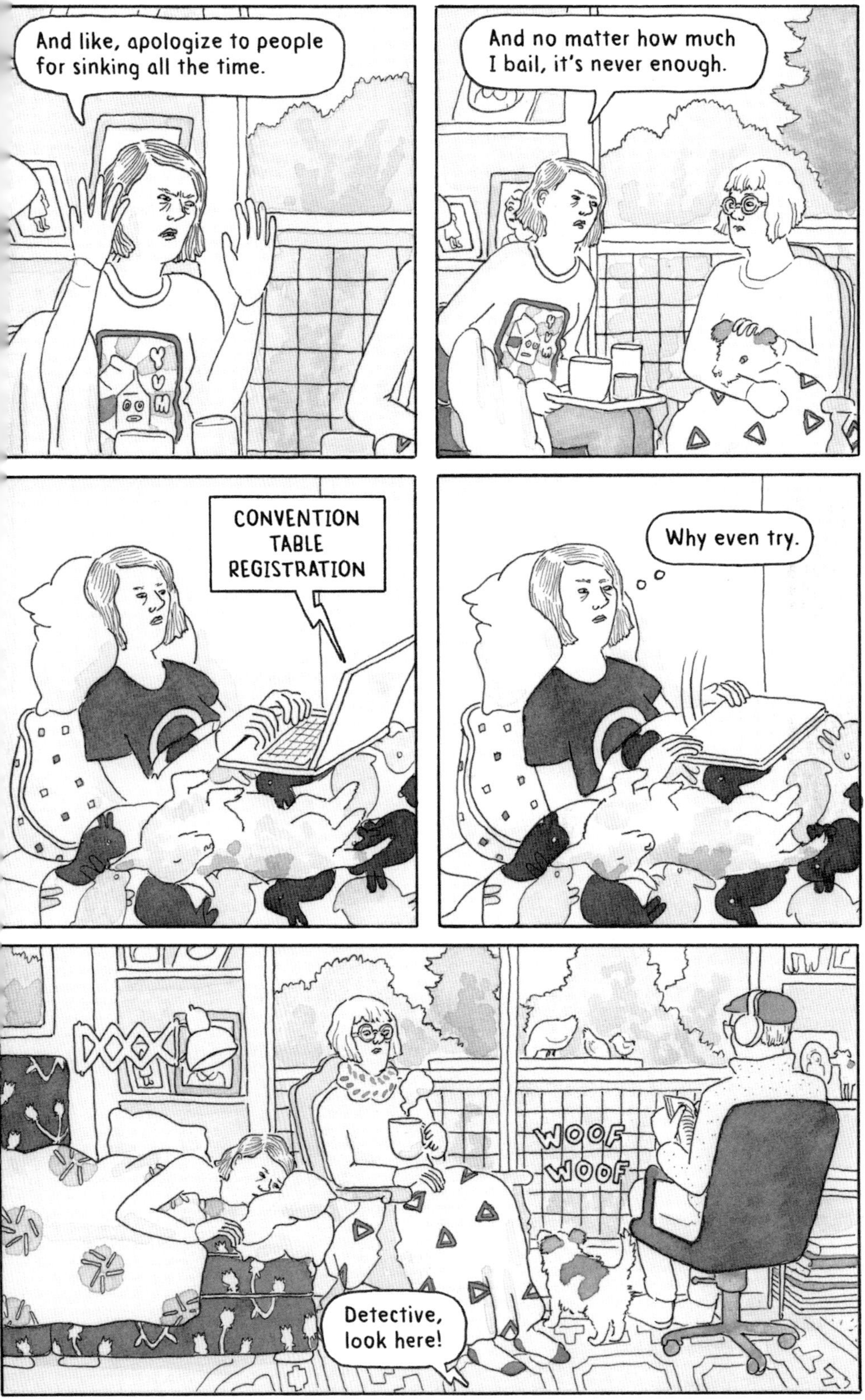
And like, apologize to people for sinking all the time.
And no matter how much I bail, it's never enough.
CONVENTION TABLE REGISTRATION
Why even try.
WOOF
WOOF
Detective, look here!

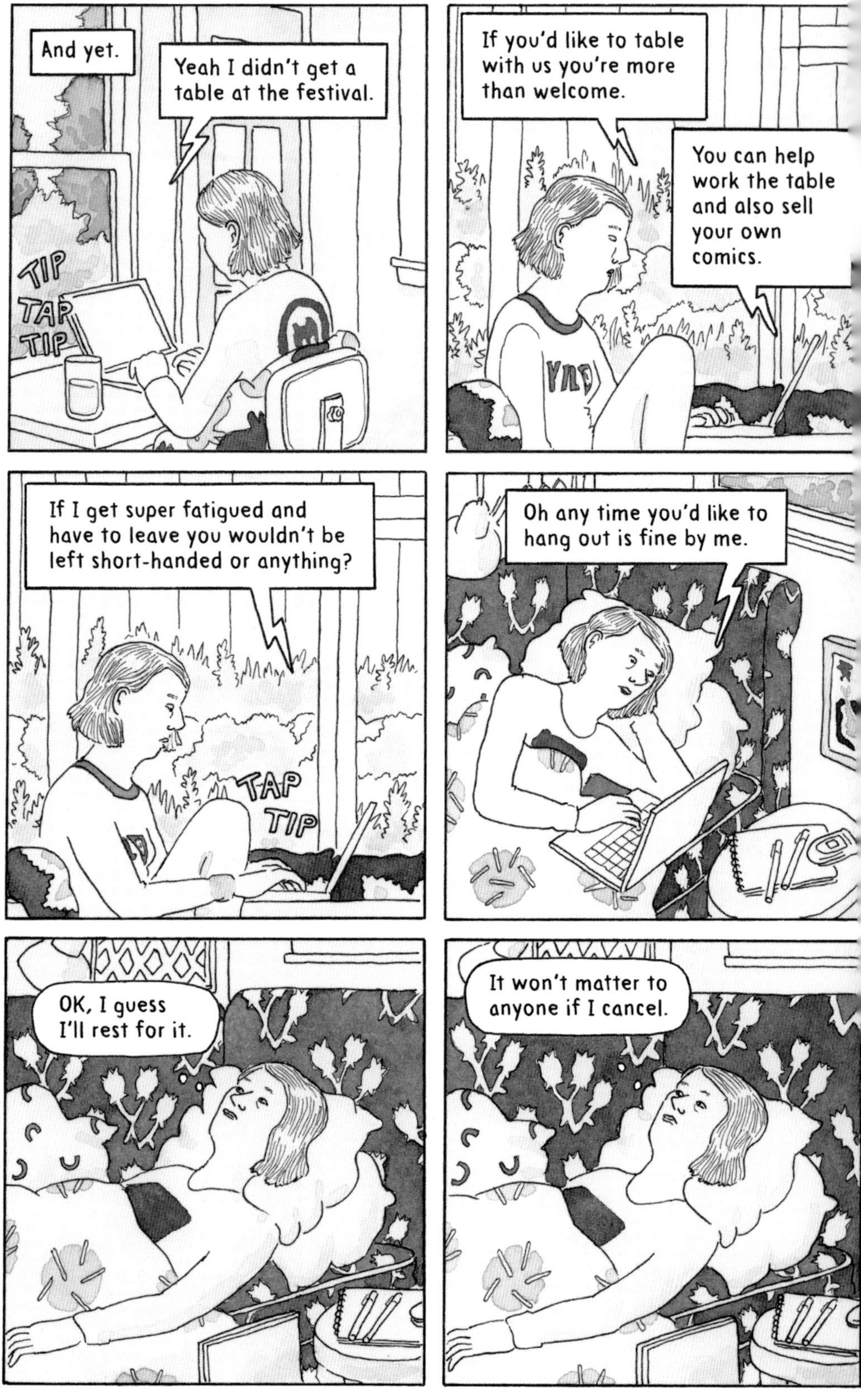
And yet.
Yeah I didn't get a table at the festival.
TIP TAP TIP
If you'd like to table with us you're more than welcome.
You can help work the table and also sell your own comics.
If I get super fatigued and have to leave you wouldn't be left short-handed or anything?
TAP TIP
Oh any time you'd like to hang out is fine by me.
OK, I guess I'll rest for it.
It won't matter to anyone if I cancel.

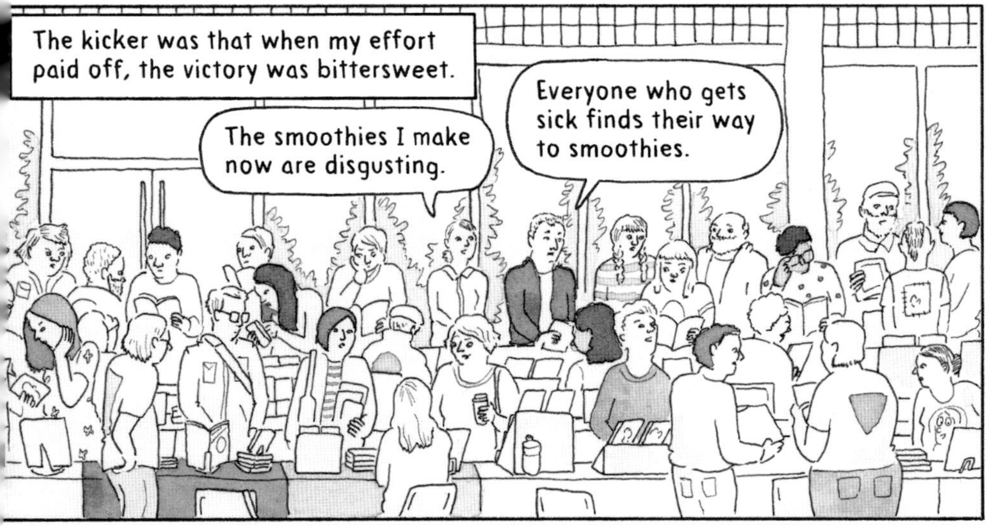
The kicker was that when my effort paid off, the victory was bittersweet.
The smoothies I make now are disgusting.
Everyone who gets sick finds their way to smoothies.

Yes, the novelty made everything vivid and exciting and precious.

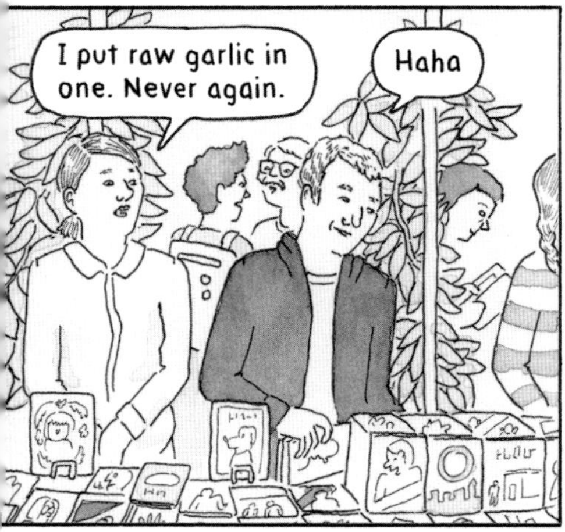
I put raw garlic in one. Never again.
Haha

Every conversation thrilling.

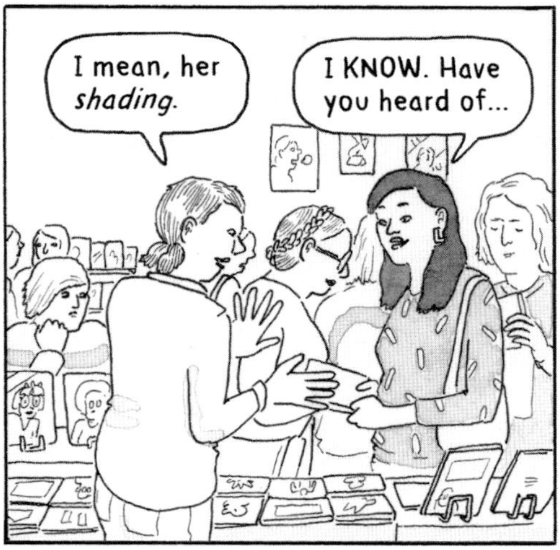
I mean, her *shading*.
I KNOW. Have you heard of...

Every stranger, a gem.

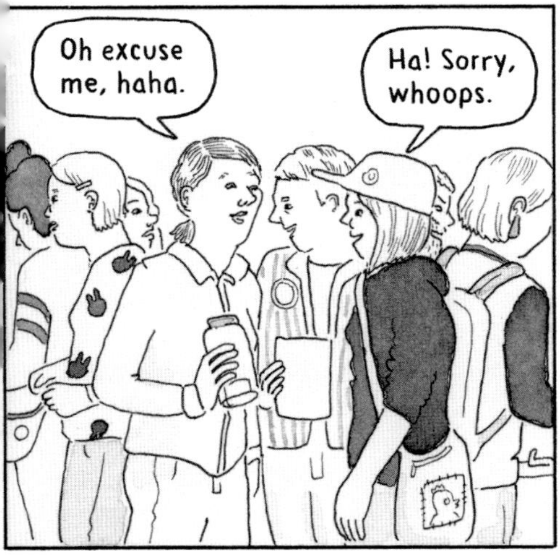
Oh excuse me, haha.
Ha! Sorry, whoops.

Every jerk, a character.

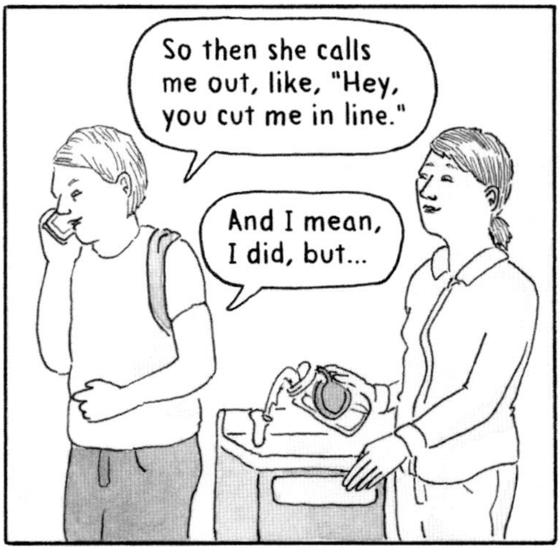
So then she calls me out, like, "Hey, you cut me in line."
And I mean, I did, but...

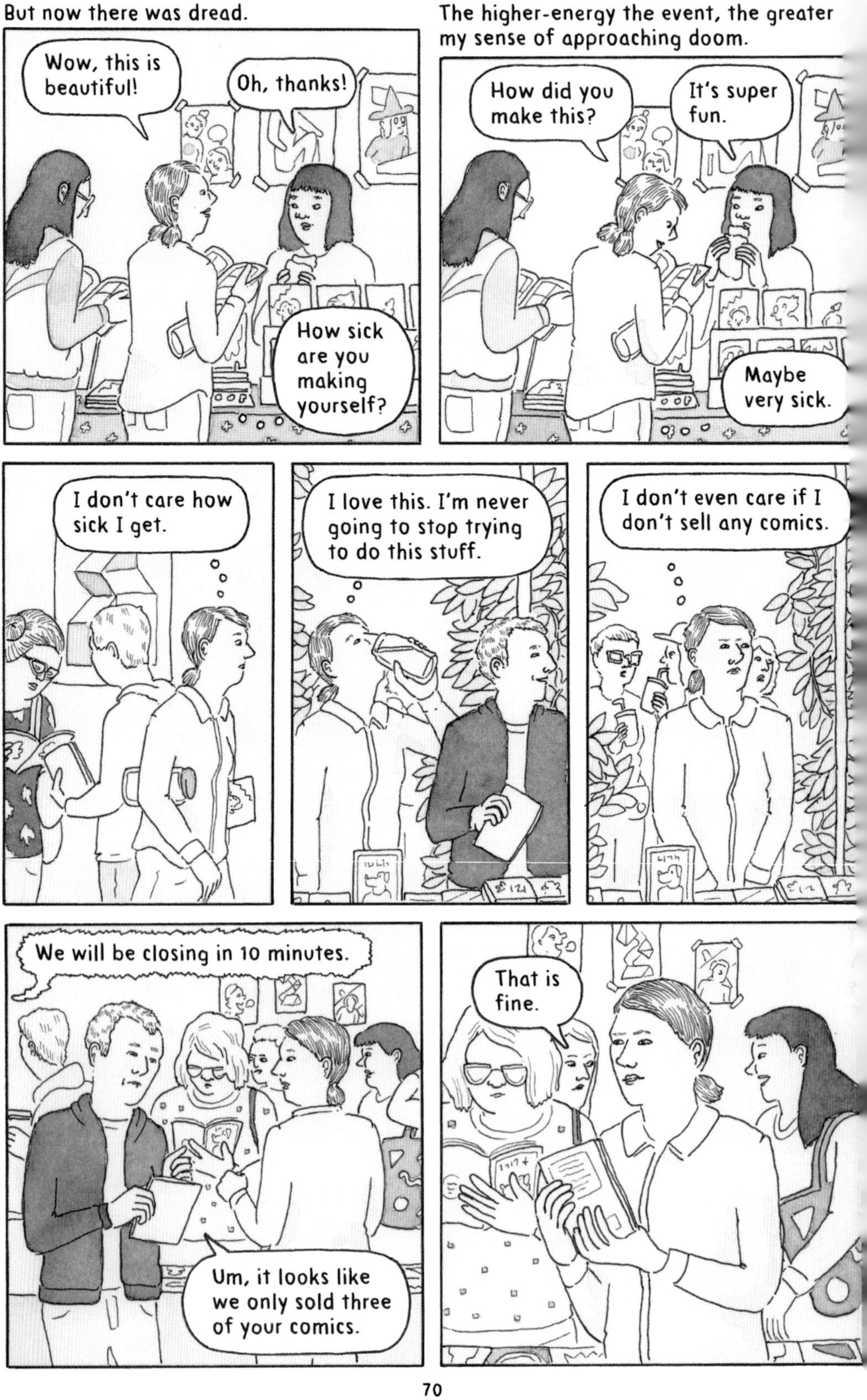
But now there was dread.
Wow, this is beautiful!
Oh, thanks!
How sick are you making yourself?
The higher-energy the event, the greater my sense of approaching doom.
How did you make this?
It's super fun.
Maybe very sick.
I don't care how sick I get.
I love this. I'm never going to stop trying to do this stuff.
I don't even care if I don't sell any comics.
We will be closing in 10 minutes.
Um, it looks like we only sold three of your comics.
That is fine.

As the years went on, the dread became present even when I was at home.

Day to day, there was a quiet, tedious vigilance.

'or example, wondering what sitting up t a desk could be costing me.

BEEP BEEP BEEP

Should I have been lying down while I worked?

Without medical advice, I'd turned to advice online for patients of a disease that *sounded* like what I could be sick with.

The advice was nothing wild like, "Buy this pricey supplement regimen."

Although I'd fallen for that a few times.

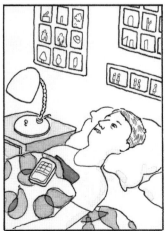

It was common-sense advice. You know, don't stand if you can sit. Don't run if you can walk.

BEEP BEEP BEEP

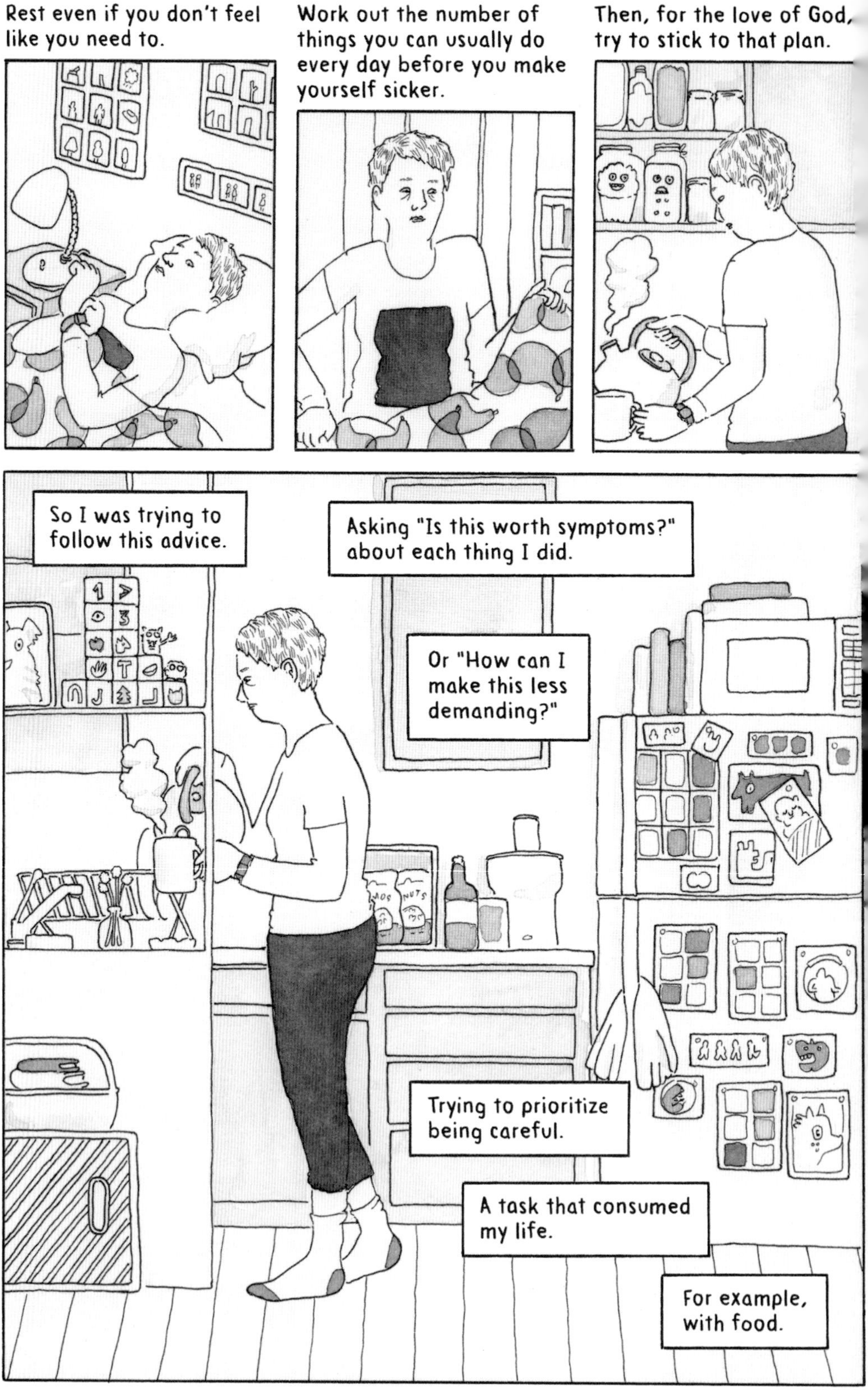
Rest even if you don't feel like you need to.
Work out the number of things you can usually do every day before you make yourself sicker.
Then, for the love of God, try to stick to that plan.
So I was trying to follow this advice.
Asking "Is this worth symptoms?" about each thing I did.
Or "How can I make this less demanding?"
Trying to prioritize being careful.
A task that consumed my life.
For example, with food.

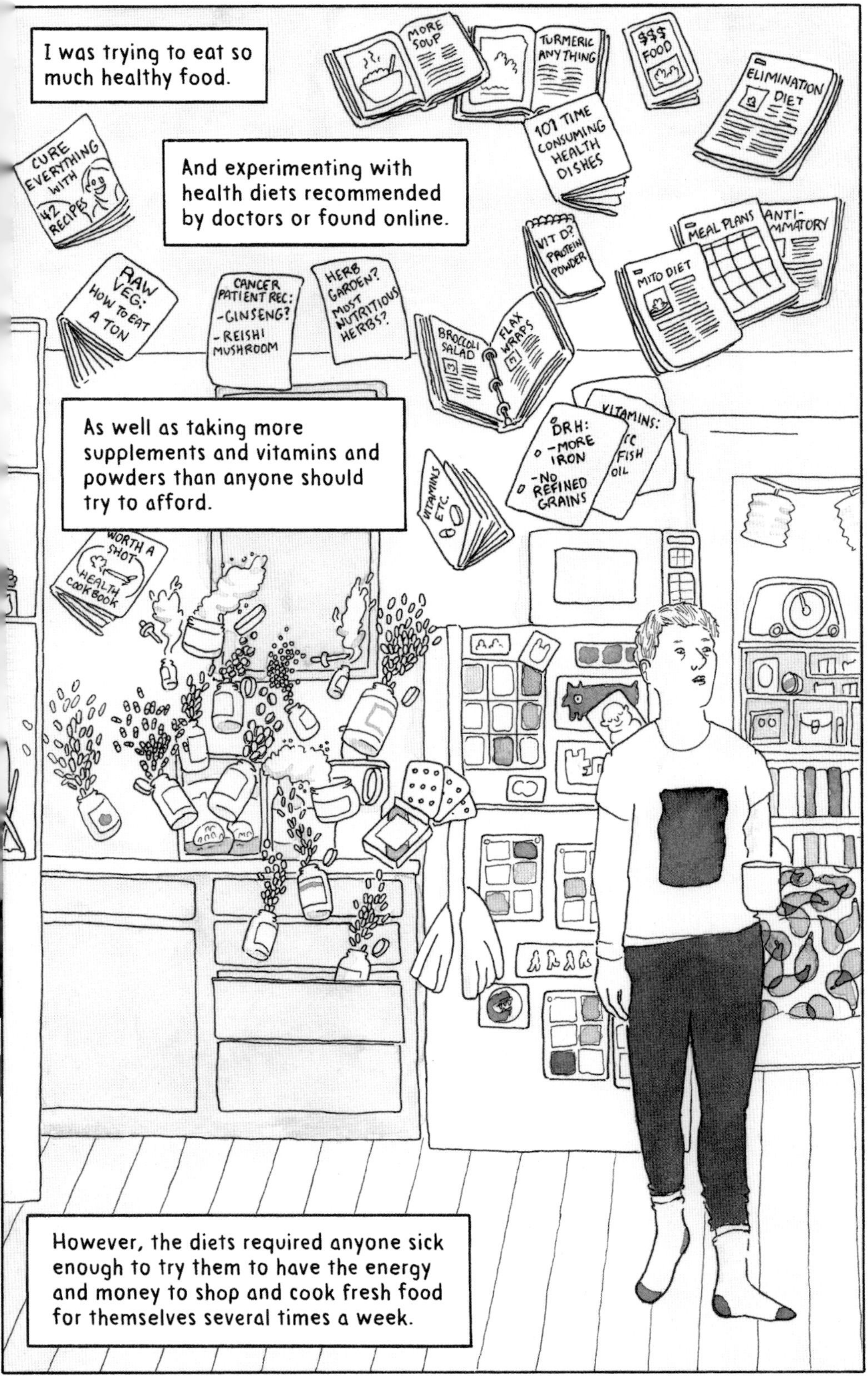

I was trying to eat so much healthy food.
MORE SOUP
TURMERIC ANYTHING
$$$ FOOD
ELIMINATION DIET
101 TIME CONSUMING HEALTH DISHES
CURE EVERYTHING WITH 42 RECIPES
And experimenting with health diets recommended by doctors or found online.
VIT D? PROTEIN POWDER
MEAL PLANS
MITO DIET
RAW VEG: HOW TO EAT A TON
CANCER PATIENT REC: -GINSENG? -REISHI MUSHROOM
HERB GARDEN? MOST NUTRITIOUS HERBS?
BROCCOLI SALAD
FLAX WRAPS
DRH: -MORE IRON -NO REFINED GRAINS
VITAMINS:
FISH OIL
As well as taking more supplements and vitamins and powders than anyone should try to afford.
VITAMINS ETC.
WORTH A SHOT HEALTH COOKBOOK
However, the diets required anyone sick enough to try them to have the energy and money to shop and cook fresh food for themselves several times a week.

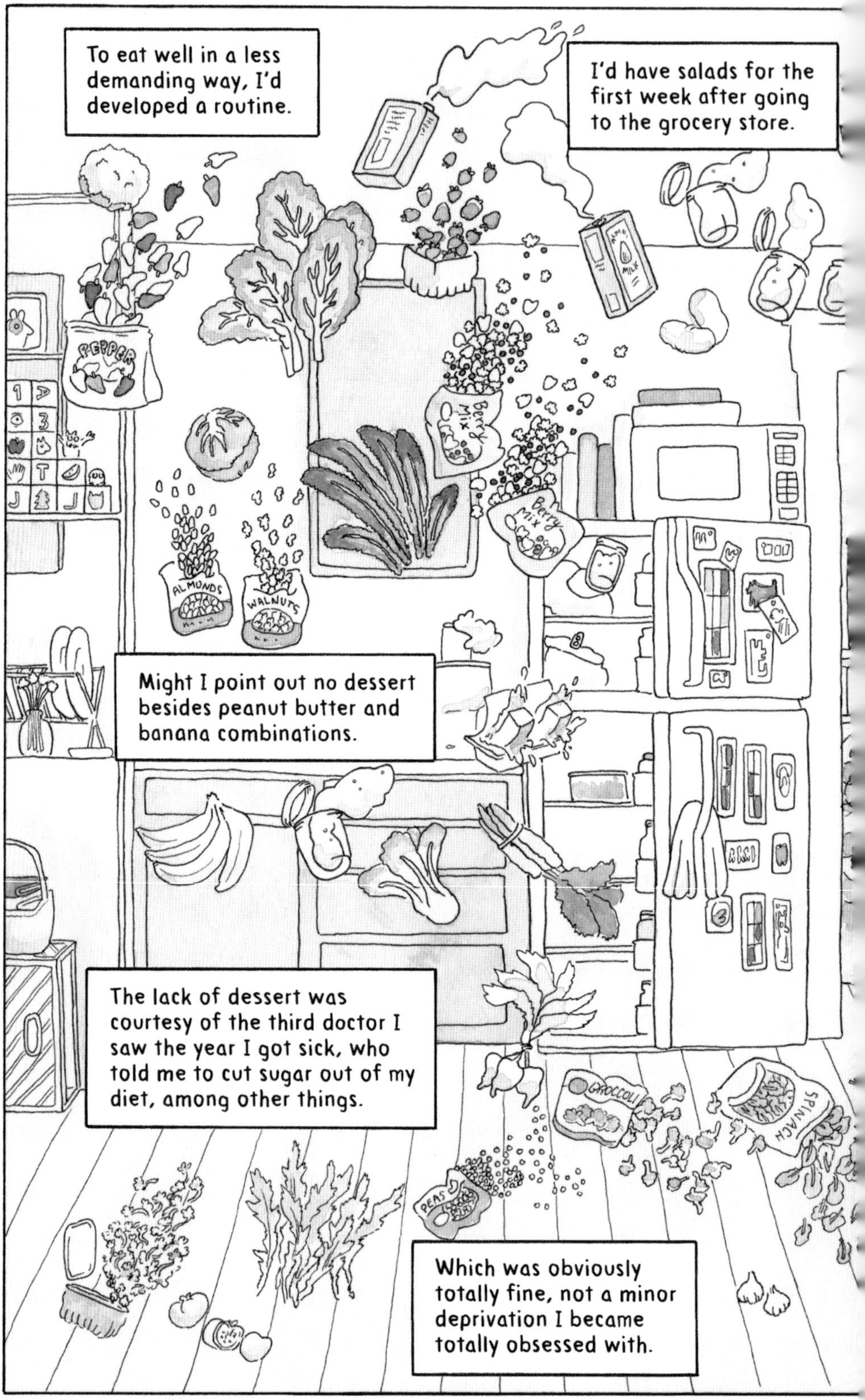

To eat well in a less demanding way, I'd developed a routine.
I'd have salads for the first week after going to the grocery store.
PEPPER
Berry Mix
Berry Mix
ALMONDS
WALNUTS
Might I point out no dessert besides peanut butter and banana combinations.
The lack of dessert was courtesy of the third doctor I saw the year I got sick, who told me to cut sugar out of my diet, among other things.
BROCCOLI
SPINACH
PEAS
Which was obviously totally fine, not a minor deprivation I became totally obsessed with.

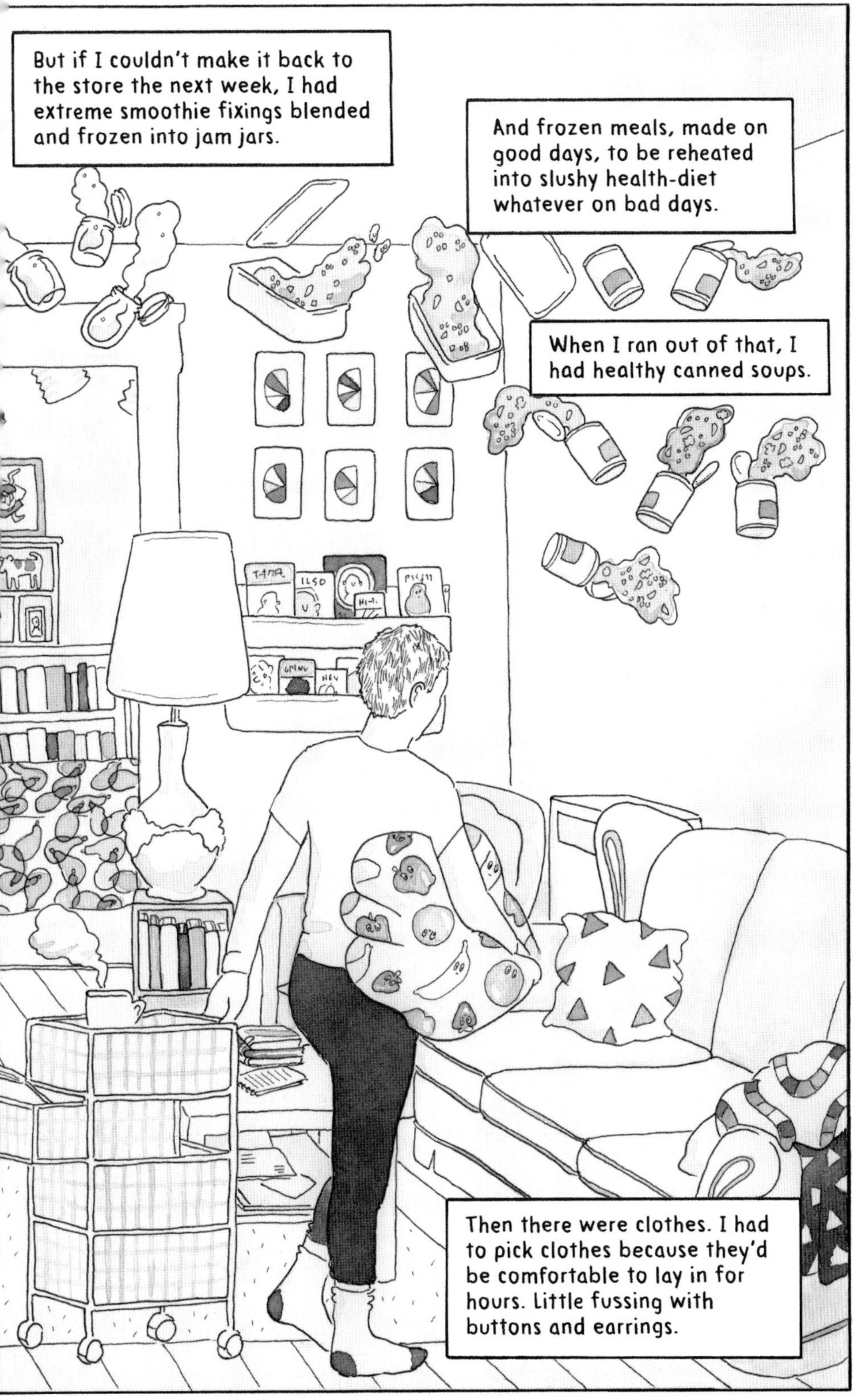
But if I couldn't make it back to the store the next week, I had extreme smoothie fixings blended and frozen into jam jars.
And frozen meals, made on good days, to be reheated into slushy health-diet whatever on bad days.
When I ran out of that, I had healthy canned soups.
Then there were clothes. I had to pick clothes because they'd be comfortable to lay in for hours. Little fussing with buttons and earrings.

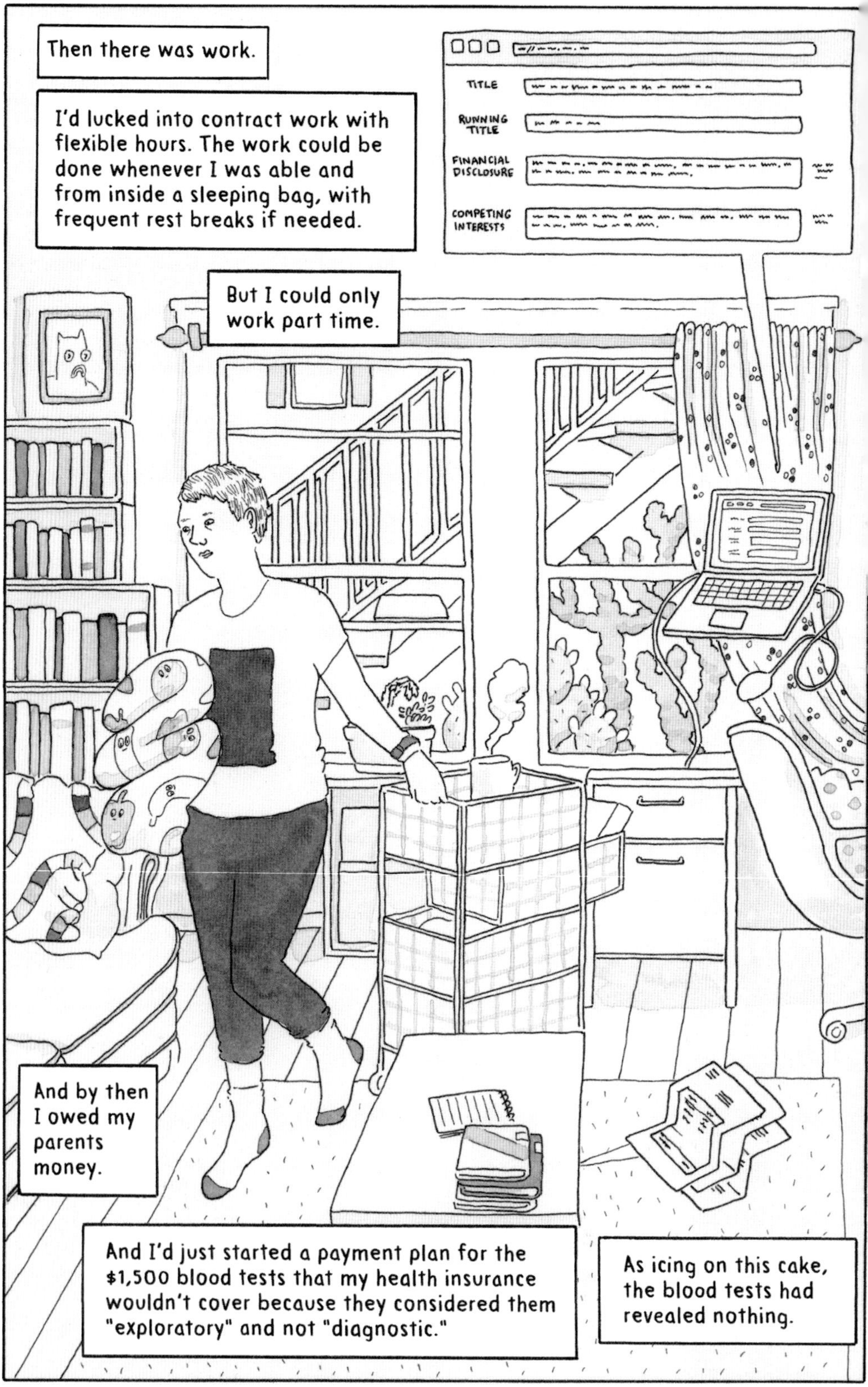
Then there was work.
I'd lucked into contract work with flexible hours. The work could be done whenever I was able and from inside a sleeping bag, with frequent rest breaks if needed.
TITLE
RUNNING TITLE
FINANCIAL DISCLOSURE
COMPETING INTERESTS
But I could only work part time.
And by then I owed my parents money.
And I'd just started a payment plan for the $1,500 blood tests that my health insurance wouldn't cover because they considered them "exploratory" and not "diagnostic."
As icing on this cake, the blood tests had revealed nothing.

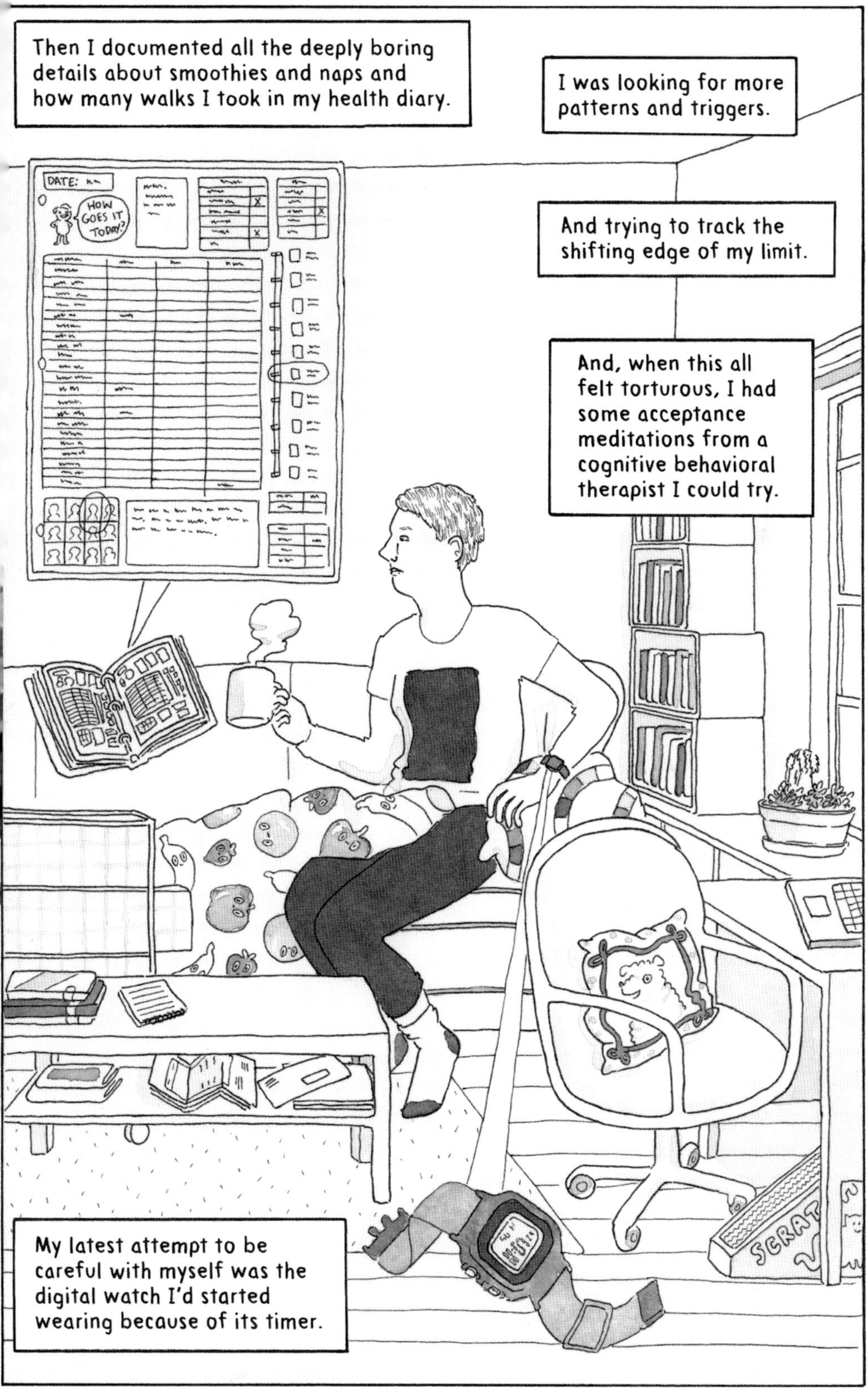
Then I documented all the deeply boring details about smoothies and naps and how many walks I took in my health diary.
I was looking for more patterns and triggers.
And trying to track the shifting edge of my limit.
And, when this all felt torturous, I had some acceptance meditations from a cognitive behavioral therapist I could try.
DATE:
HOW GOES IT TODAY?
SCRAT
My latest attempt to be careful with myself was the digital watch I'd started wearing because of its timer.

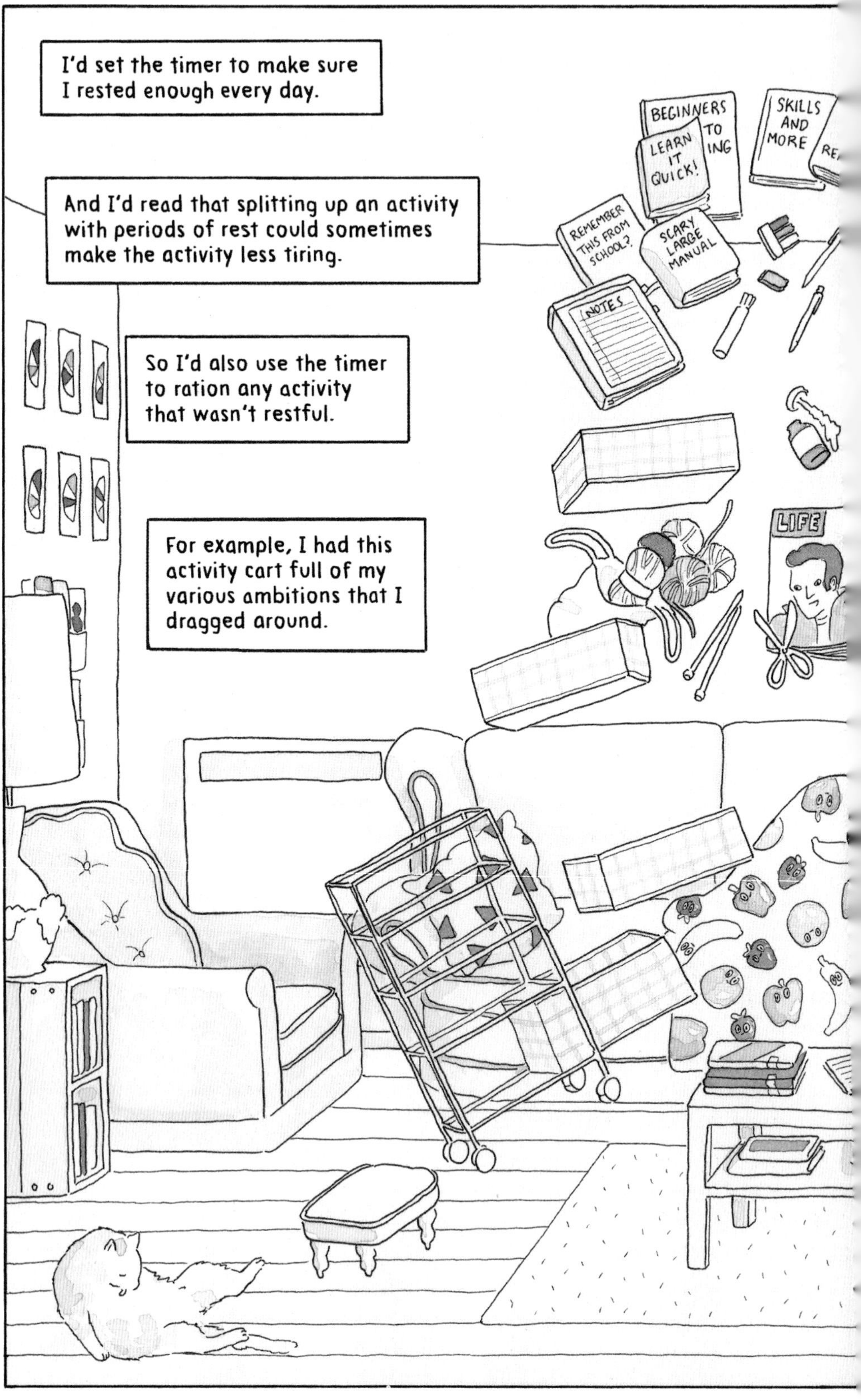
I'd set the timer to make sure I rested enough every day.
And I'd read that splitting up an activity with periods of rest could sometimes make the activity less tiring.
So I'd also use the timer to ration any activity that wasn't restful.
For example, I had this activity cart full of my various ambitions that I dragged around.
BEGINNERS
LEARN IT QUICK!
SKILLS AND MORE
REMEMBER THIS FROM SCHOOL?
SCARY LARGE MANUAL
NOTES
LIFE

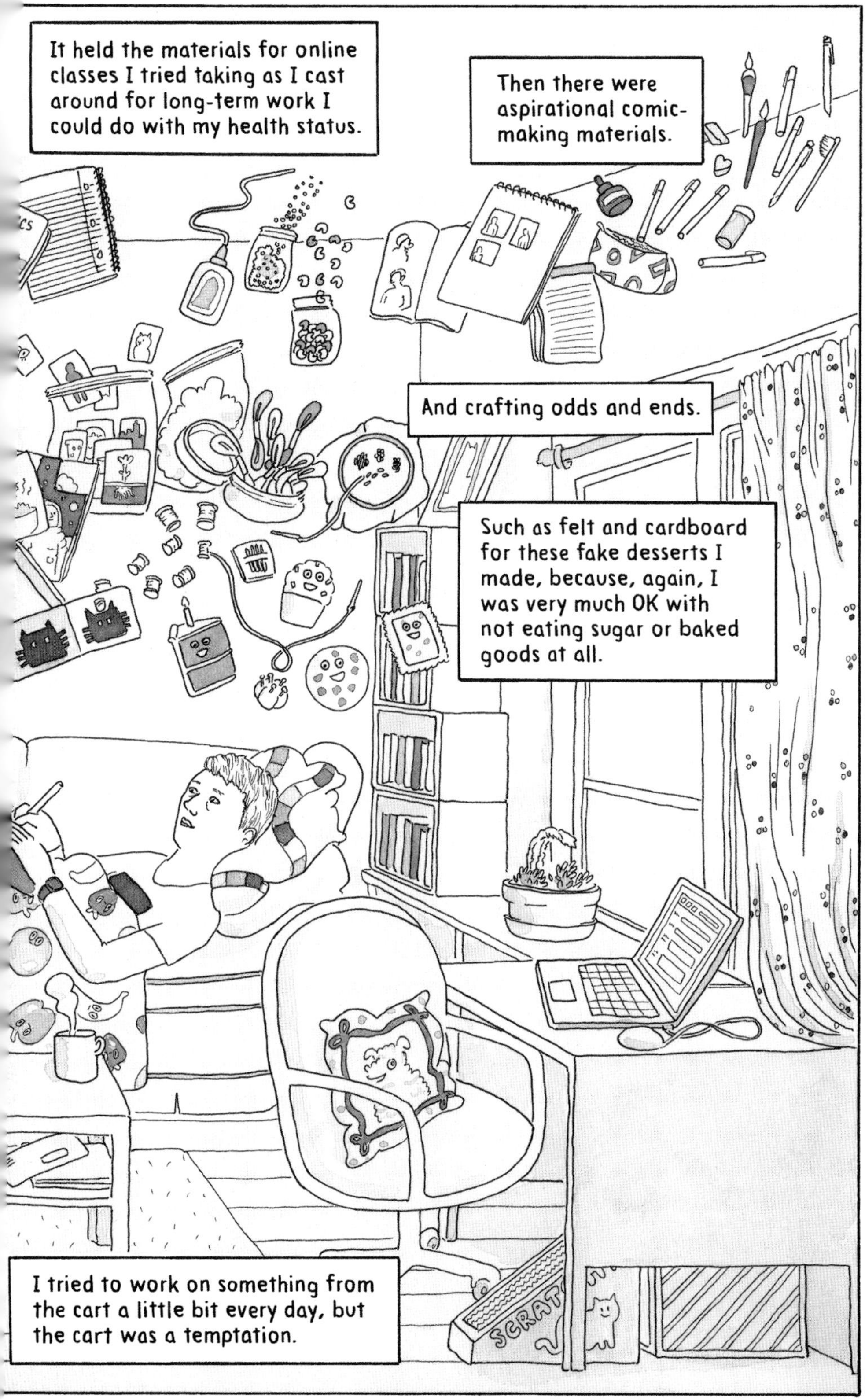

It held the materials for online classes I tried taking as I cast around for long-term work I could do with my health status.
Then there were aspirational comic-making materials.
And crafting odds and ends.
Such as felt and cardboard for these fake desserts I made, because, again, I was very much OK with not eating sugar or baked goods at all.
I tried to work on something from the cart a little bit every day, but the cart was a temptation.

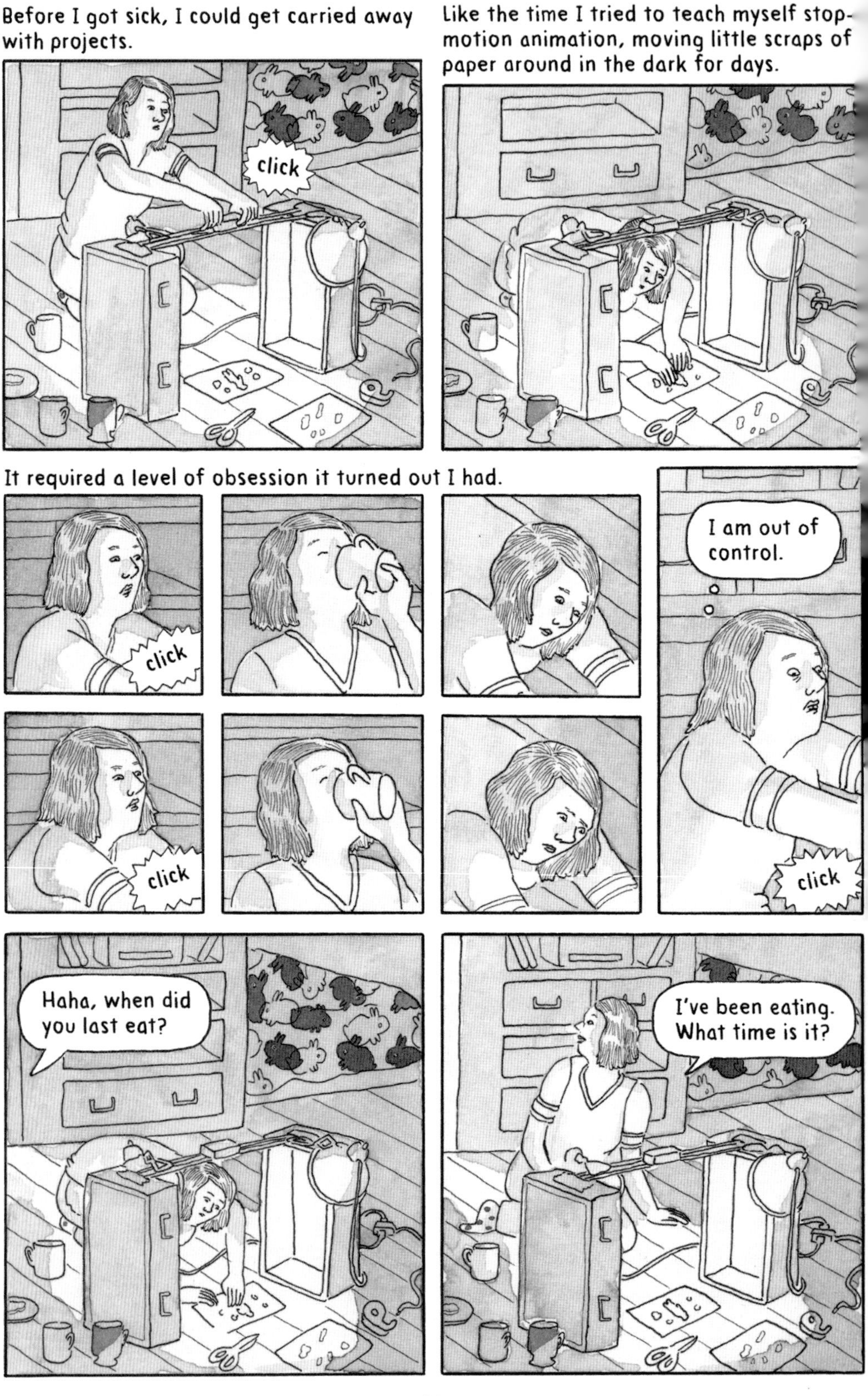
Before I got sick, I could get carried away with projects.
click
Like the time I tried to teach myself stop-motion animation, moving little scraps of paper around in the dark for days.
It required a level of obsession it turned out I had.
click
click
I am out of control.
click
Haha, when did you last eat?
I've been eating. What time is it?

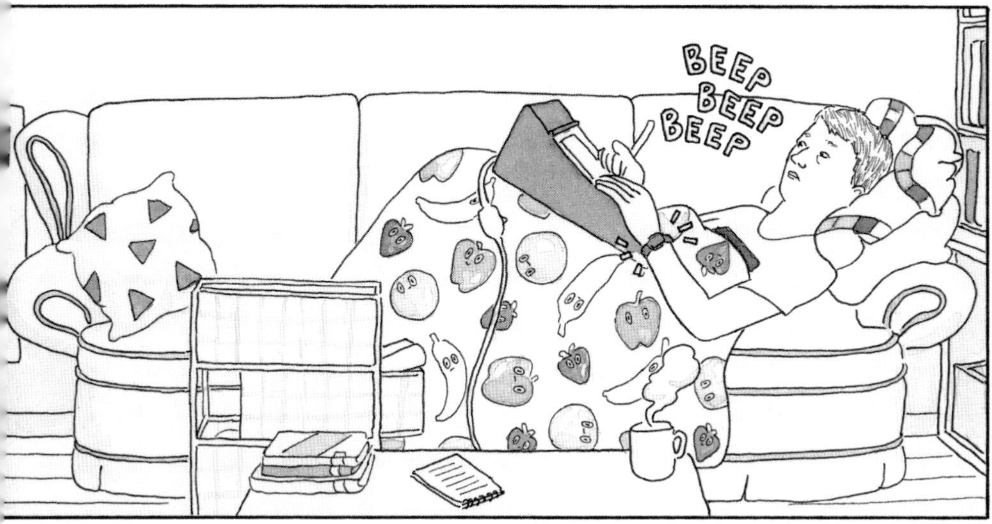
BEEP
BEEP
BEEP

The problem was the timer just notified me when it was time to stop.

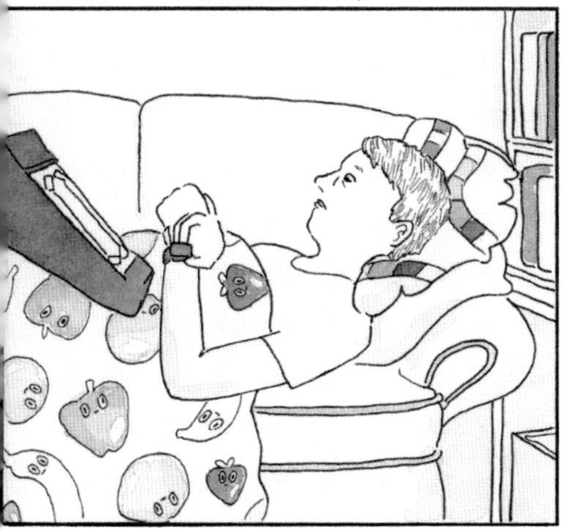

The whole system actually depended on my virtuous self-denial.

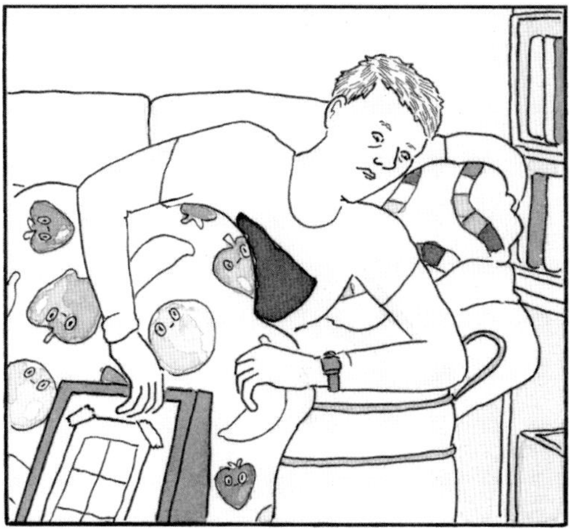

And whether I could sustain it day in, day out.

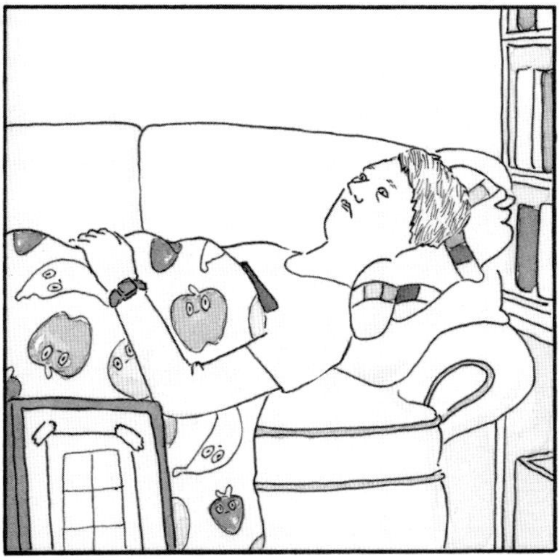

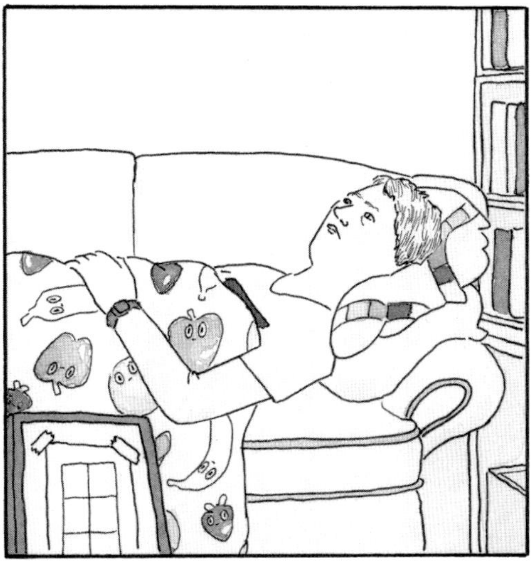

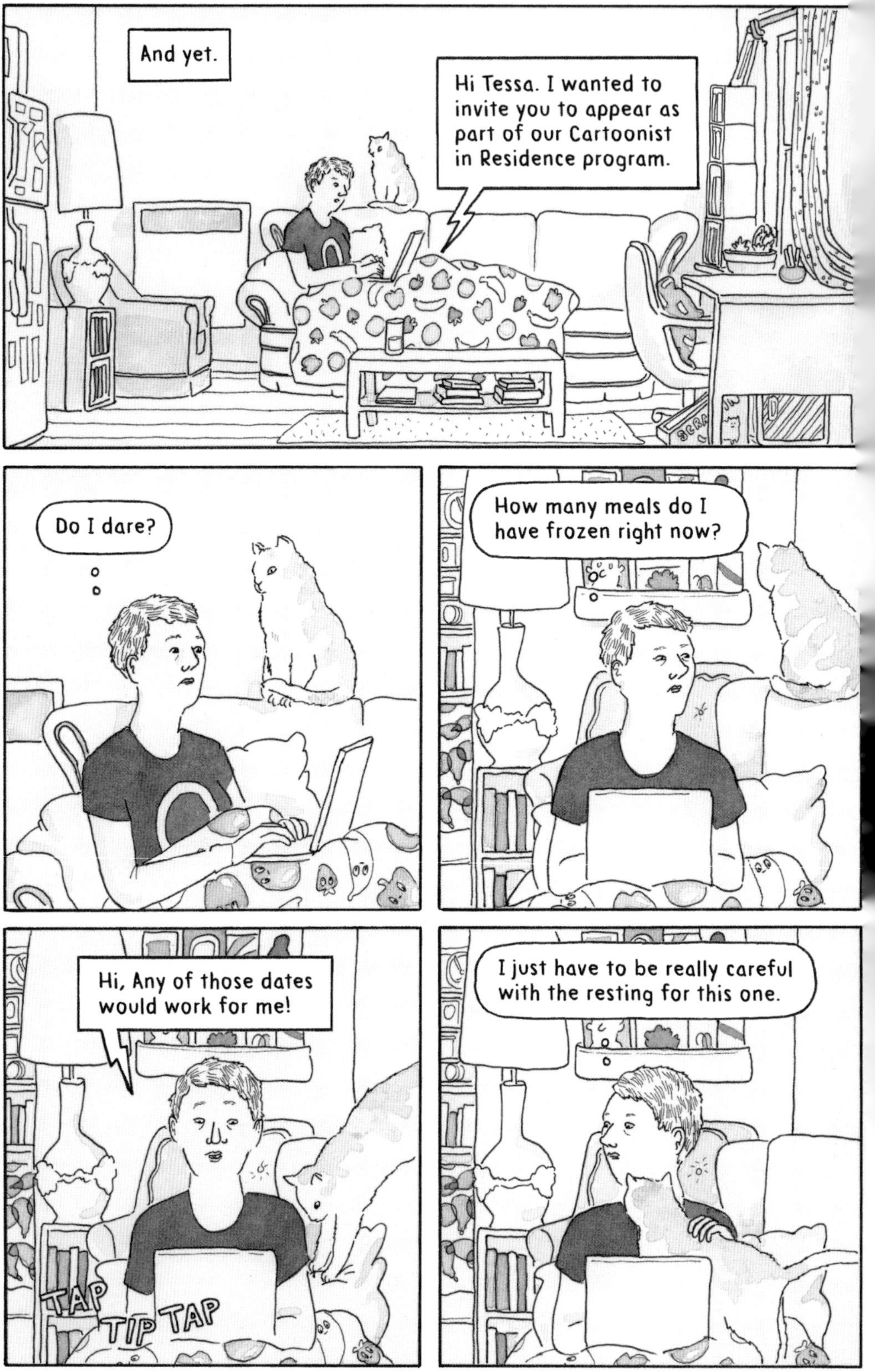
And yet.
Hi Tessa. I wanted to invite you to appear as part of our Cartoonist in Residence program.
Do I dare?
How many meals do I have frozen right now?
Hi, Any of those dates would work for me!
TAP TIP TAP
I just have to be really careful with the resting for this one.

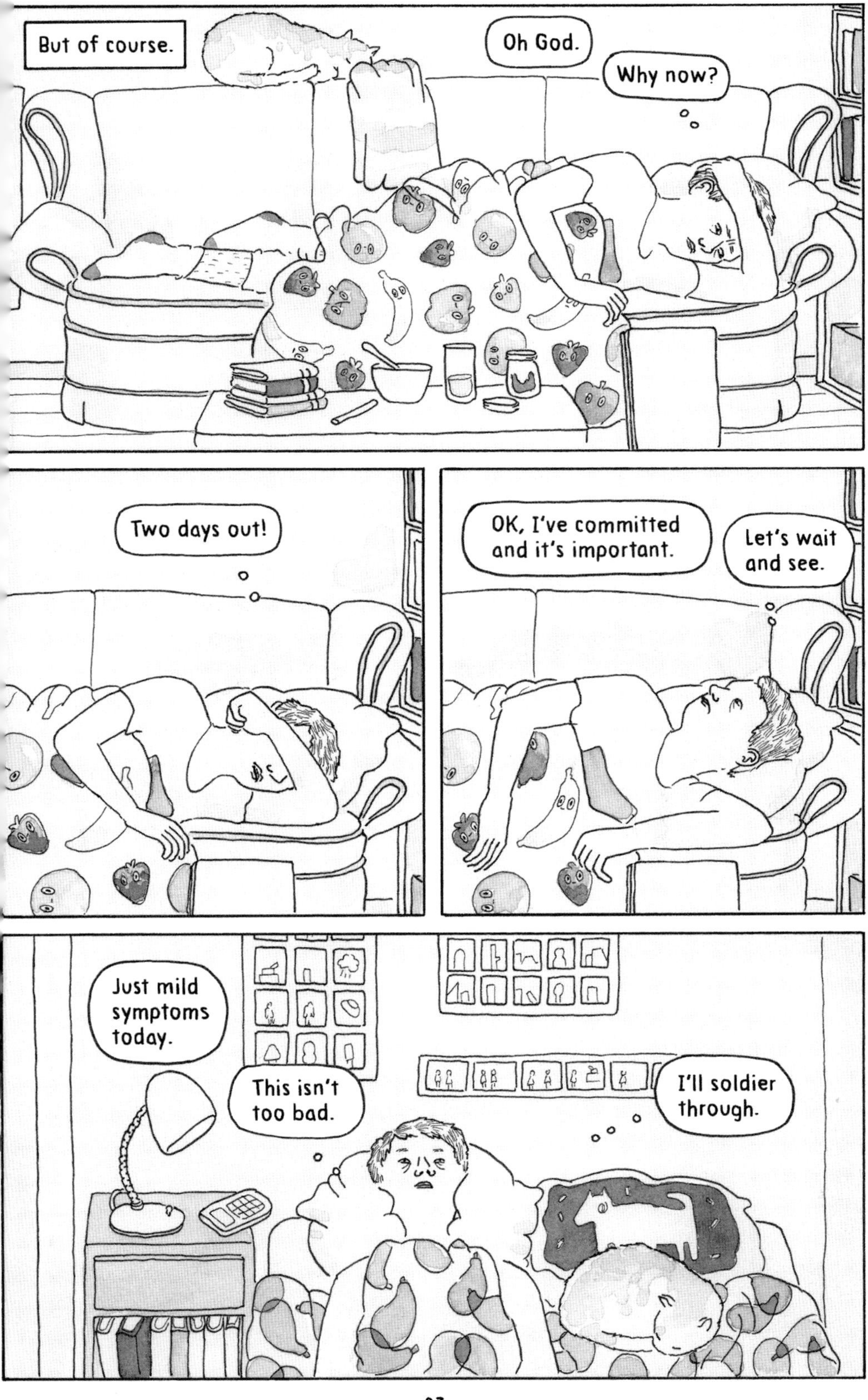
But of course.
Oh God.
Why now?
Two days out!
OK, I've committed and it's important.
Let's wait and see.
Just mild symptoms today.
This isn't too bad.
I'll soldier through.

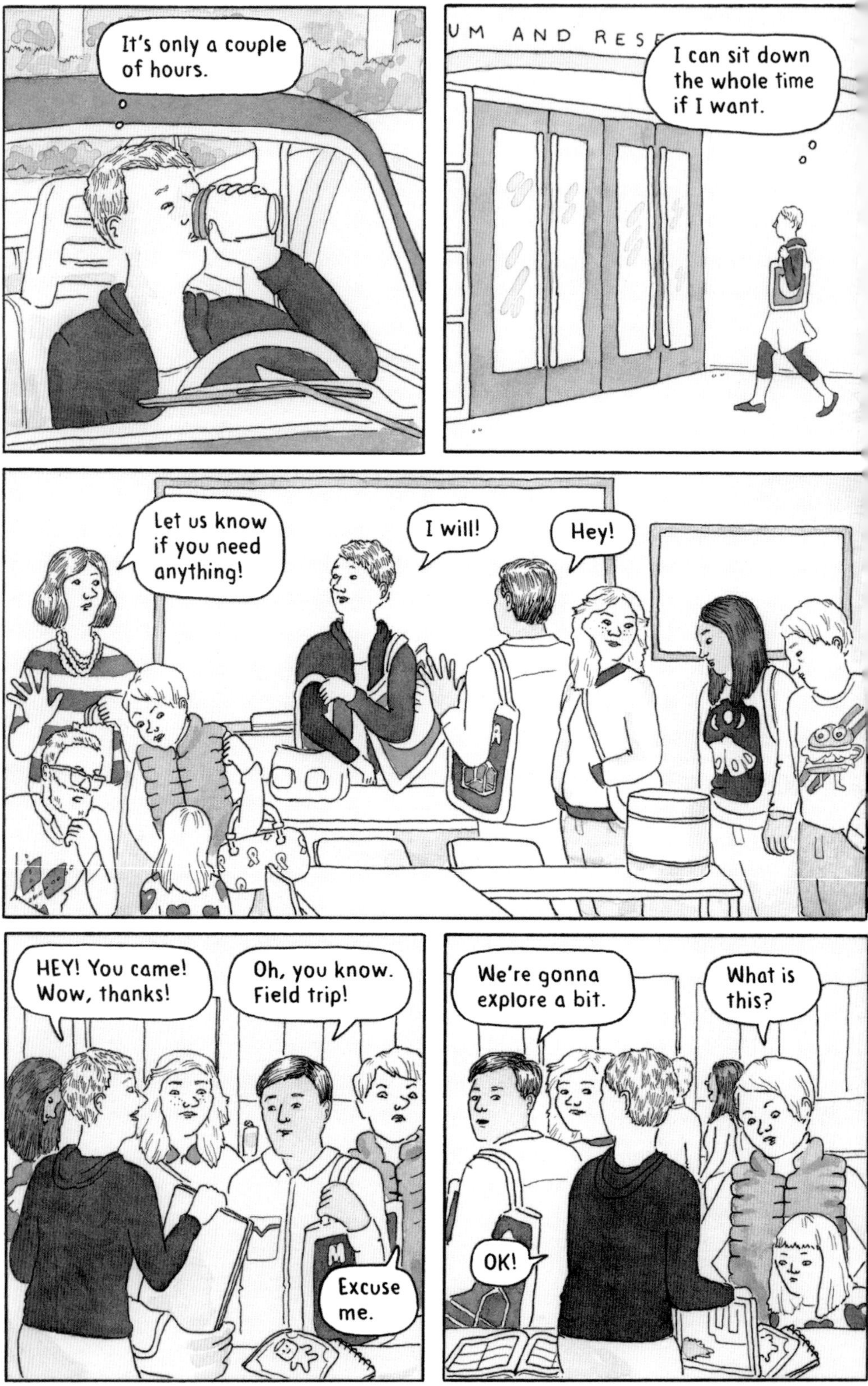
It's only a couple of hours.
UM AND RESE
I can sit down the whole time if I want.
Let us know if you need anything!
I will!
Hey!
HEY! You came! Wow, thanks!
Oh, you know. Field trip!
Excuse me.
We're gonna explore a bit.
What is this?
OK!

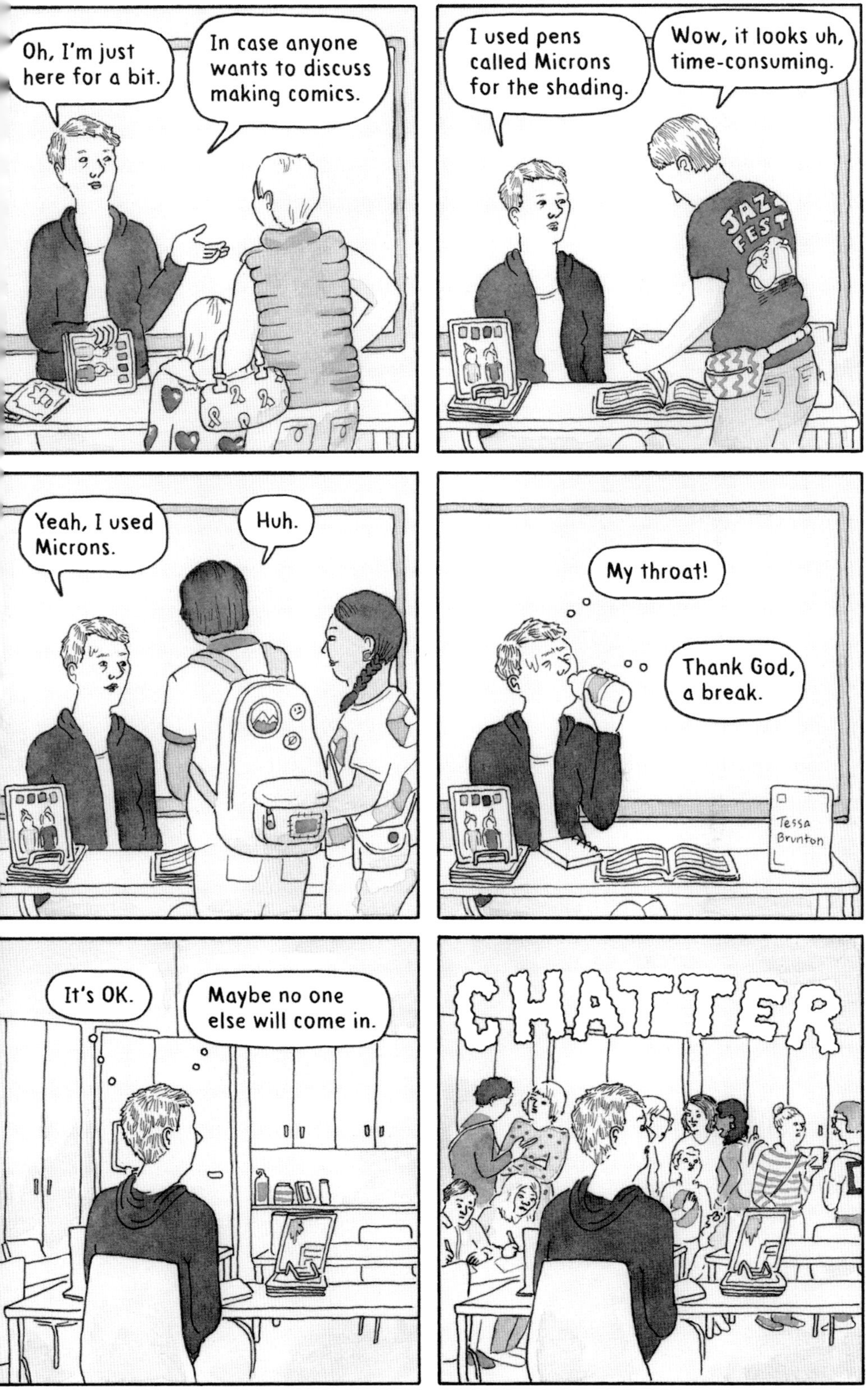
Oh, I'm just here for a bit.
In case anyone wants to discuss making comics.
I used pens called Microns for the shading.
Wow, it looks uh, time-consuming.
Yeah, I used Microns.
Huh.
My throat!
Thank God, a break.
Tessa Brunton
It's OK.
Maybe no one else will come in.
CHATTER

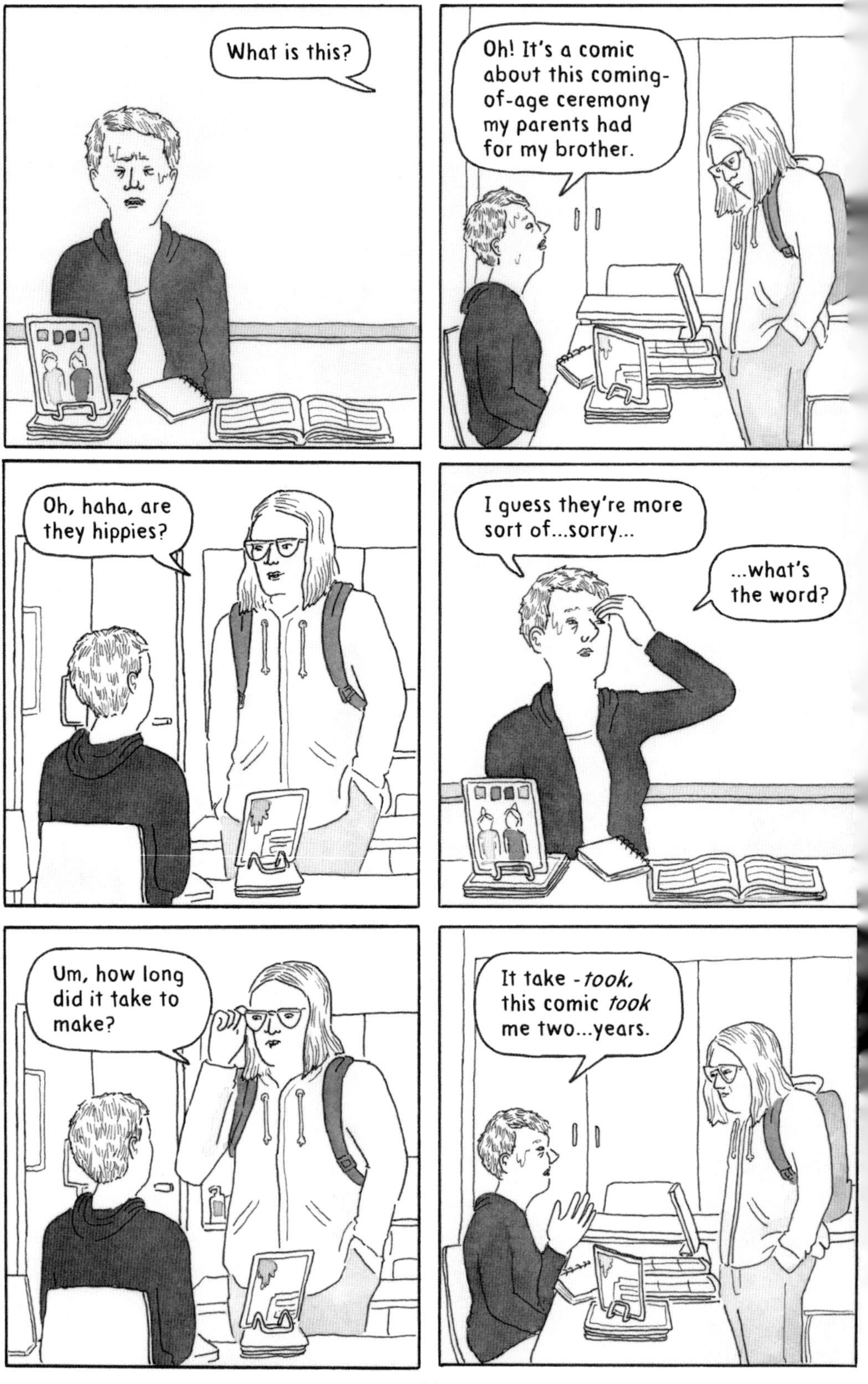
What is this?
Oh! It's a comic about this coming-of-age ceremony my parents had for my brother.
Oh, haha, are they hippies?
I guess they're more sort of...sorry...
...what's the word?
Um, how long did it take to make?
It take -*took*, this comic *took* me two...years.

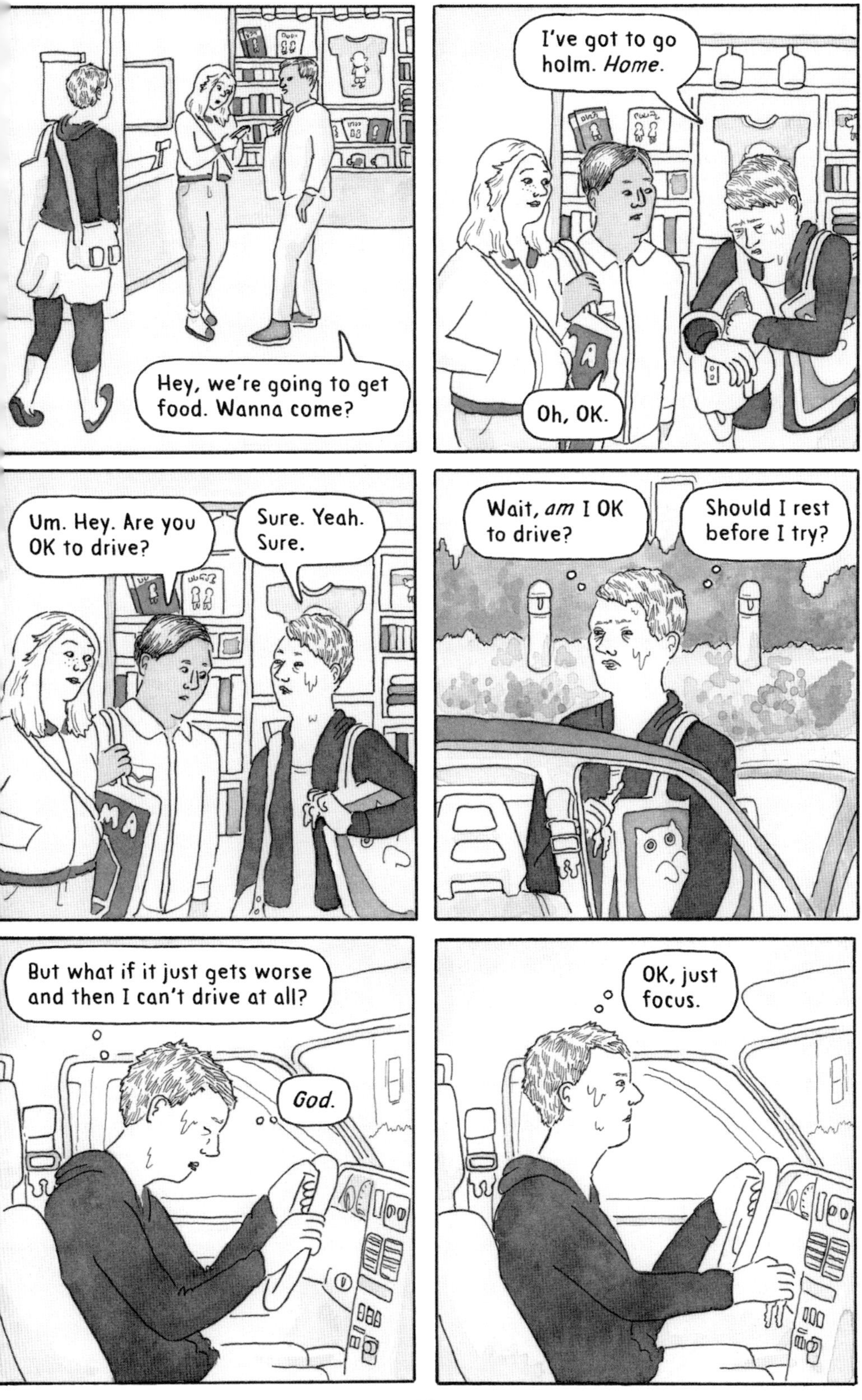
Hey, we're going to get food. Wanna come?
I've got to go holm. *Home*.
Oh, OK.
Um. Hey. Are you OK to drive?
Sure. Yeah. Sure.
Wait, *am* I OK to drive?
Should I rest before I try?
But what if it just gets worse and then I can't drive at all?
God.
OK, just focus.

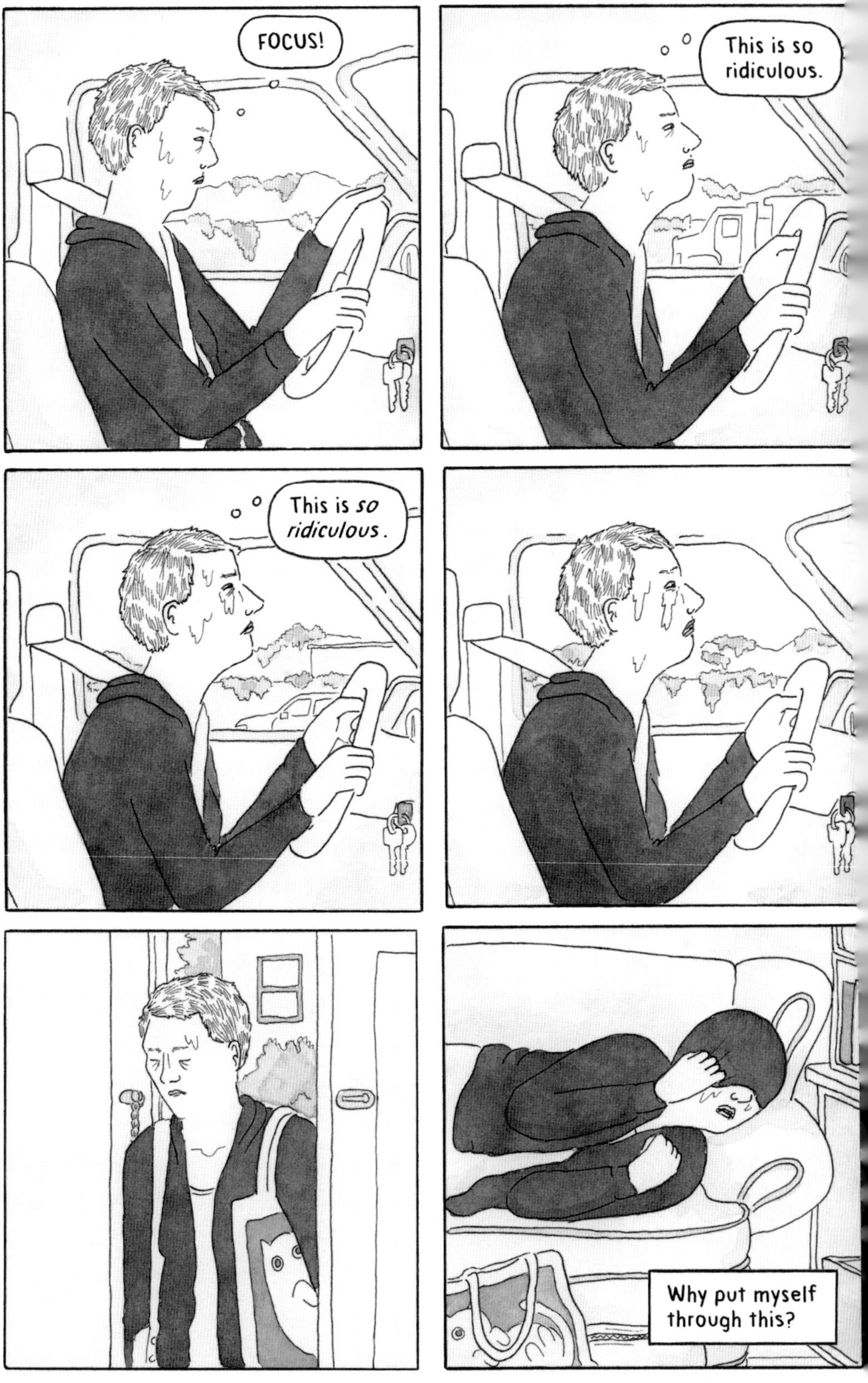
FOCUS!
This is so ridiculous.
This is *so ridiculous*.
Why put myself through this?

king "Is this worth more symptoms?" out each thing I did sorted my life, but ways I couldn't easily explain to myself.

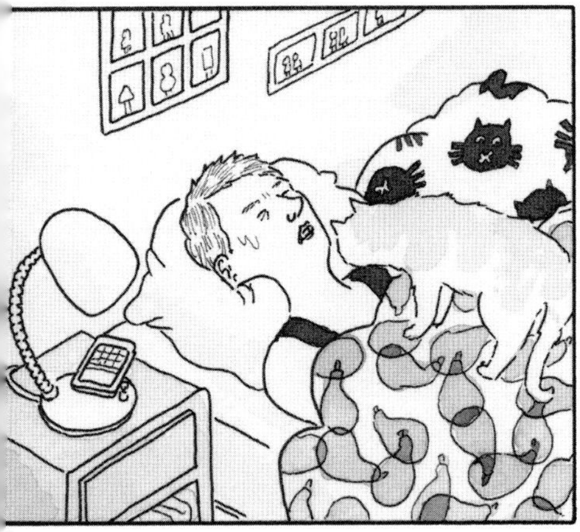

Why did I still have my bike in my apartment, taking up precious floor space?

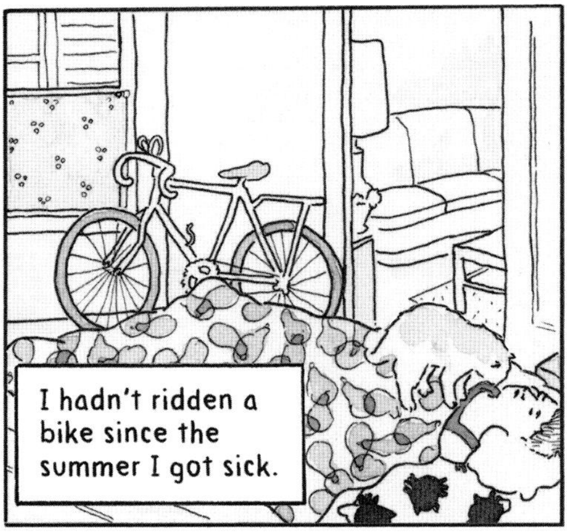
I hadn't ridden a bike since the summer I got sick.

r that matter, why was I spending my mited energy making fake desserts and en putting them around my apartment?

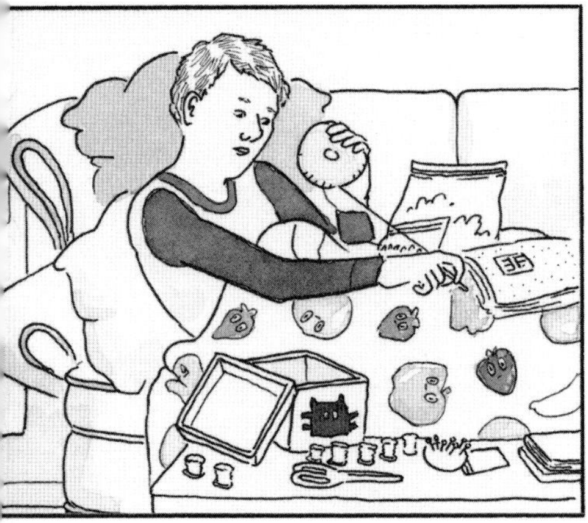

Did I want to remind myself of what I couldn't have?

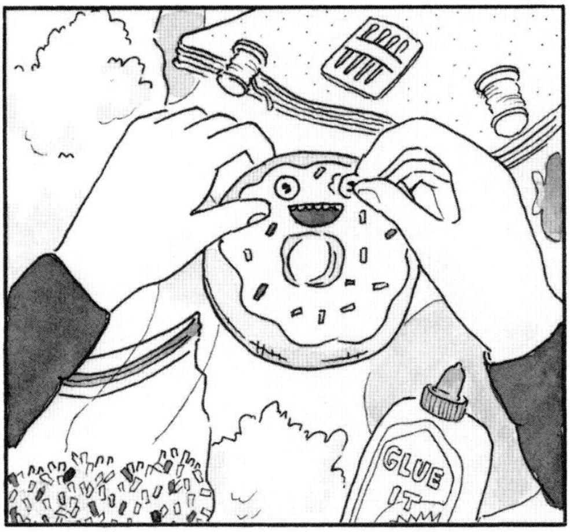
GLUE IT

nd say I was having a good day, which neant I felt like I was on the last day of flu: not vigorous, but not actively uffering, and able to act well.

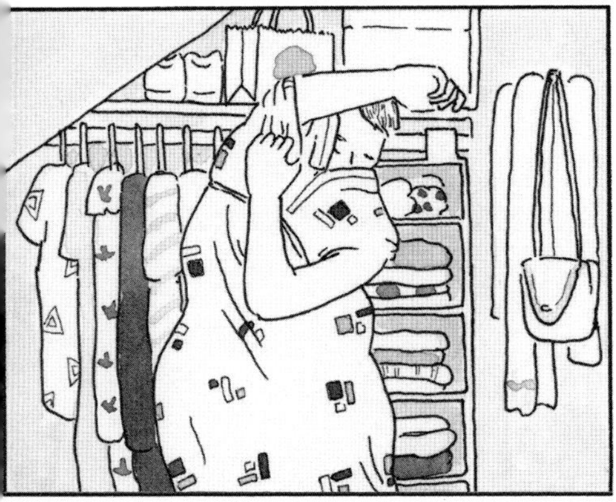

Why would I try to go to a party? Did I want to just drop a bomb on my body?

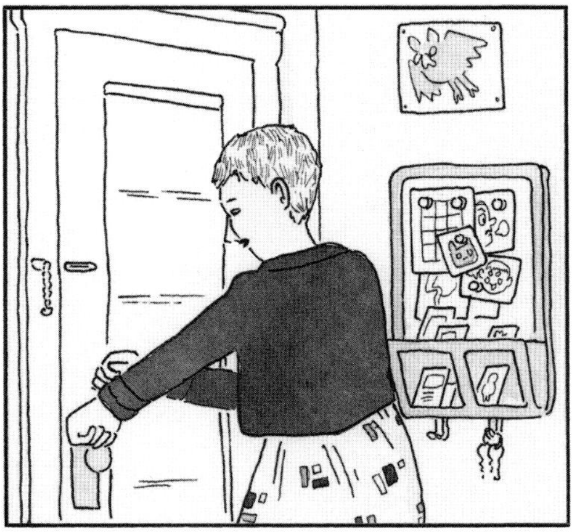

If I was going to use precious energy to leave my apartment, there were so many things I *needed* to do.

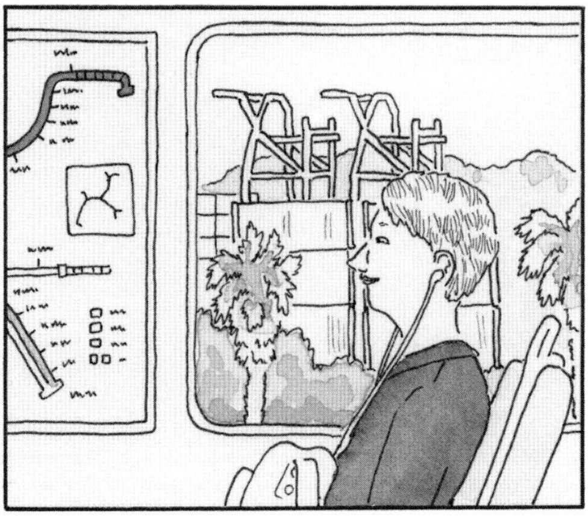

And if I insisted on seeing people instead of getting my tail light fixed, why couldn I at least make it illness-friendly?

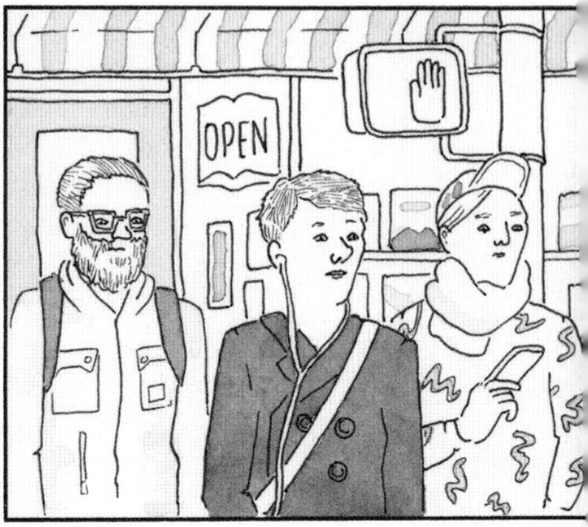
OPEN

You know, why not have a short, low-key visit with a friend in my apartment?

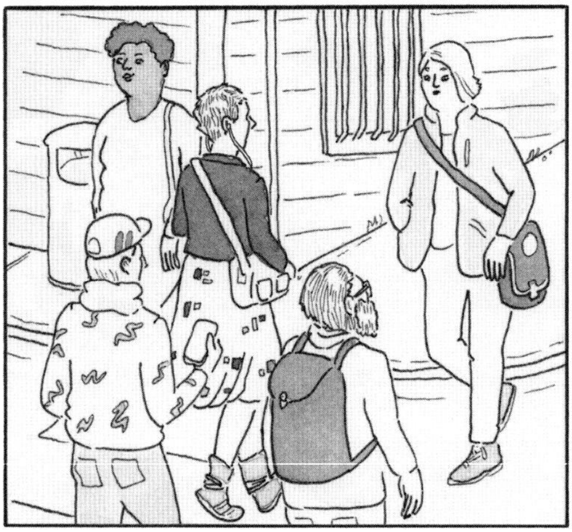

Just drinking decaffeinated tea for an hou on a couch followed by rest, with no noise or cold or walking.

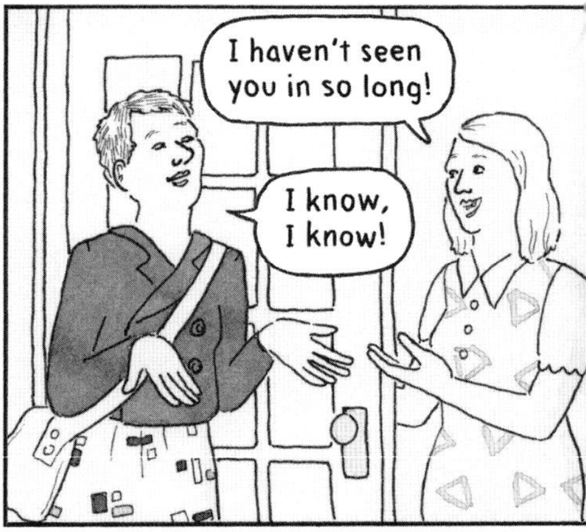
I haven't seen you in so long!
I know, I know!

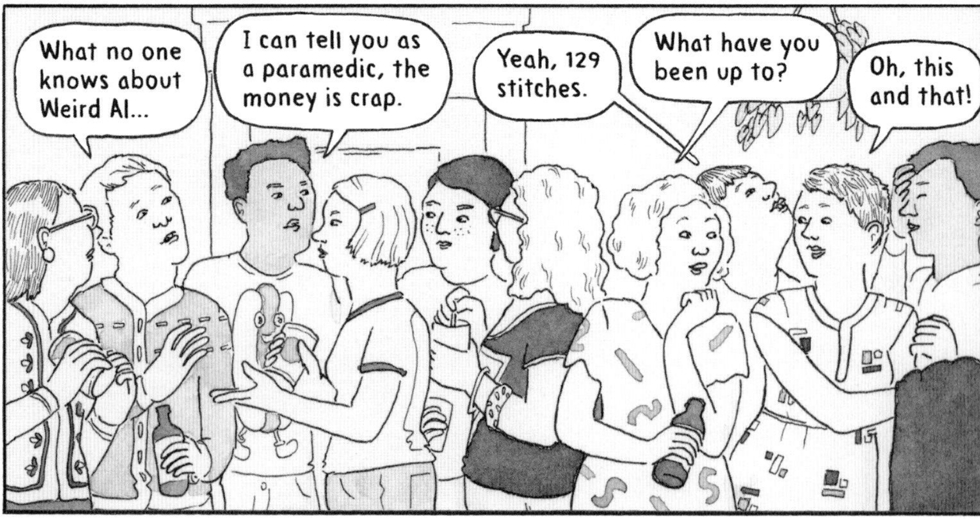
What no one knows about Weird Al...
I can tell you as a paramedic, the money is crap.
Yeah, 129 stitches.
What have you been up to?
Oh, this and that!

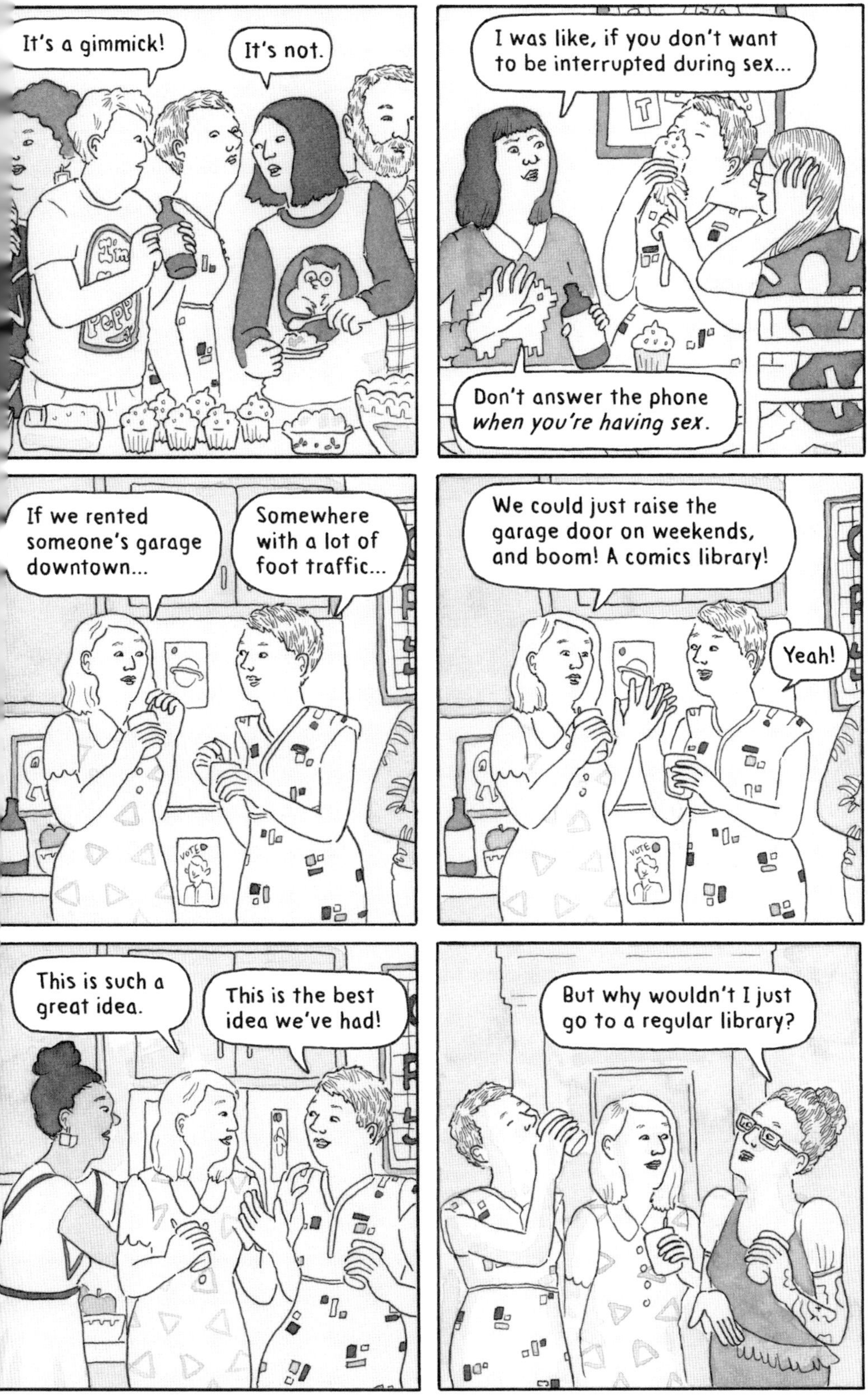
It's a gimmick!
It's not.
I'm Pepp
I was like, if you don't want to be interrupted during sex...
Don't answer the phone *when you're having sex*.
If we rented someone's garage downtown...
Somewhere with a lot of foot traffic...
We could just raise the garage door on weekends, and boom! A comics library!
Yeah!
This is such a great idea.
This is the best idea we've had!
But why wouldn't I just go to a regular library?

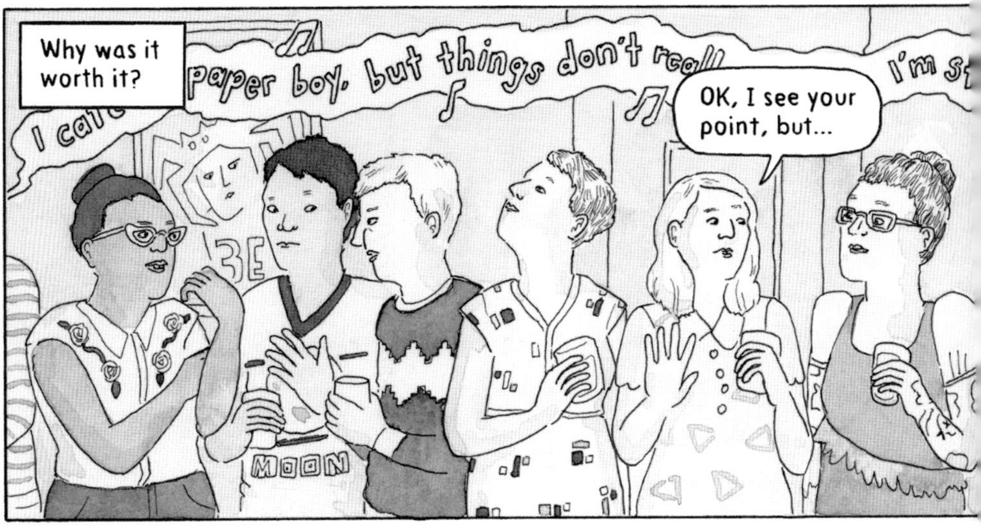
Why was it worth it?
paper boy, but things don't
OK, I see your point, but...
MOON

It wasn't just fun for the sake of fun.

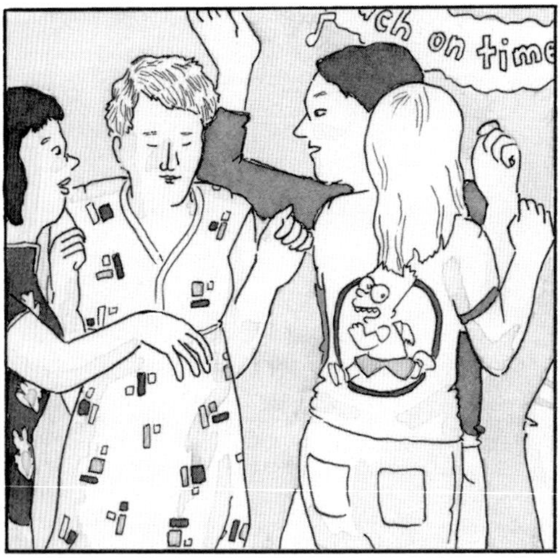
on time

It felt good to do something on my terms

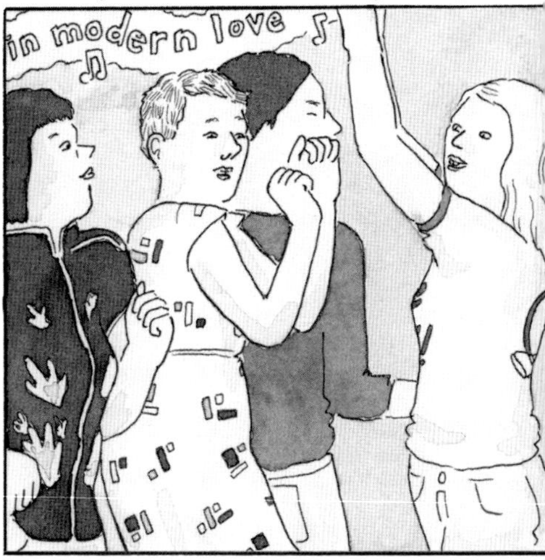
in modern love

As in, I felt like my "old self."

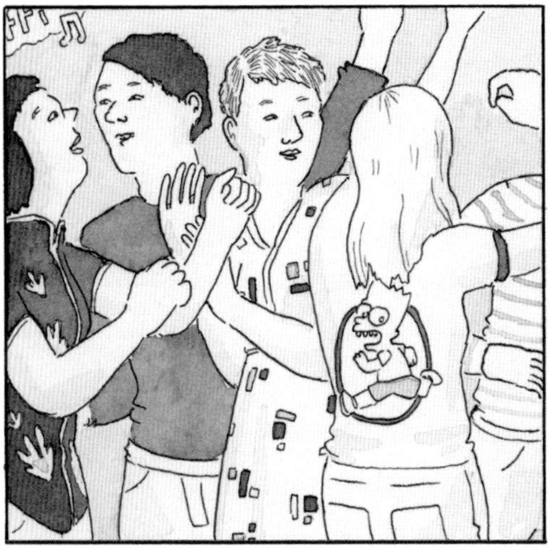

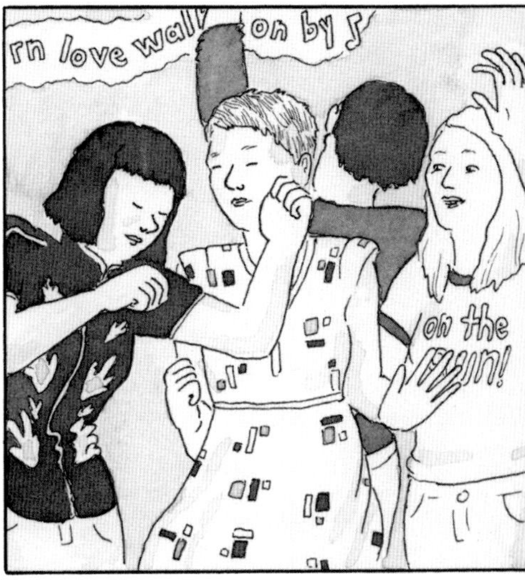
rn love wal
on by
on the

y last healthy year was 25. It was not
ome banner year of my life, full of
aditions I wanted to carry on.

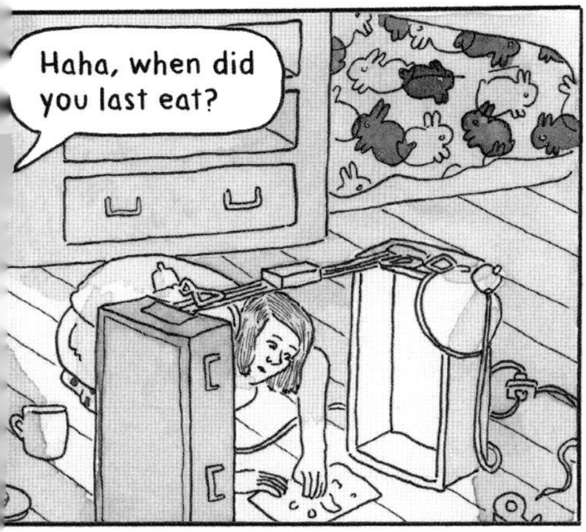
Haha, when did you last eat?

The best thing I can say about that year is I was becoming good friends with my housemate.

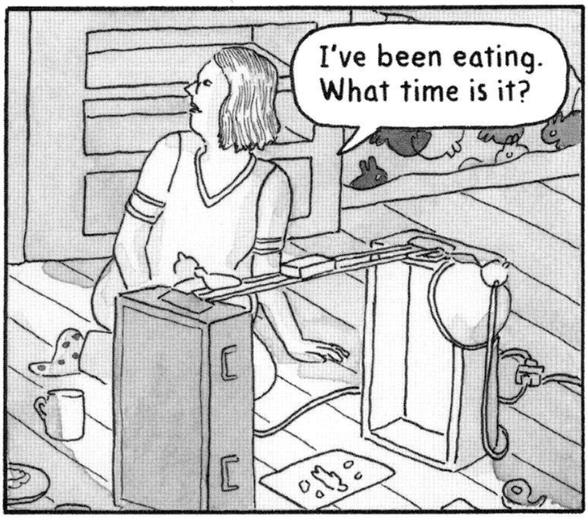
I've been eating. What time is it?

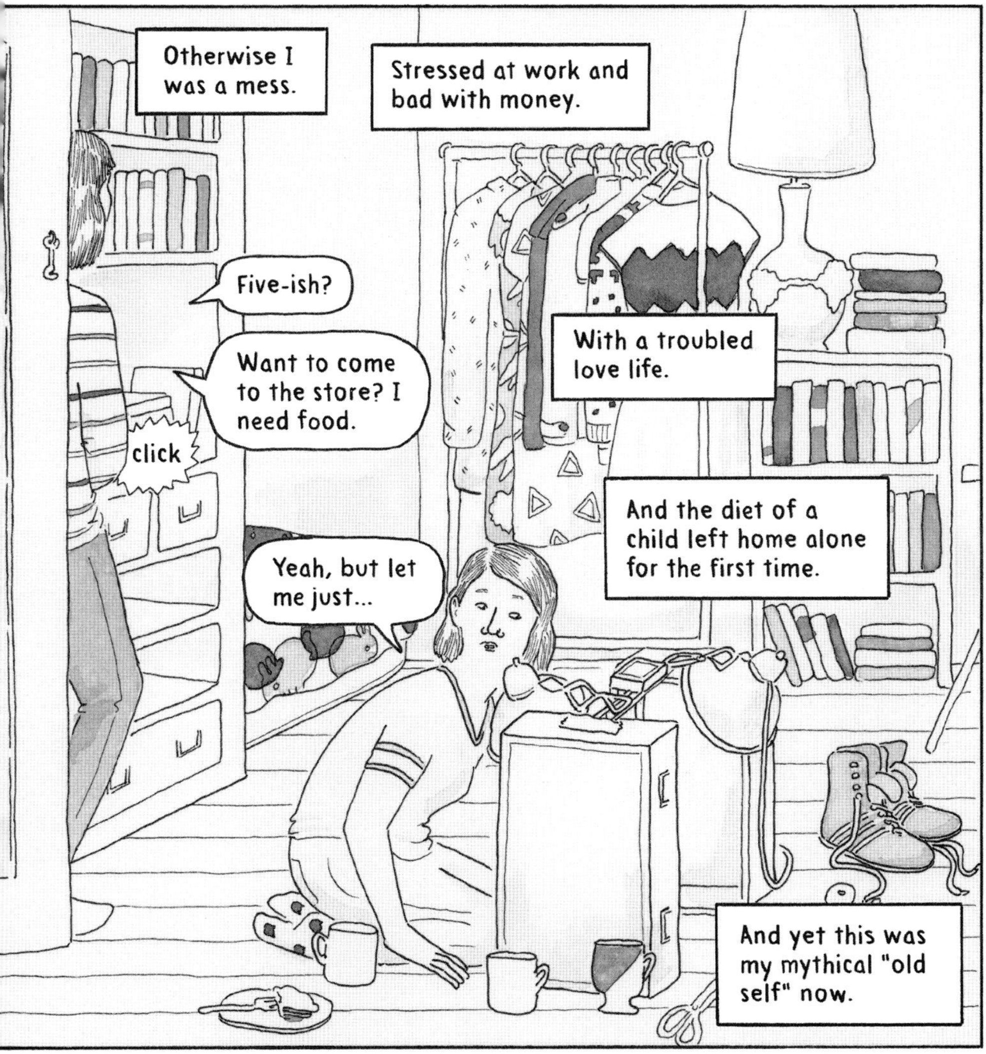
Otherwise I was a mess.
Stressed at work and bad with money.
Five-ish?
Want to come to the store? I need food.
click
With a troubled love life.
Yeah, but let me just...
And the diet of a child left home alone for the first time.
And yet this was my mythical "old self" now.

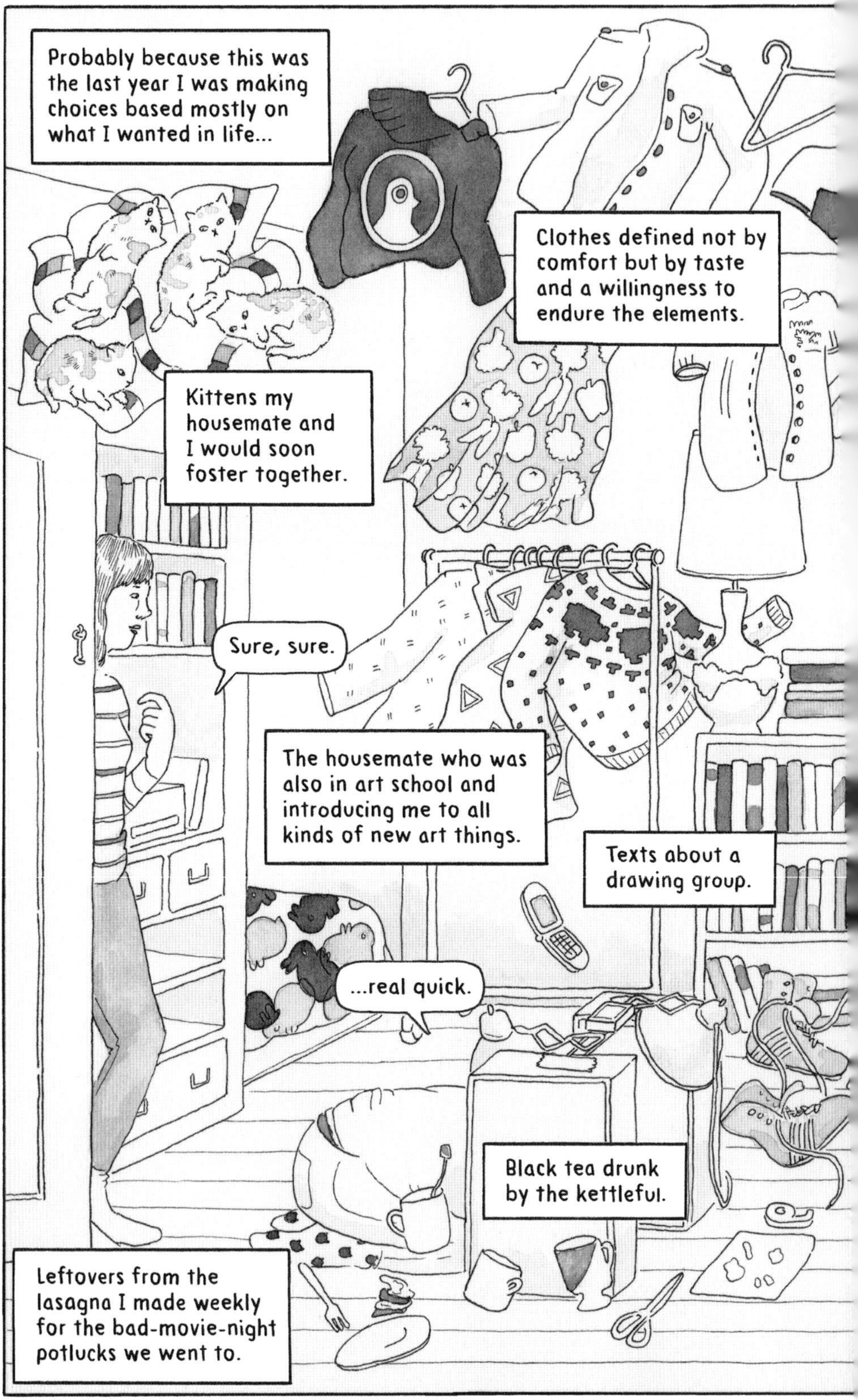
Probably because this was the last year I was making choices based mostly on what I wanted in life...
Clothes defined not by comfort but by taste and a willingness to endure the elements.
Kittens my housemate and I would soon foster together.
Sure, sure.
The housemate who was also in art school and introducing me to all kinds of new art things.
Texts about a drawing group.
...real quick.
Black tea drunk by the kettleful.
Leftovers from the lasagna I made weekly for the bad-movie-night potlucks we went to.

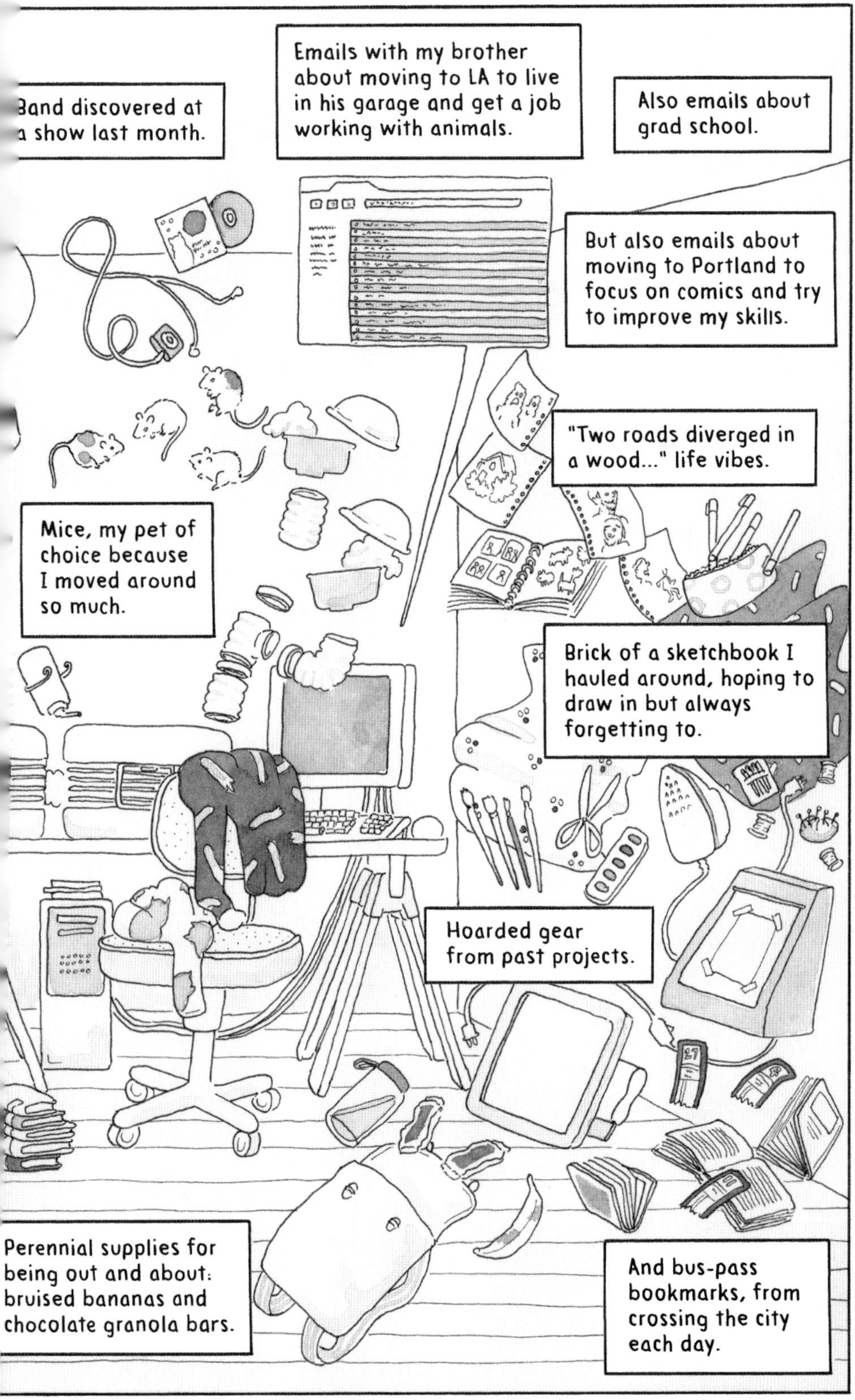

Band discovered at a show last month.
Emails with my brother about moving to LA to live in his garage and get a job working with animals.
Also emails about grad school.
But also emails about moving to Portland to focus on comics and try to improve my skills.
Mice, my pet of choice because I moved around so much.
"Two roads diverged in a wood..." life vibes.
Brick of a sketchbook I hauled around, hoping to draw in but always forgetting to.
Hoarded gear from past projects.
Perennial supplies for being out and about: bruised bananas and chocolate granola bars.
And bus-pass bookmarks, from crossing the city each day.

Instead of making seemingly every choice based on the nightmare rules of the illness.

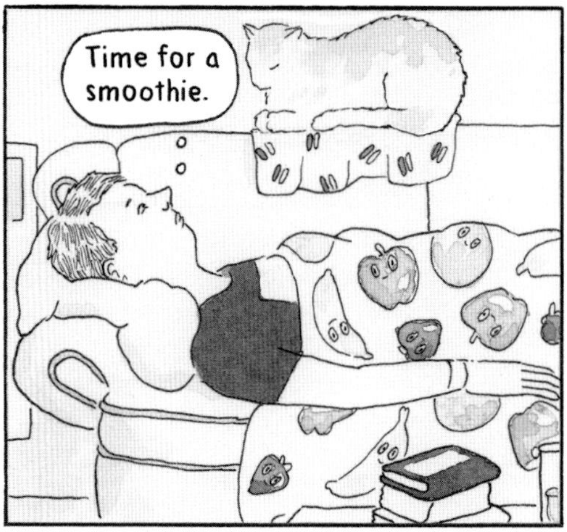
Time for a smoothie.

When you start asking "Is this worth it?" about each thing you do every day, it has an effect over time.

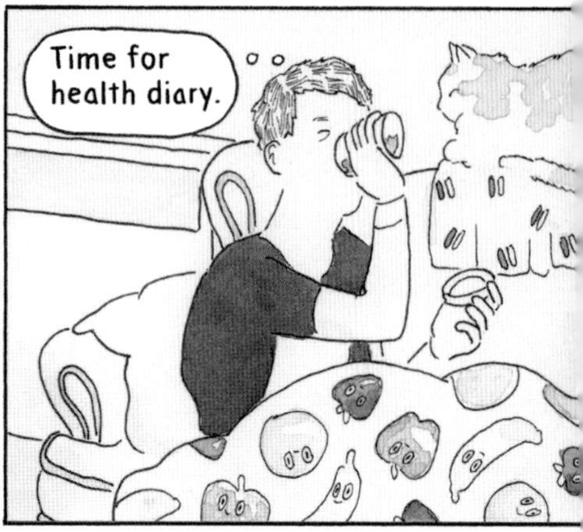
Time for health diary.

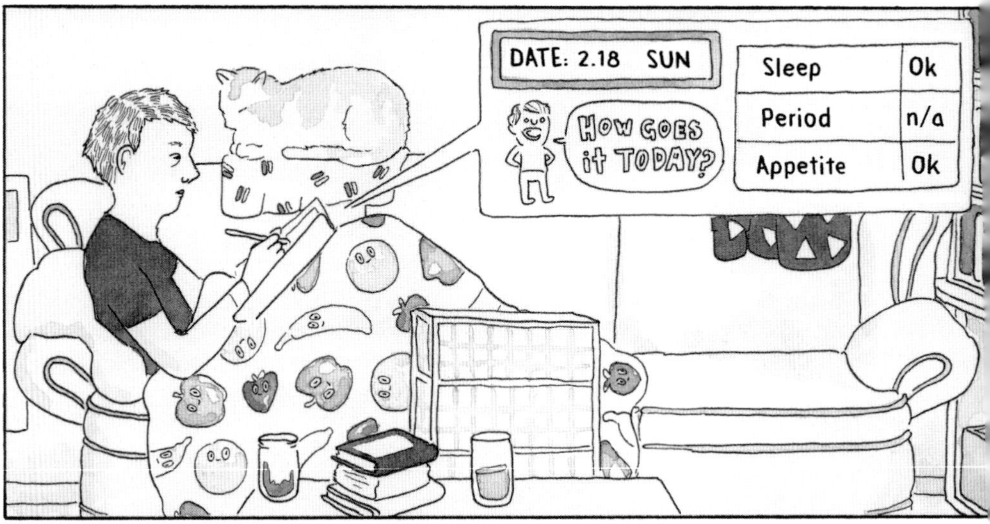
DATE: 2.18 SUN
HOW GOES it TODAY?
Sleep Ok
Period n/a
Appetite Ok

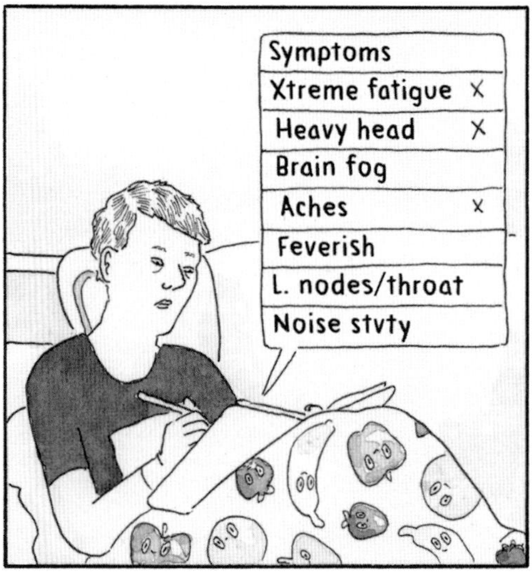
Symptoms
Xtreme fatigue X
Heavy head X
Brain fog
Aches X
Feverish
L. nodes/throat
Noise stvty

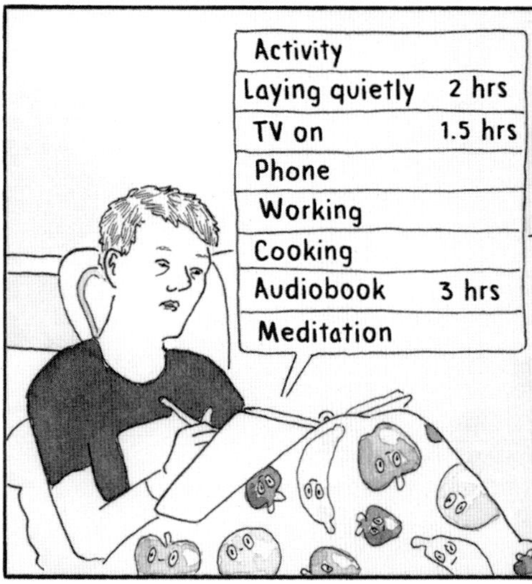
Activity
Laying quietly 2 hrs
TV on 1.5 hrs
Phone
Working
Cooking
Audiobook 3 hrs
Meditation

e illness didn't erase who I was.

But I felt so muted.

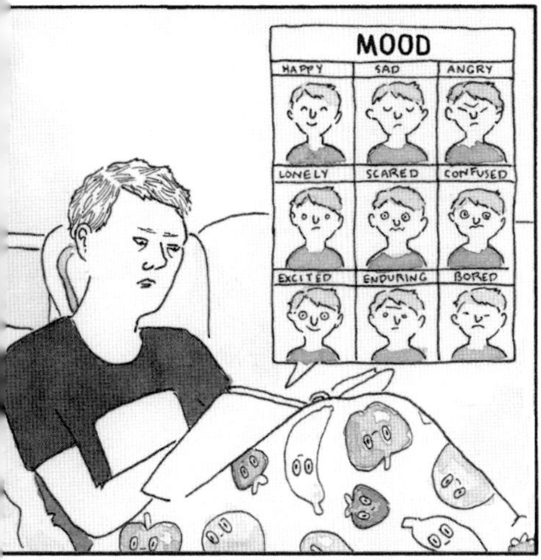
MOOD
HAPPY
SAD
ANGRY
LONELY
SCARED
CONFUSED
EXCITED
ENDURING
BORED

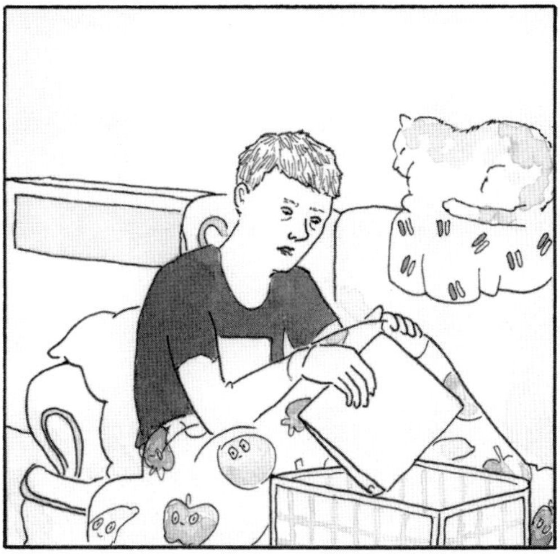

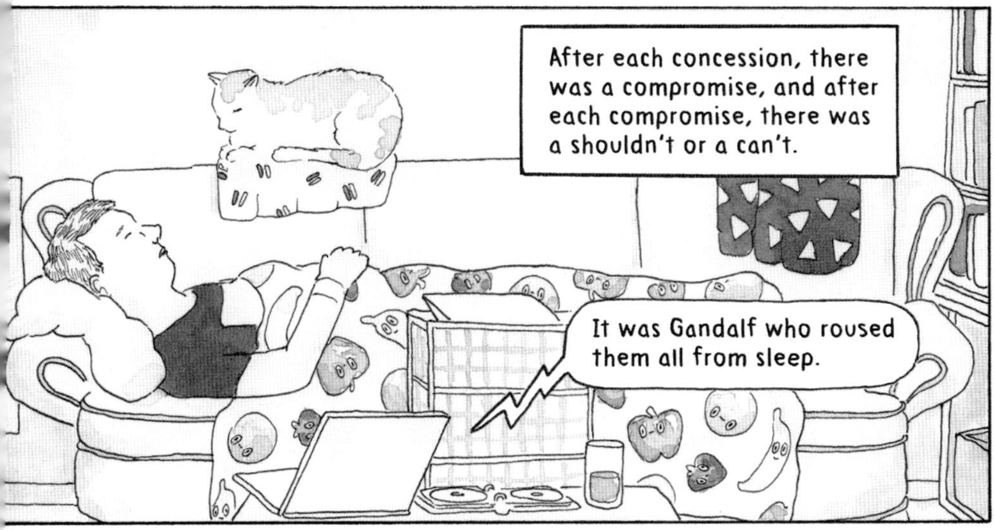
After each concession, there was a compromise, and after each compromise, there was a shouldn't or a can't.
It was Gandalf who roused them all from sleep.

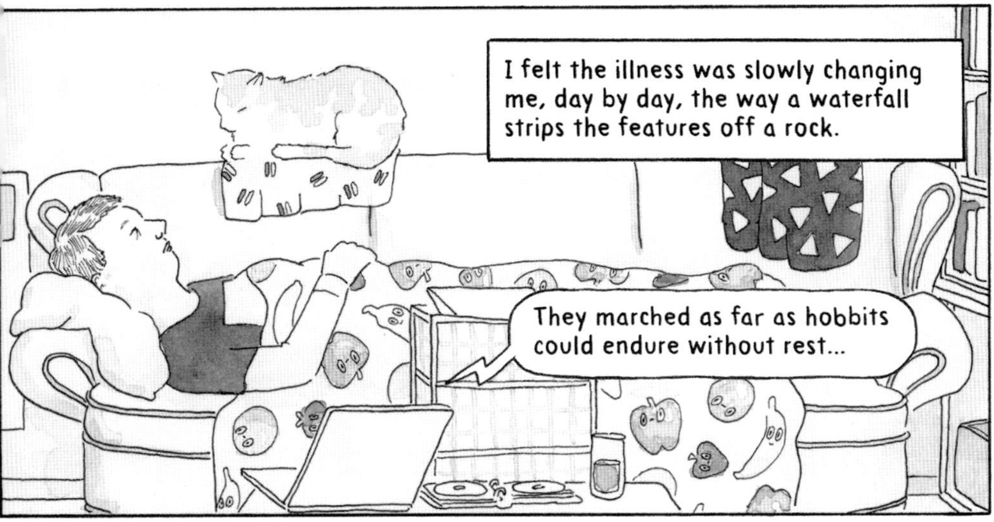
I felt the illness was slowly changing me, day by day, the way a waterfall strips the features off a rock.
They marched as far as hobbits could endure without rest...

I knew there were sick people who had adapted well to the radical change illness brought to their lives.

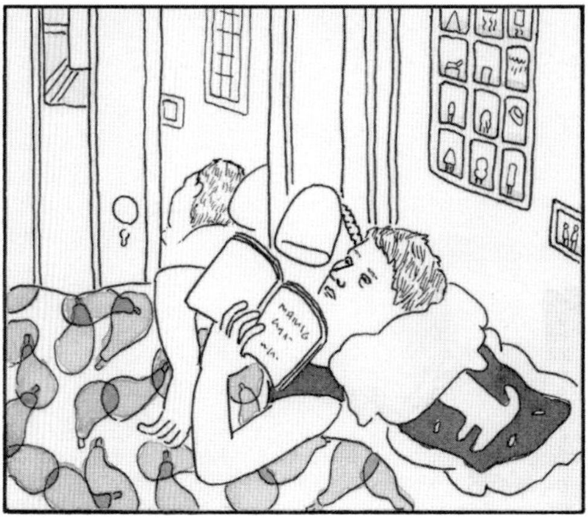

I had read about them.

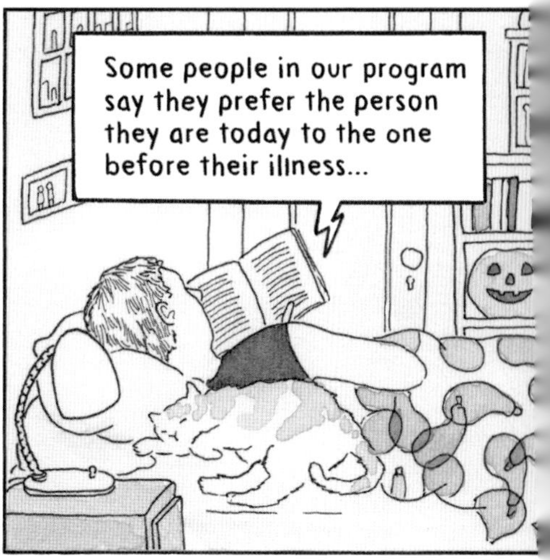
Some people in our program say they prefer the person they are today to the one before their illness...

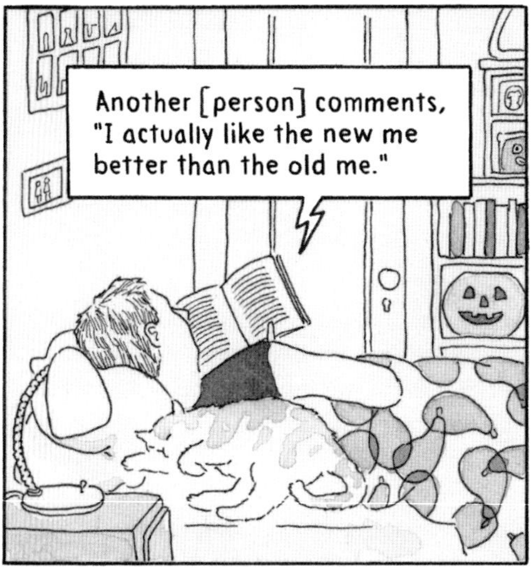
Another [person] comments, "I actually like the new me better than the old me."

They would not self-describe as eroding rocks.

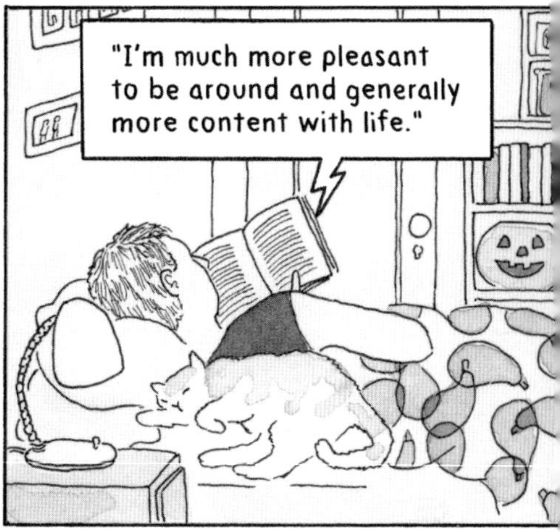
"I'm much more pleasant to be around and generally more content with life."

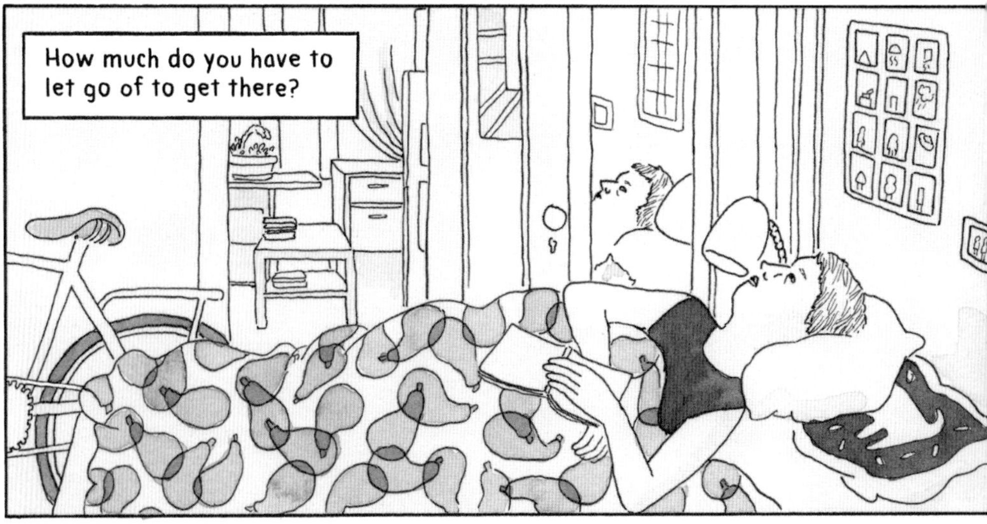
How much do you have to let go of to get there?

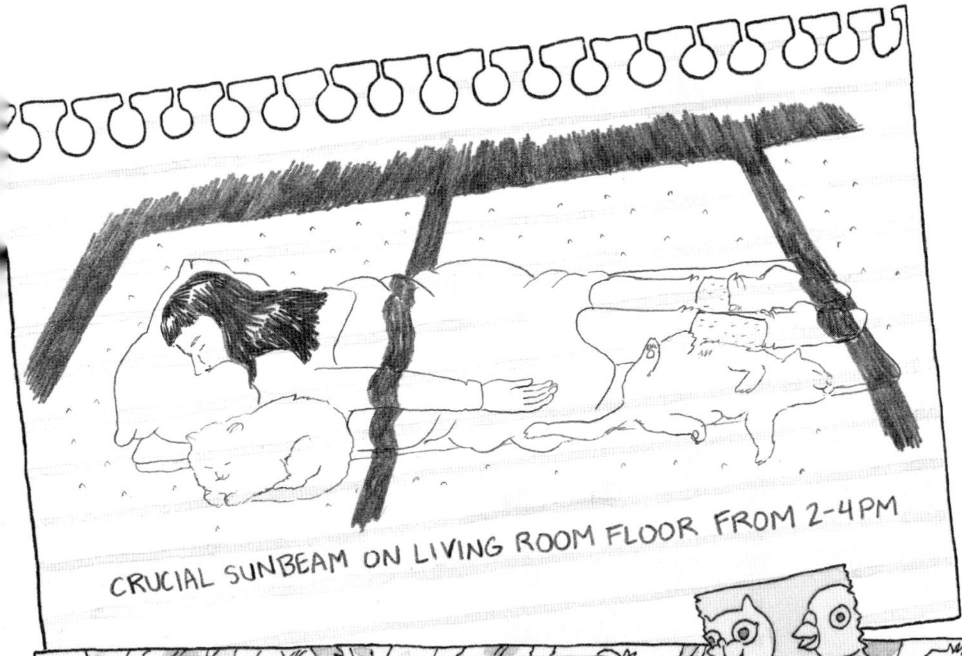
CRUCIAL SUNBEAM ON LIVING ROOM FLOOR FROM 2-4PM

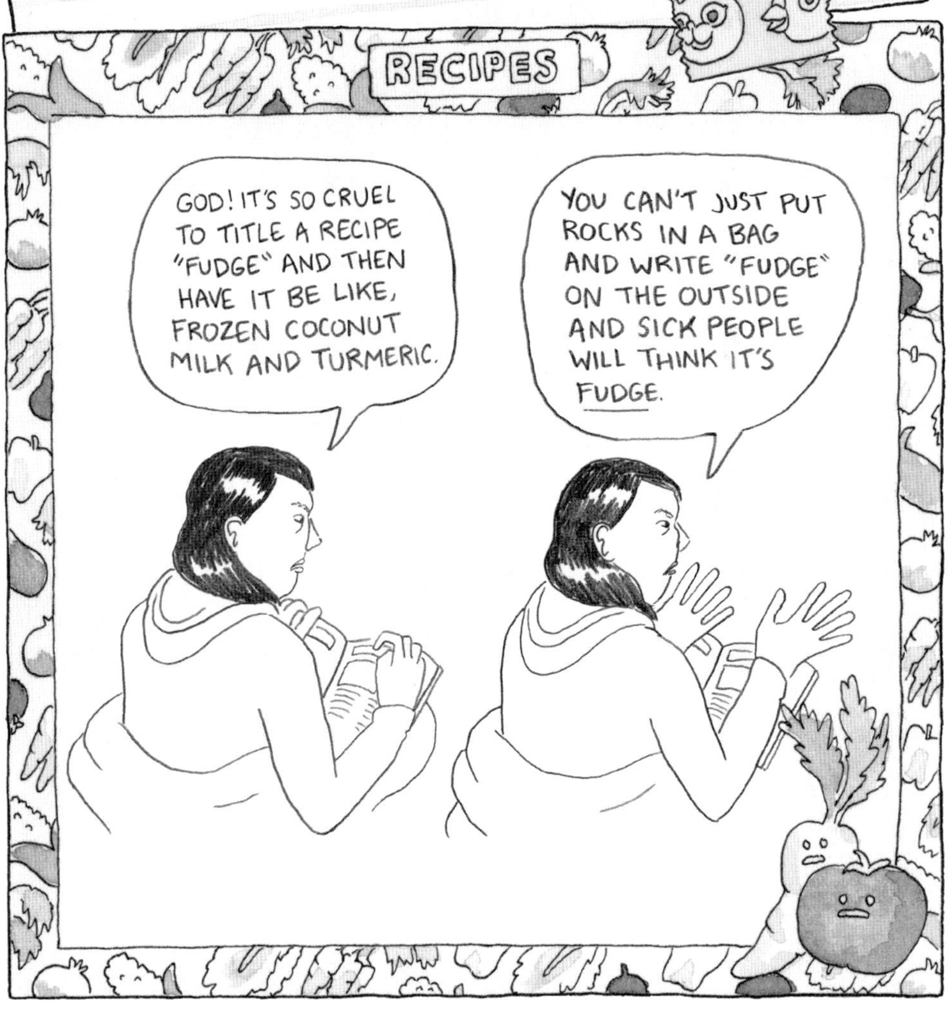
RECIPES
GOD! IT'S SO CRUEL TO TITLE A RECIPE "FUDGE" AND THEN HAVE IT BE LIKE, FROZEN COCONUT MILK AND TURMERIC.
YOU CAN'T JUST PUT ROCKS IN A BAG AND WRITE "FUDGE" ON THE OUTSIDE AND SICK PEOPLE WILL THINK IT'S FUDGE.

Dark Rides

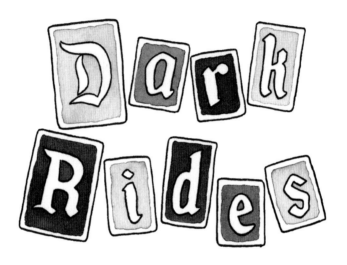

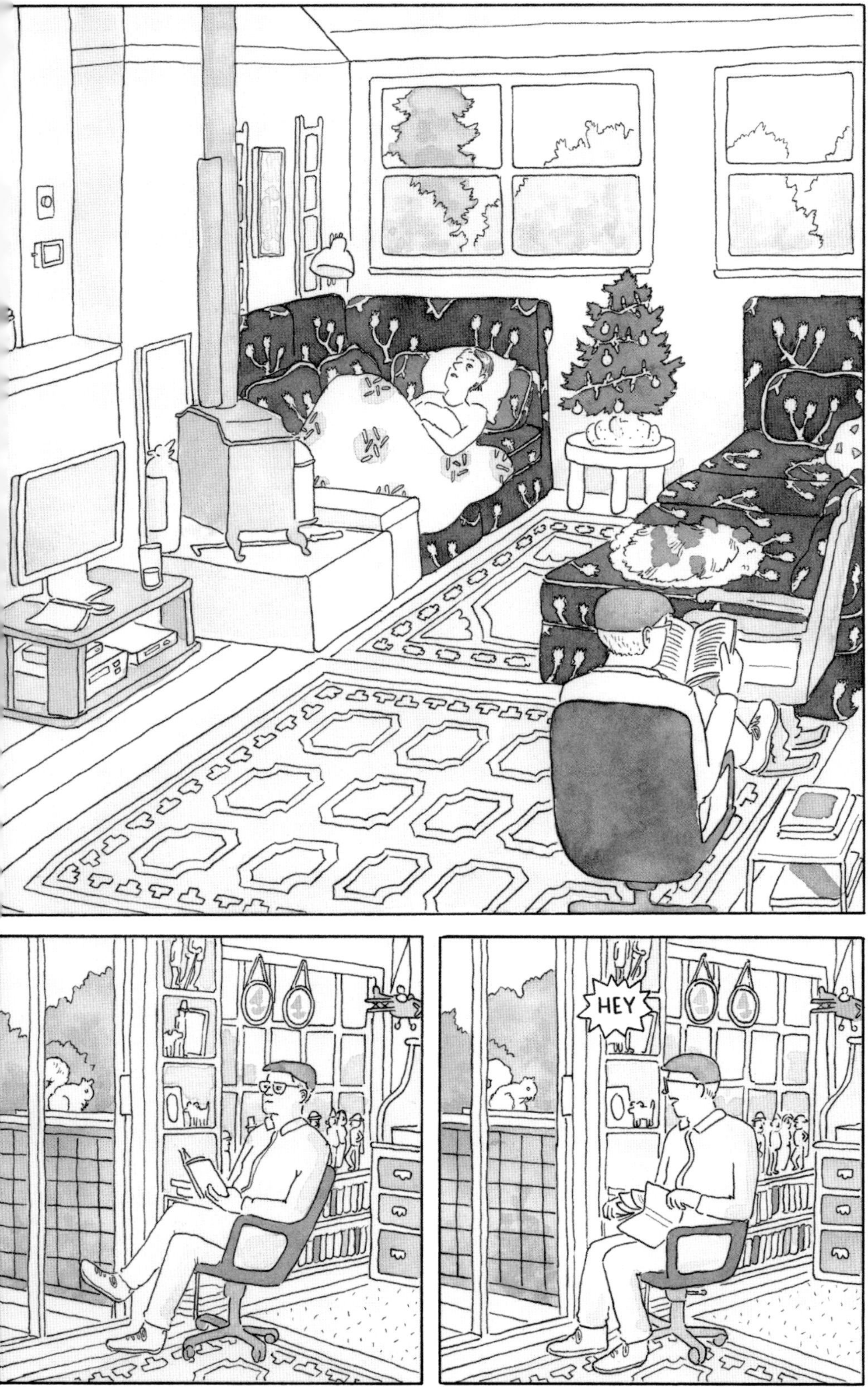
HEY

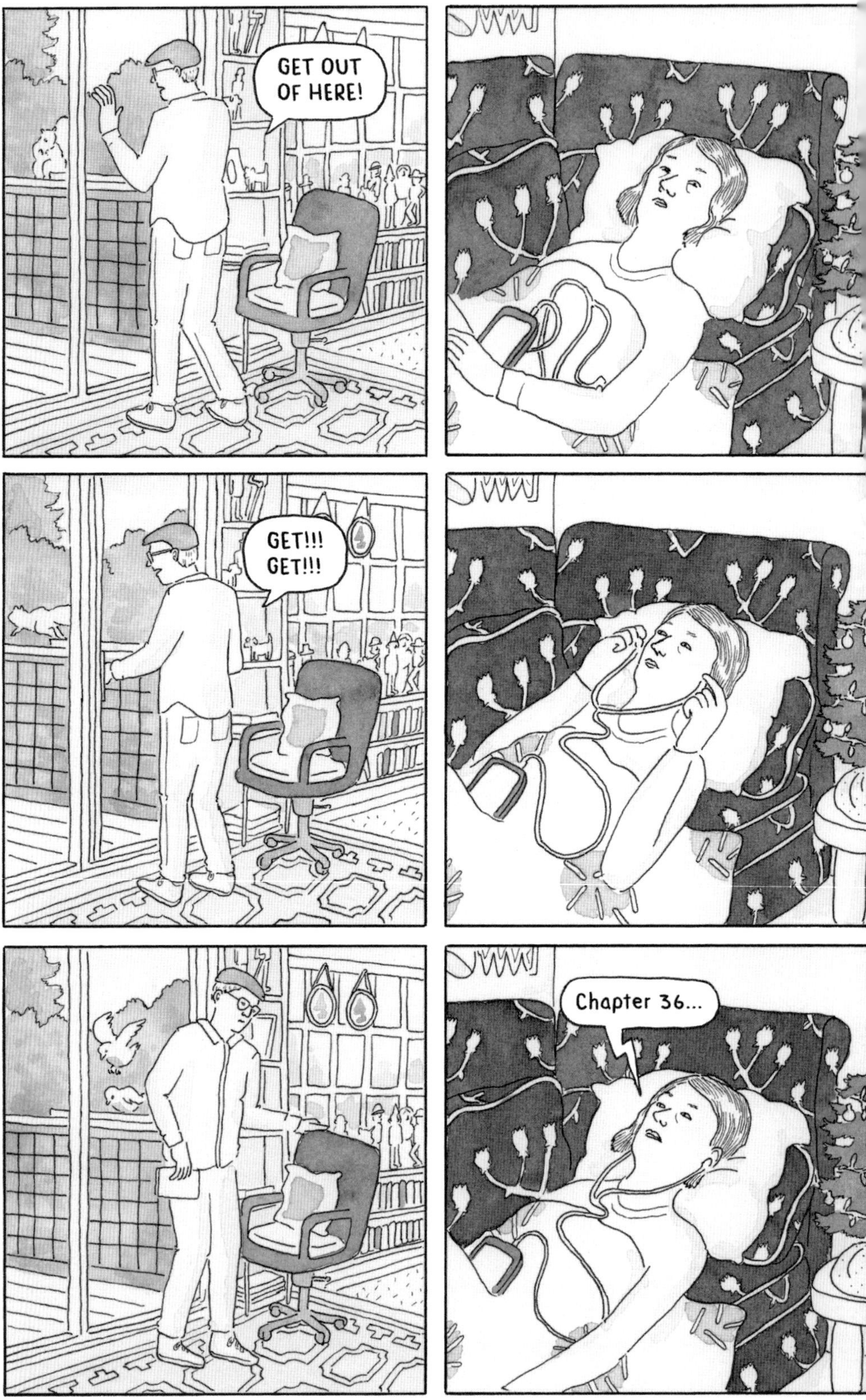
GET OUT OF HERE!
GET!!! GET!!!
Chapter 36...

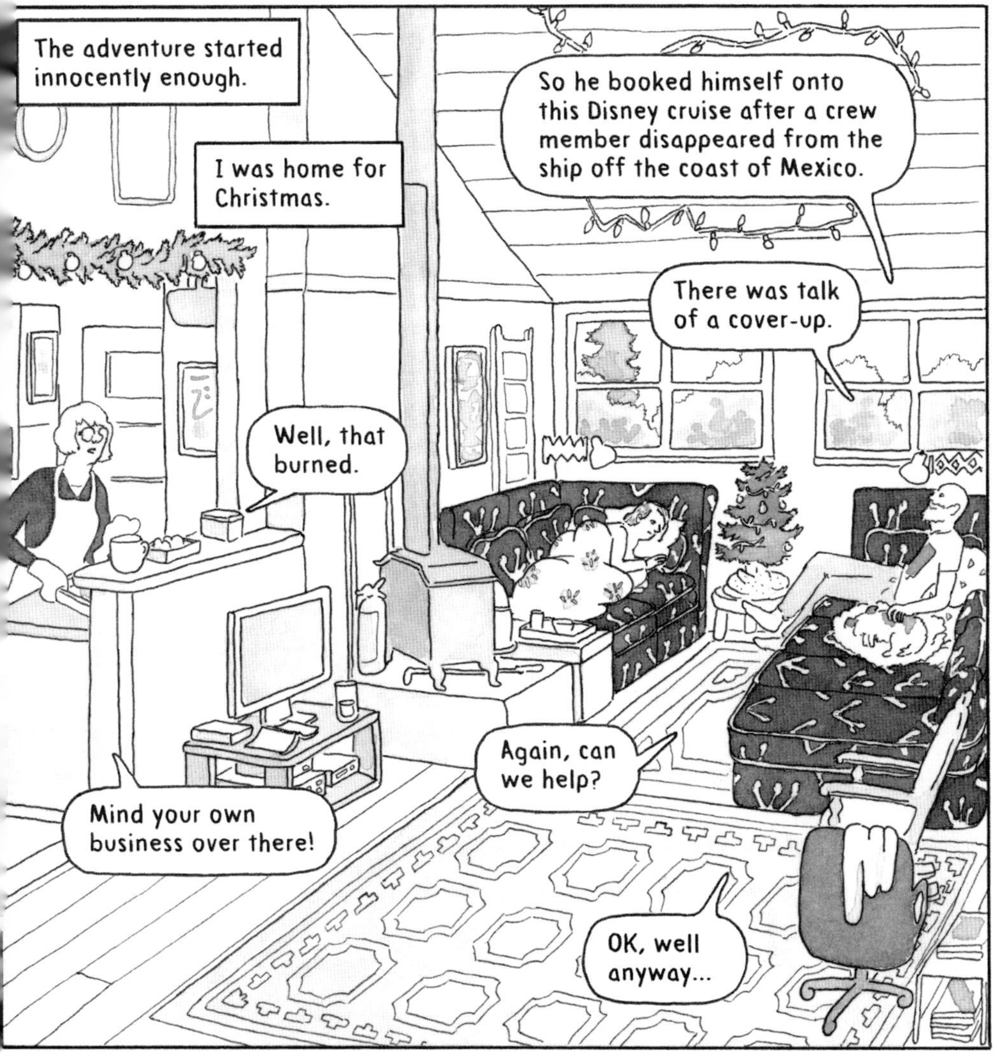
The adventure started innocently enough.
I was home for Christmas.
So he booked himself onto this Disney cruise after a crew member disappeared from the ship off the coast of Mexico.
There was talk of a cover-up.
Well, that burned.
Mind your own business over there!
Again, can we help?
OK, well anyway...

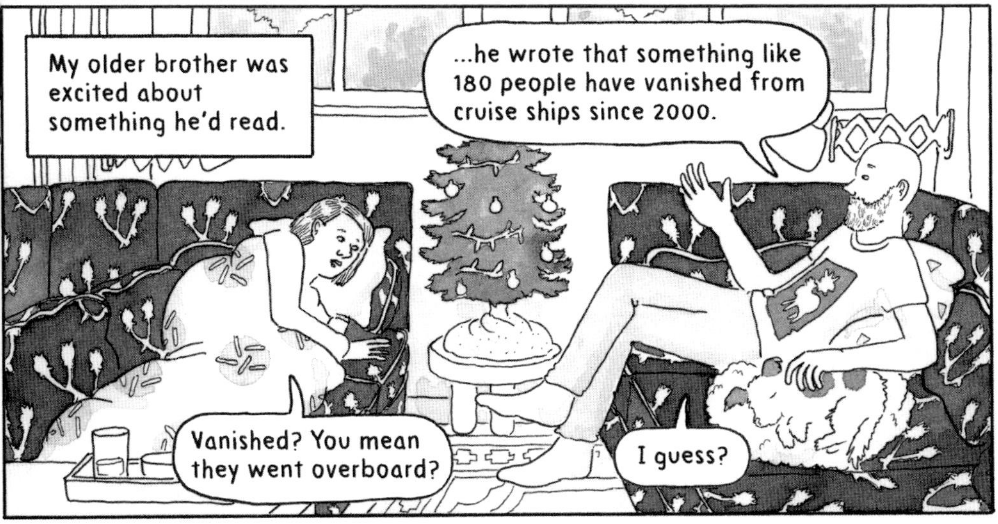
My older brother was excited about something he'd read.
...he wrote that something like 180 people have vanished from cruise ships since 2000.
Vanished? You mean they went overboard?
I guess?

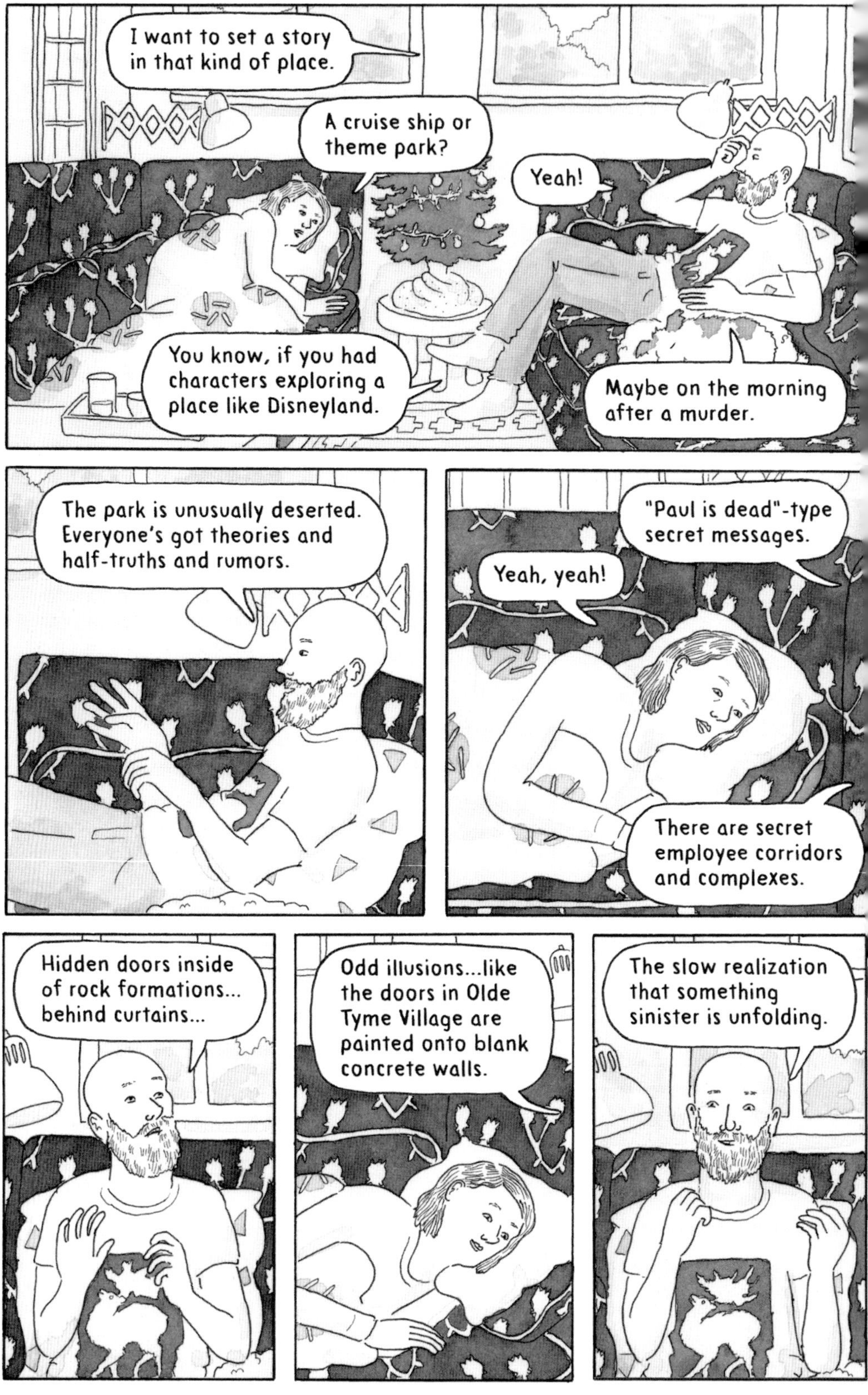
I want to set a story in that kind of place.
A cruise ship or theme park?
Yeah!
You know, if you had characters exploring a place like Disneyland.
Maybe on the morning after a murder.
The park is unusually deserted. Everyone's got theories and half-truths and rumors.
"Paul is dead"-type secret messages.
Yeah, yeah!
There are secret employee corridors and complexes.
Hidden doors inside of rock formations... behind curtains...
Odd illusions...like the doors in Olde Tyme Village are painted onto blank concrete walls.
The slow realization that something sinister is unfolding.

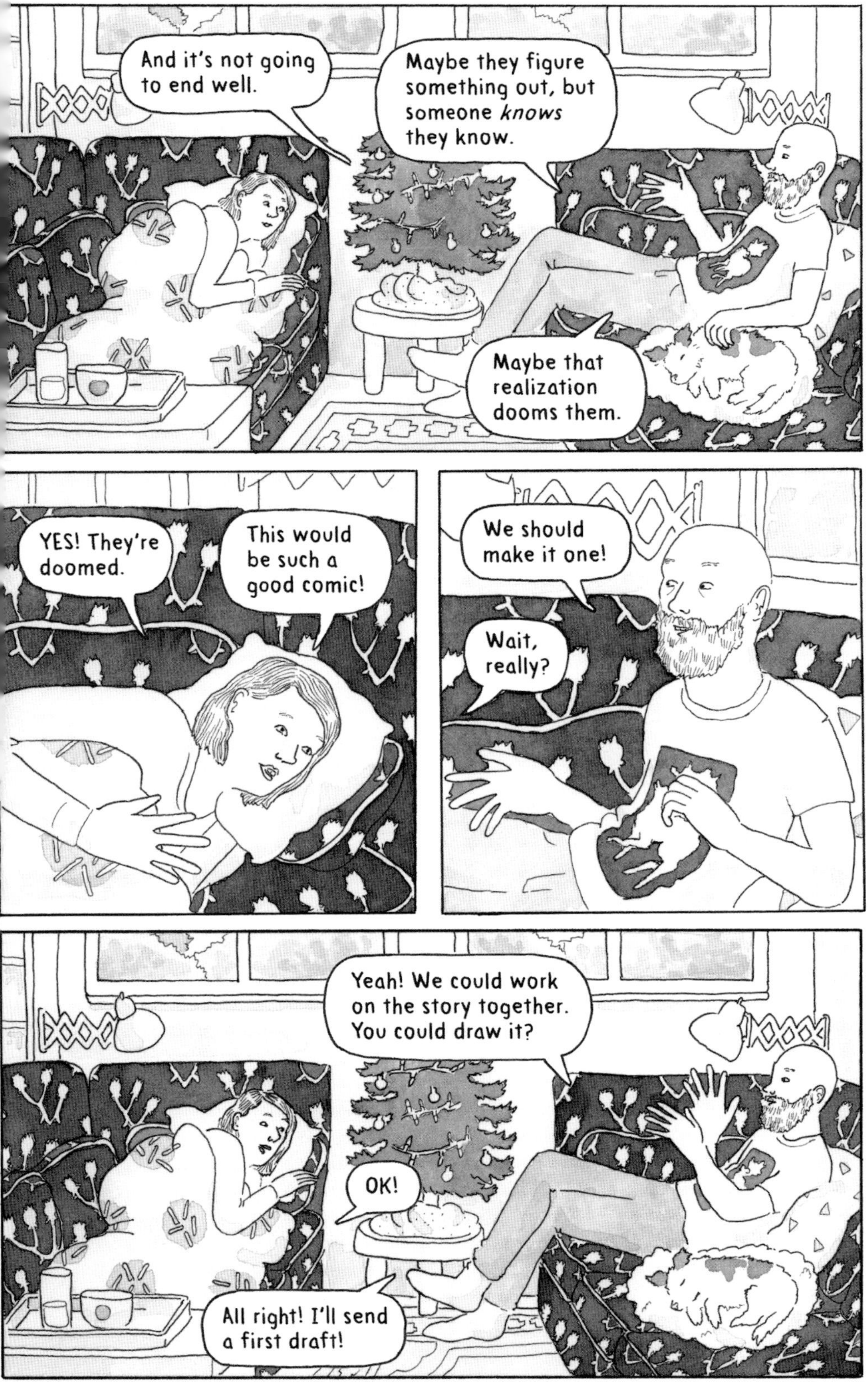
And it's not going to end well.
Maybe they figure something out, but someone *knows* they know.
Maybe that realization dooms them.
YES! They're doomed.
This would be such a good comic!
We should make it one!
Wait, really?
Yeah! We could work on the story together. You could draw it?
OK!
All right! I'll send a first draft!

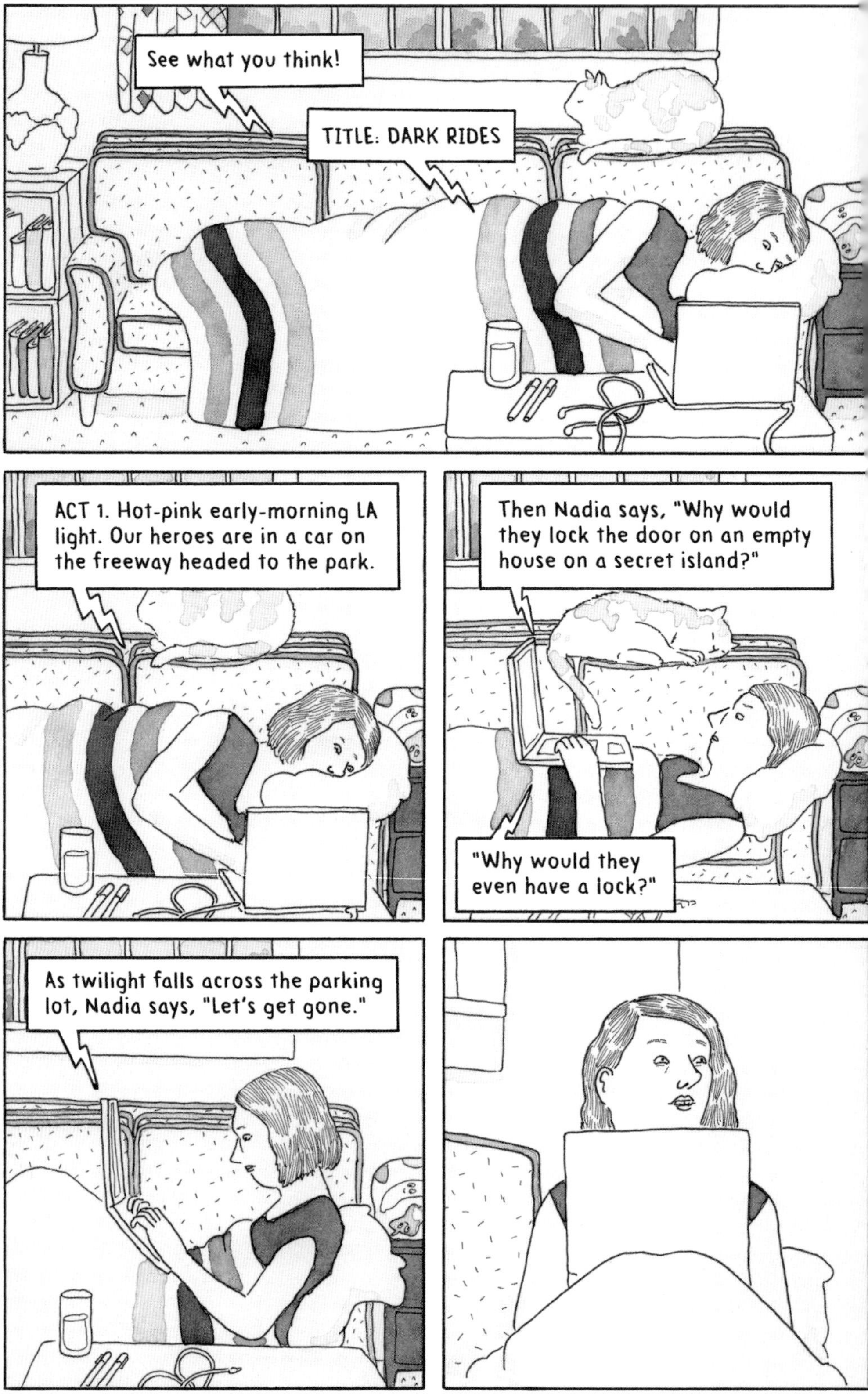
See what you think!
TITLE: DARK RIDES
ACT 1. Hot-pink early-morning LA light. Our heroes are in a car on the freeway headed to the park.
Then Nadia says, "Why would they lock the door on an empty house on a secret island?"
"Why would they even have a lock?"
As twilight falls across the parking lot, Nadia says, "Let's get gone."

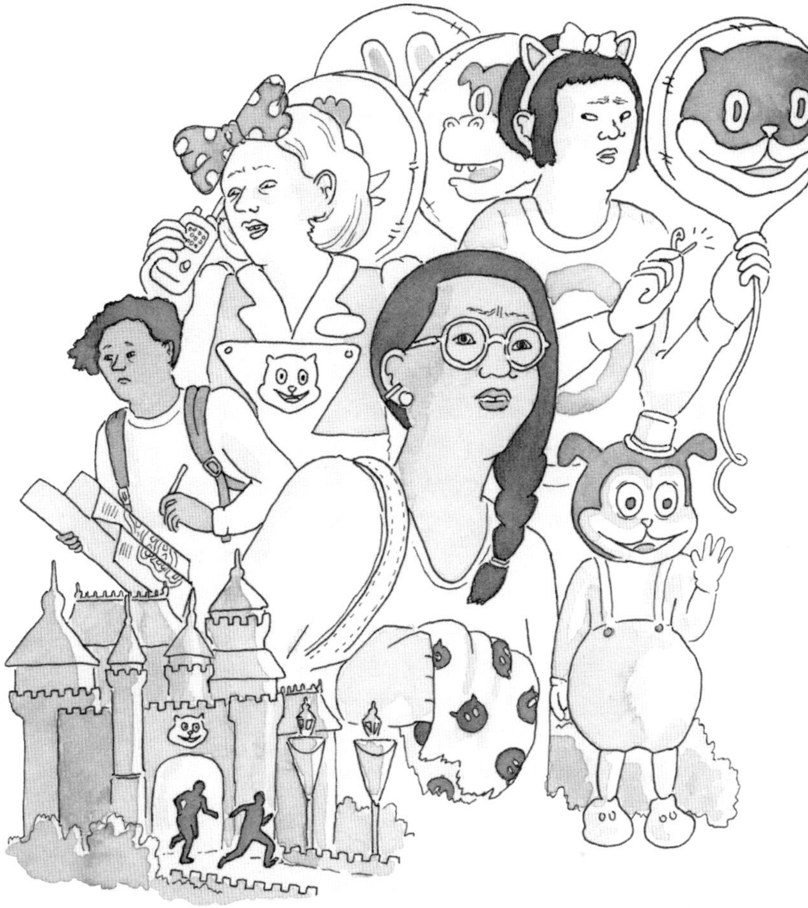

DARK RIDES

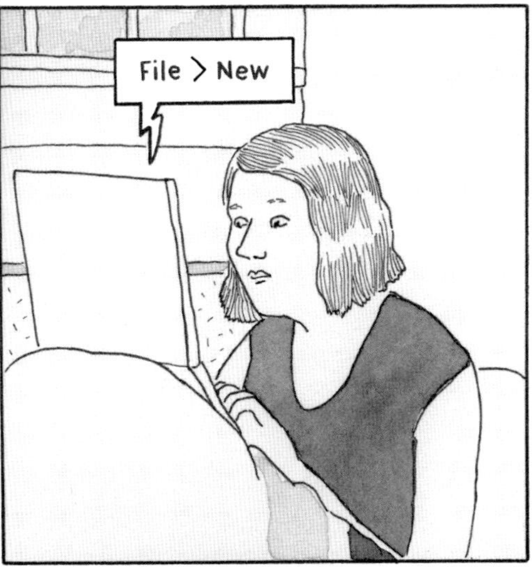
File > New

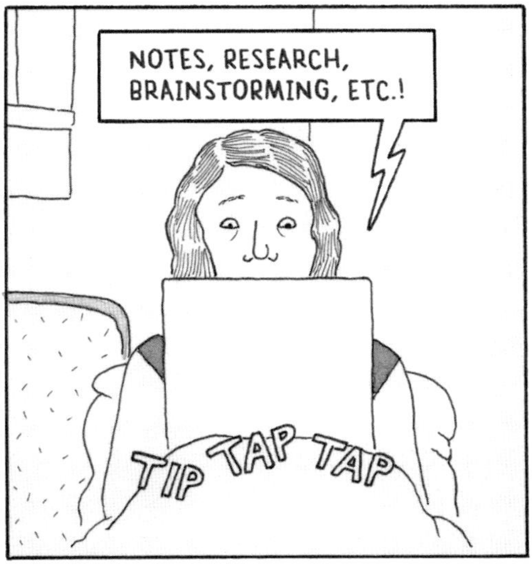
NOTES, RESEARCH, BRAINSTORMING, ETC.!
TIP TAP TAP

The story was set in a knockoff version of Disneyland, and I drew my inspiration from that wacky well.

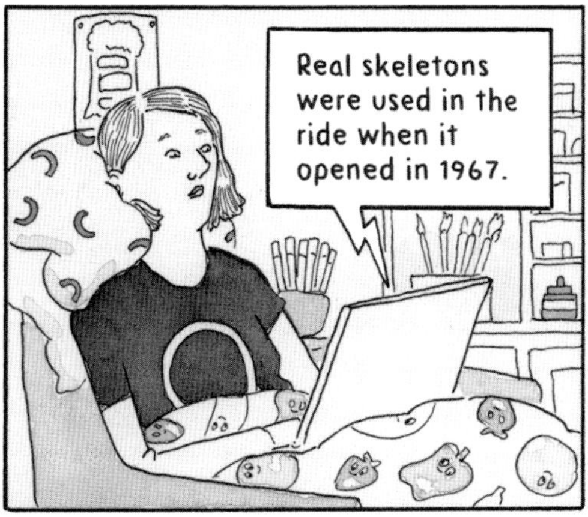
Real skeletons were used in the ride when it opened in 1967.

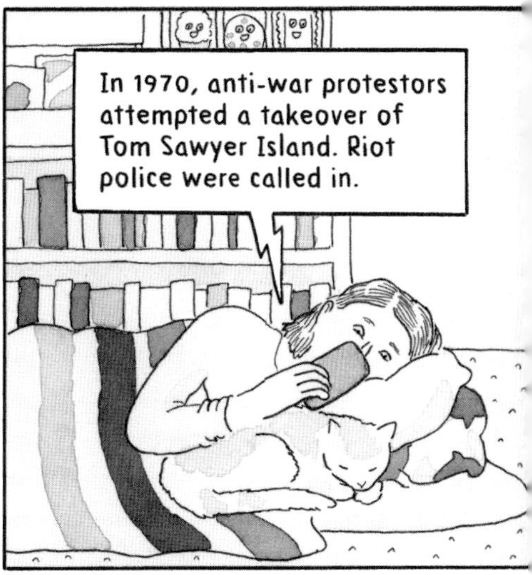
In 1970, anti-war protestors attempted a takeover of Tom Sawyer Island. Riot police were called in.

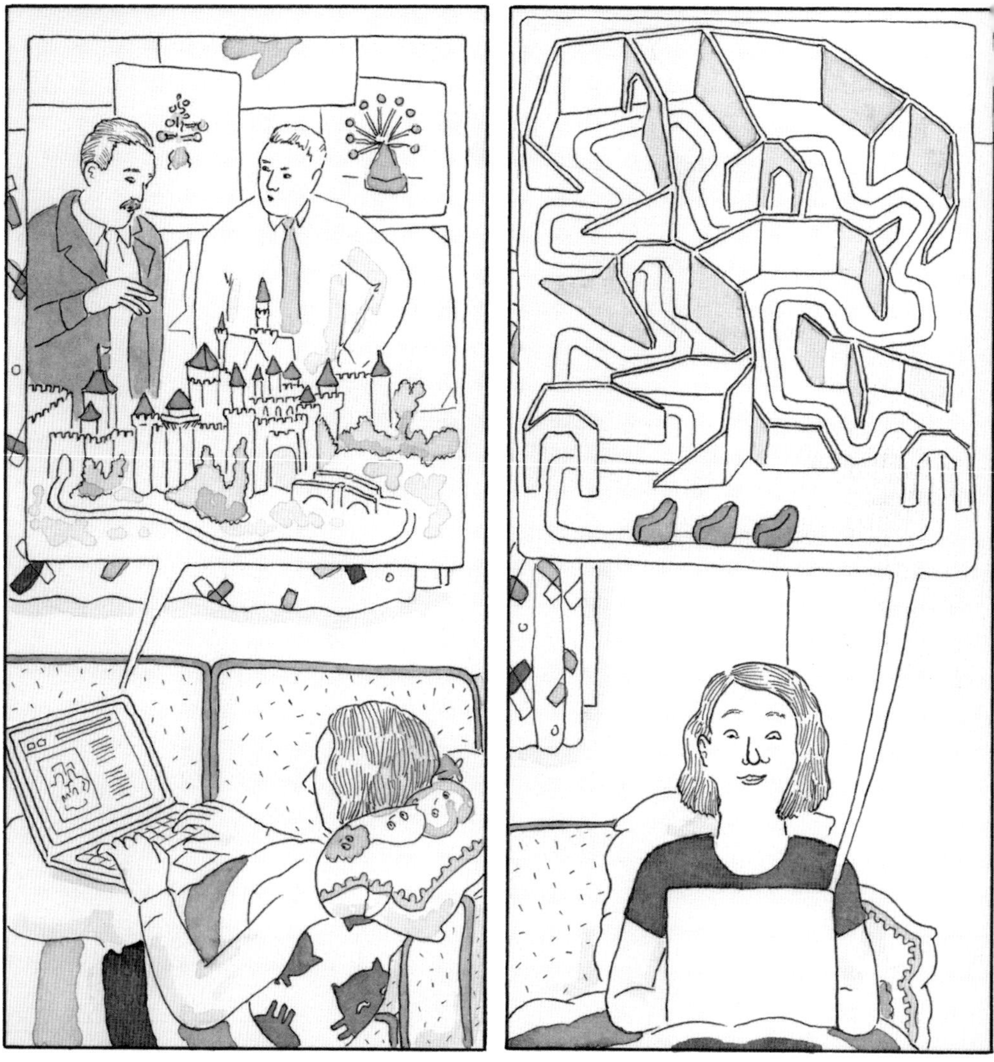

even mapped the story onto the park.

As dusk falls, they'll be on the ferry.

So the Matterhorn then becomes...

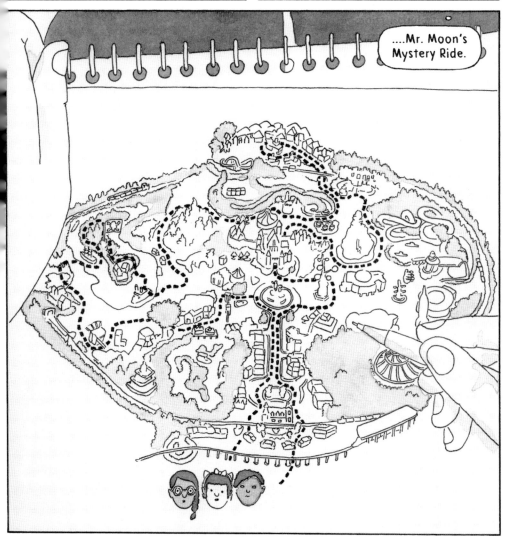

....Mr. Moon's Mystery Ride.

In the beginning, all my planning could have been considered due diligence. The story had many moving parts.

At least that's how I justified the terrifyin wall of text (my "notes") that I sent alon

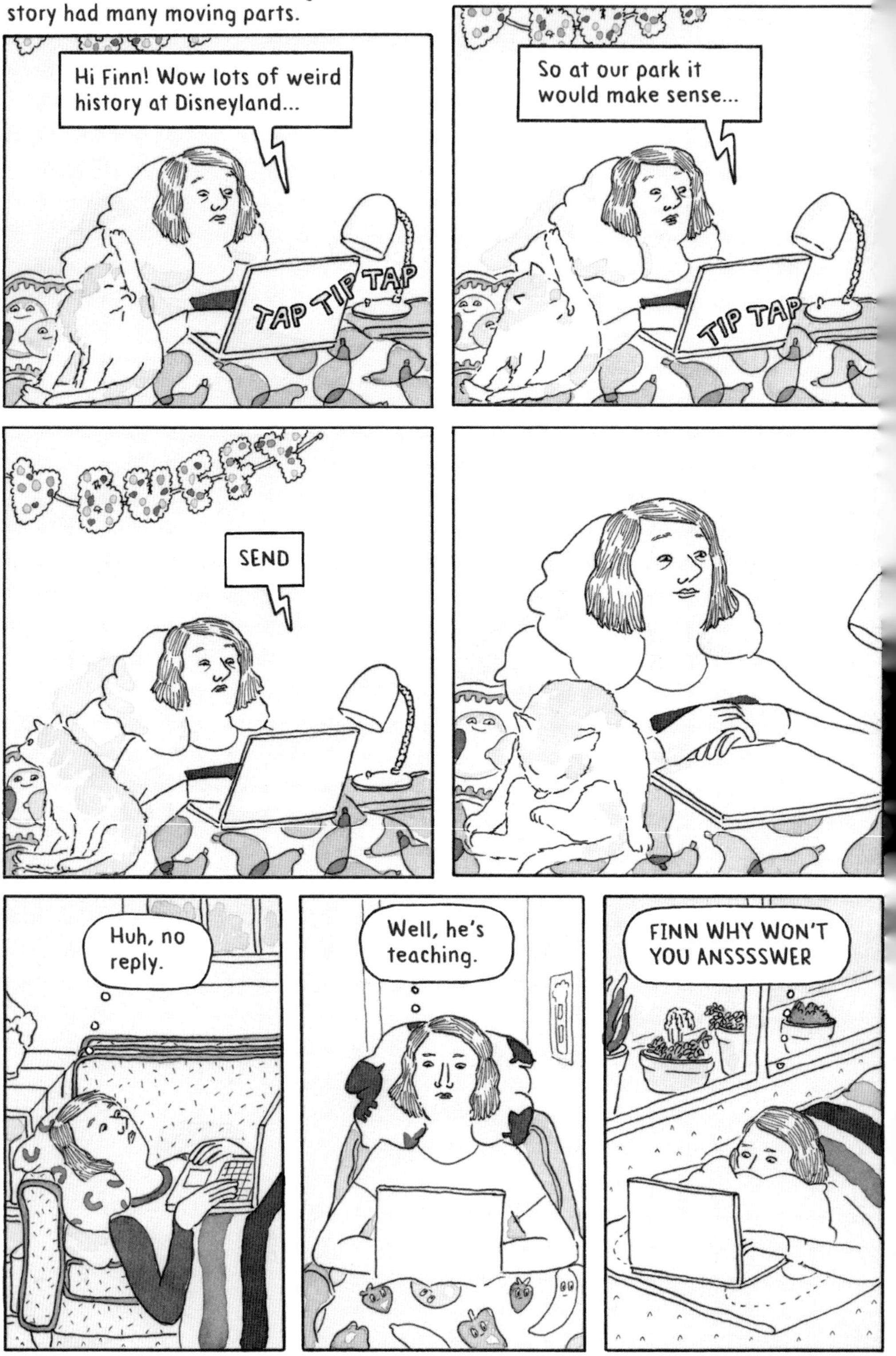
Hi Finn! Wow lots of weird history at Disneyland...
TAP TIP TAP
So at our park it would make sense...
TIP TAP
SEND
Huh, no reply.
Well, he's teaching.
FINN WHY WON'T YOU ANSSSSWER

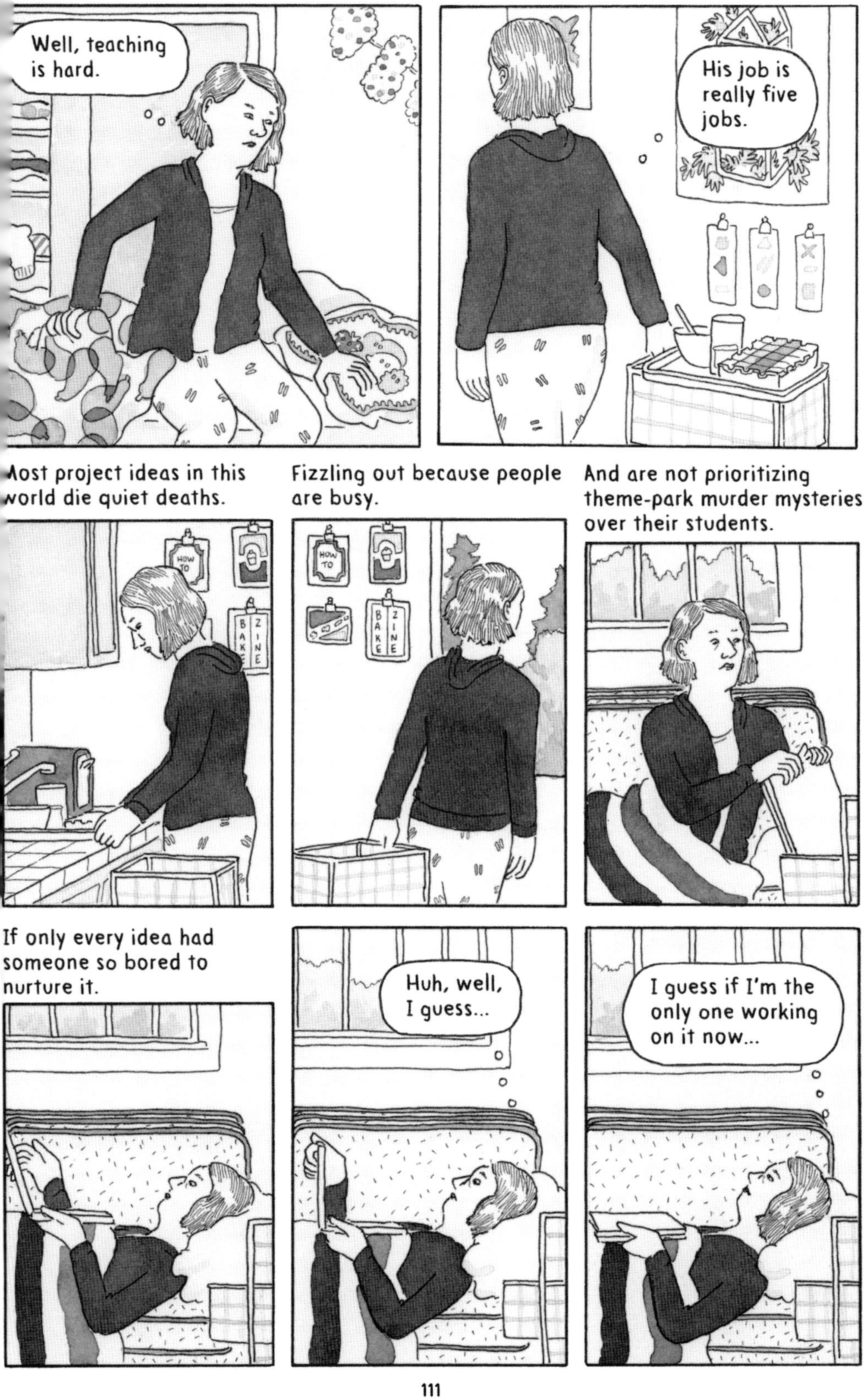
Well, teaching is hard.
His job is really five jobs.
Most project ideas in this world die quiet deaths.
Fizzling out because people are busy.
And are not prioritizing theme-park murder mysteries over their students.
HOW TO
BAKE ZINE
If only every idea had someone so bored to nurture it.
Huh, well, I guess...
I guess if I'm the only one working on it now...

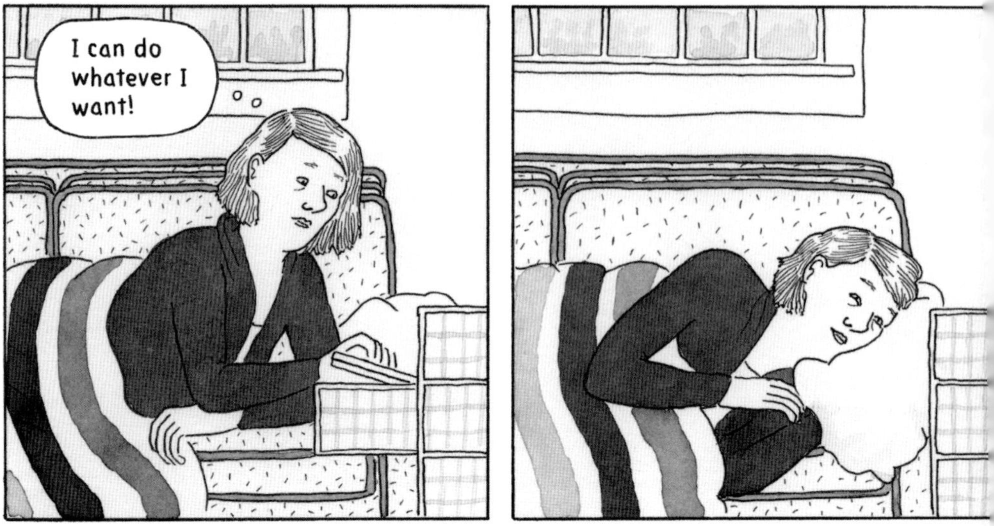
I can do whatever I want!

Now that I was the sole steward of the story, it grew and mutated.

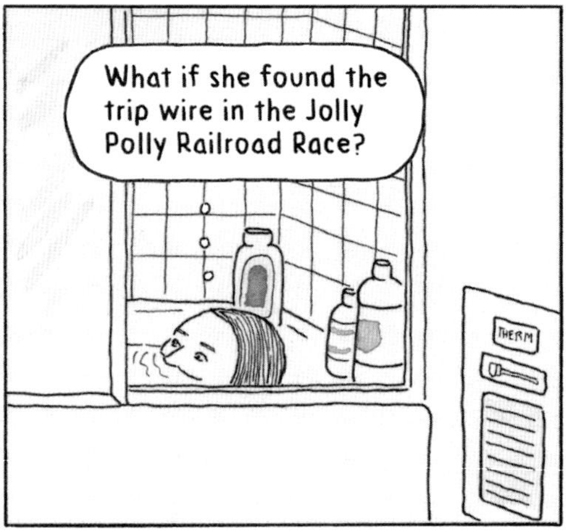
What if she found the trip wire in the Jolly Polly Railroad Race?
THERM

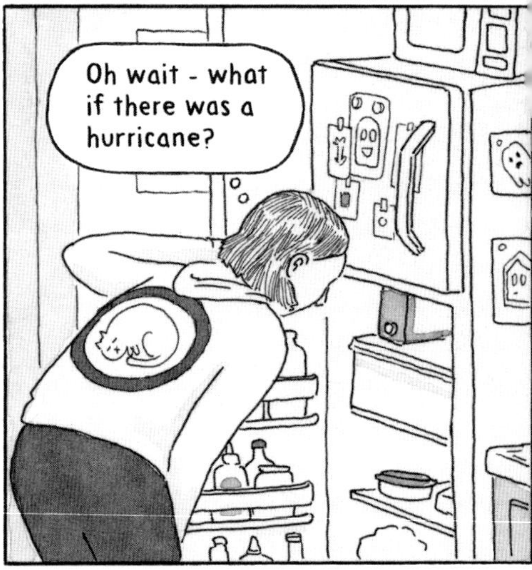
Oh wait - what if there was a hurricane?

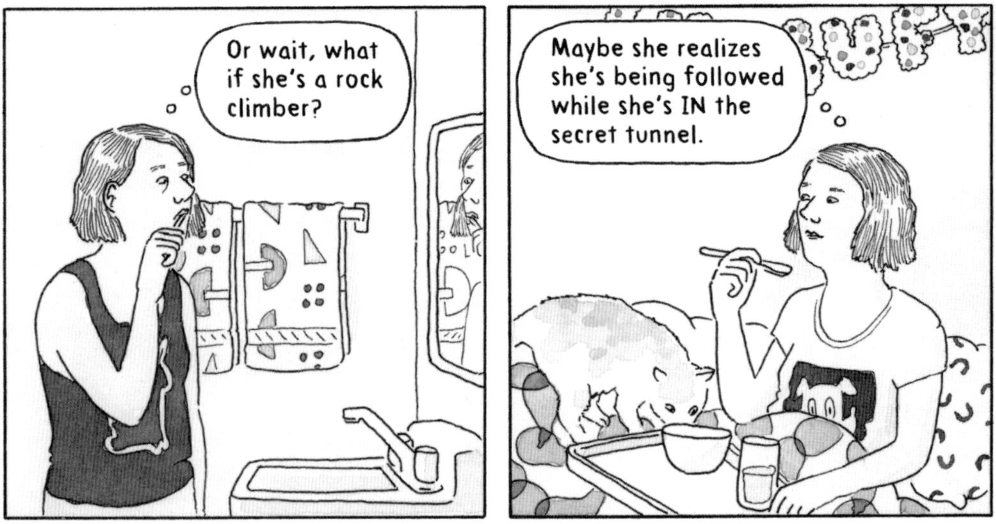
Or wait, what if she's a rock climber?
Maybe she realizes she's being followed while she's IN the secret tunnel.

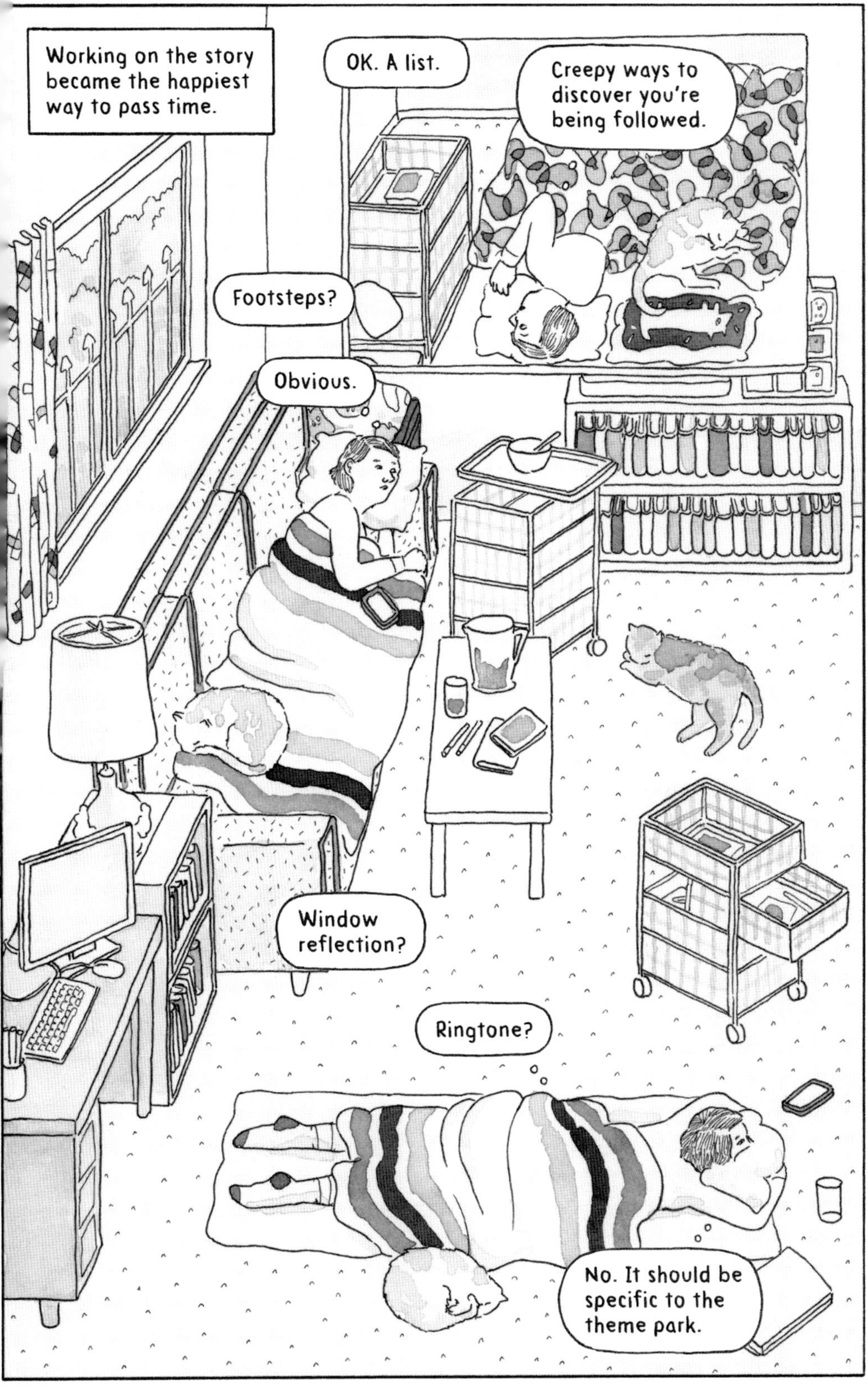

Working on the story became the happiest way to pass time.
OK. A list.
Creepy ways to discover you're being followed.
Footsteps?
Obvious.
Window reflection?
Ringtone?
No. It should be specific to the theme park.

And a choice way to distract from disappointment.

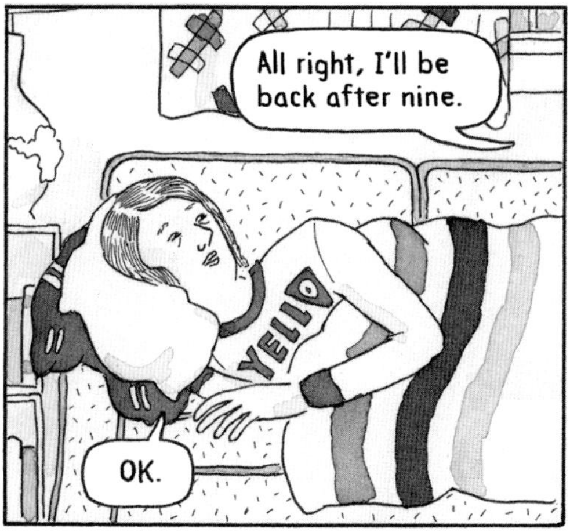
All right, I'll be back after nine.
OK.

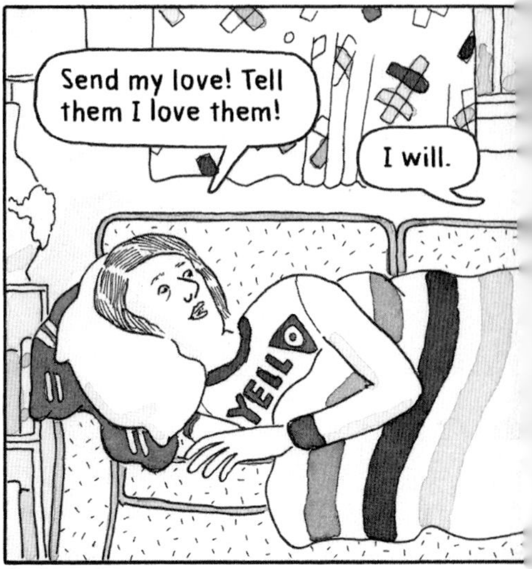
Send my love! Tell them I love them!
I will.

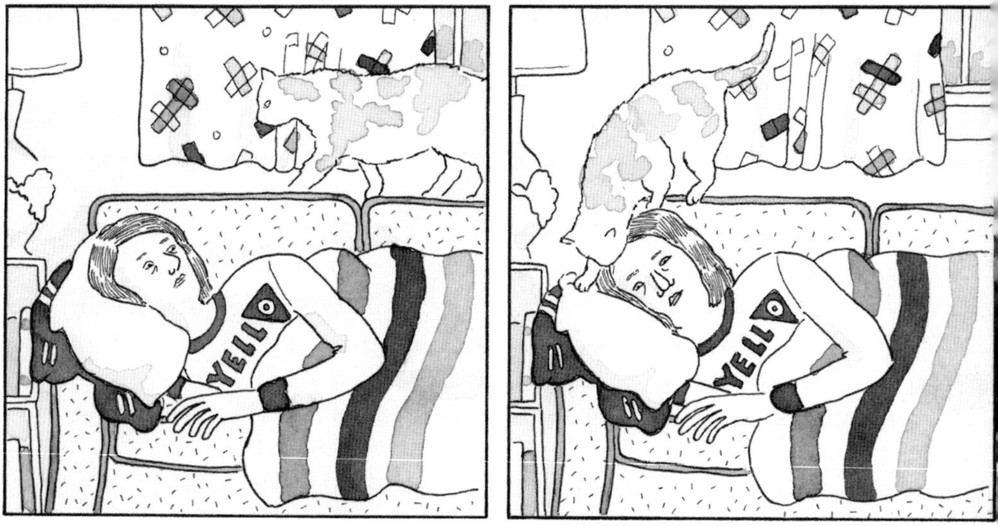

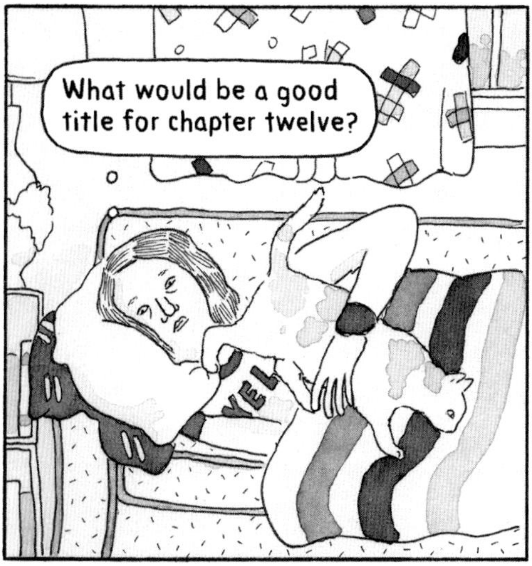
What would be a good title for chapter twelve?

But the more I built a bizarro Disneyland...

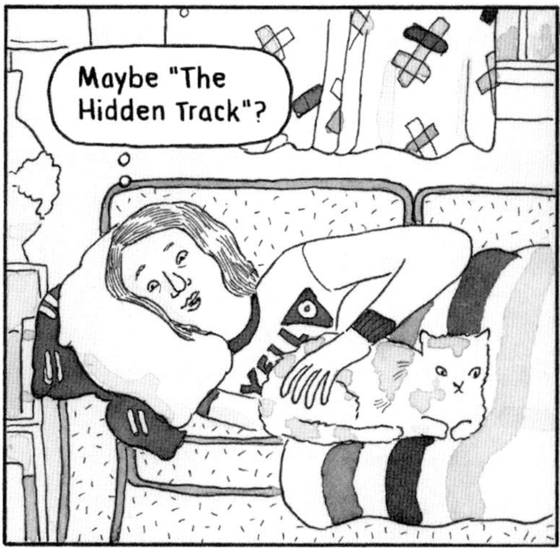
Maybe "The Hidden Track"?

the darker it became.

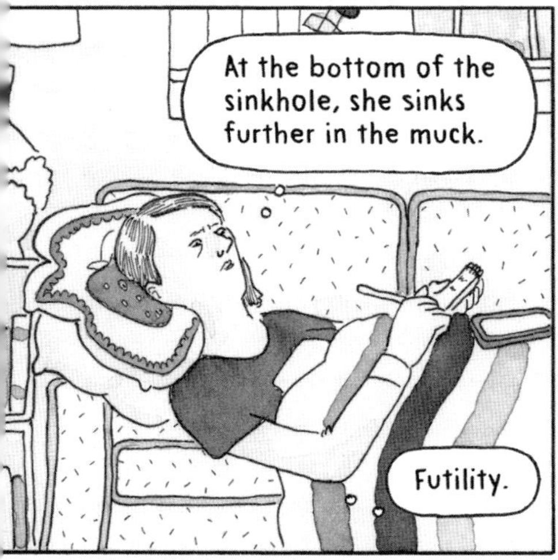
At the bottom of the sinkhole, she sinks further in the muck.
Futility.

I couldn't resist doom.

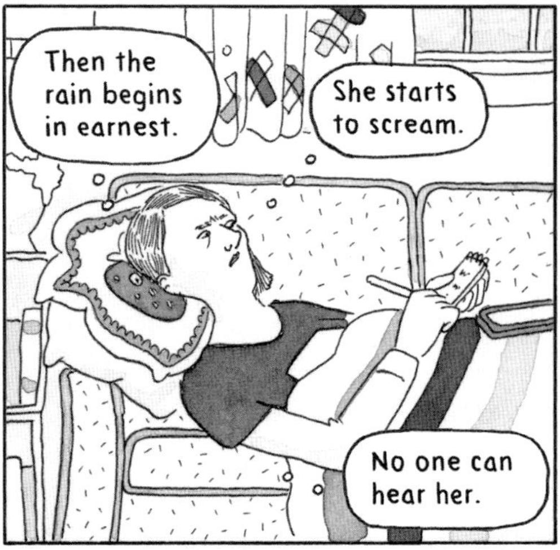
Then the rain begins in earnest.
She starts to scream.
No one can hear her.

wasn't aware of how cathartic the story was becoming for me.

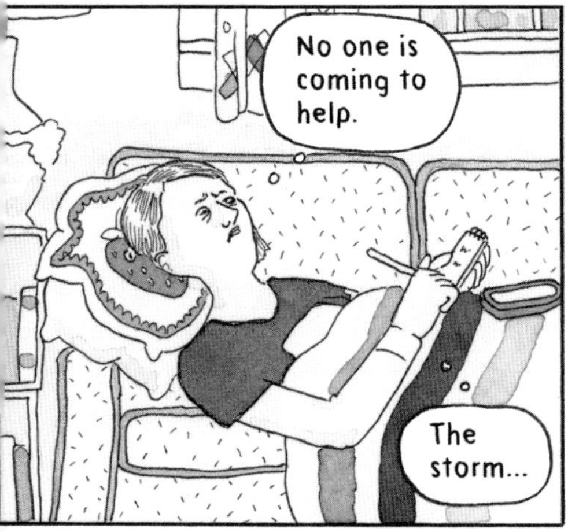
No one is coming to help.
The storm...

And how unfeasible.

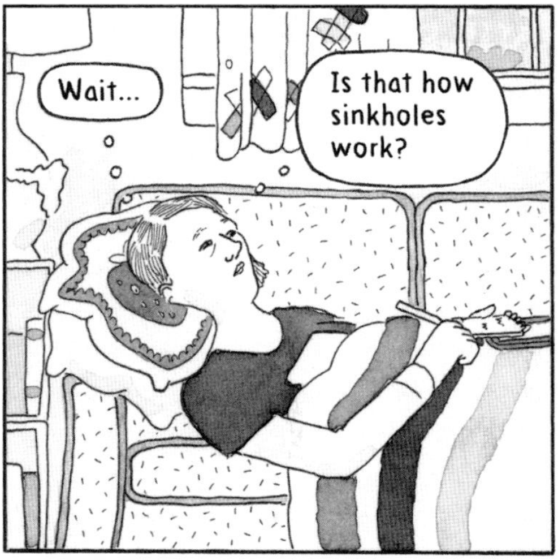
Wait...
Is that how sinkholes work?

Most years I had only been able to complete a few pages of comics.

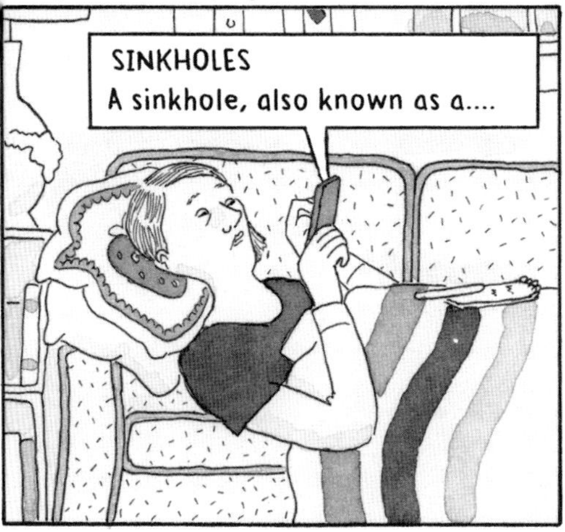
SINKHOLES
A sinkhole, also known as a....

And this story had bloated. It would need hundreds of pages of art.

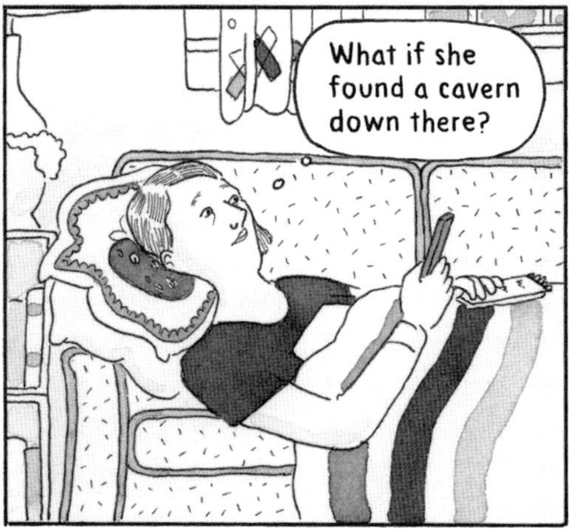
What if she found a cavern down there?

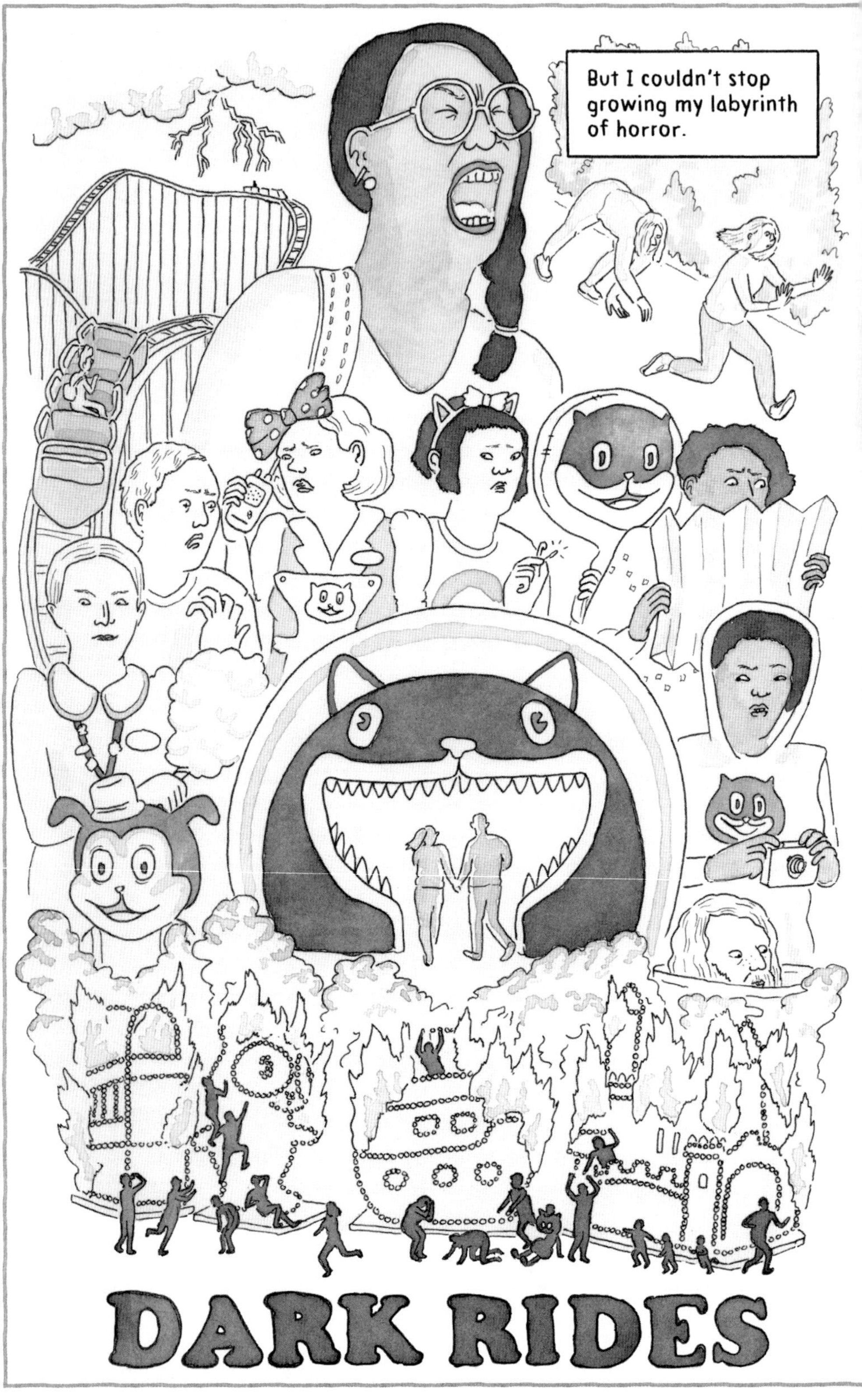
But I couldn't stop growing my labyrinth of horror.
DARK RIDES

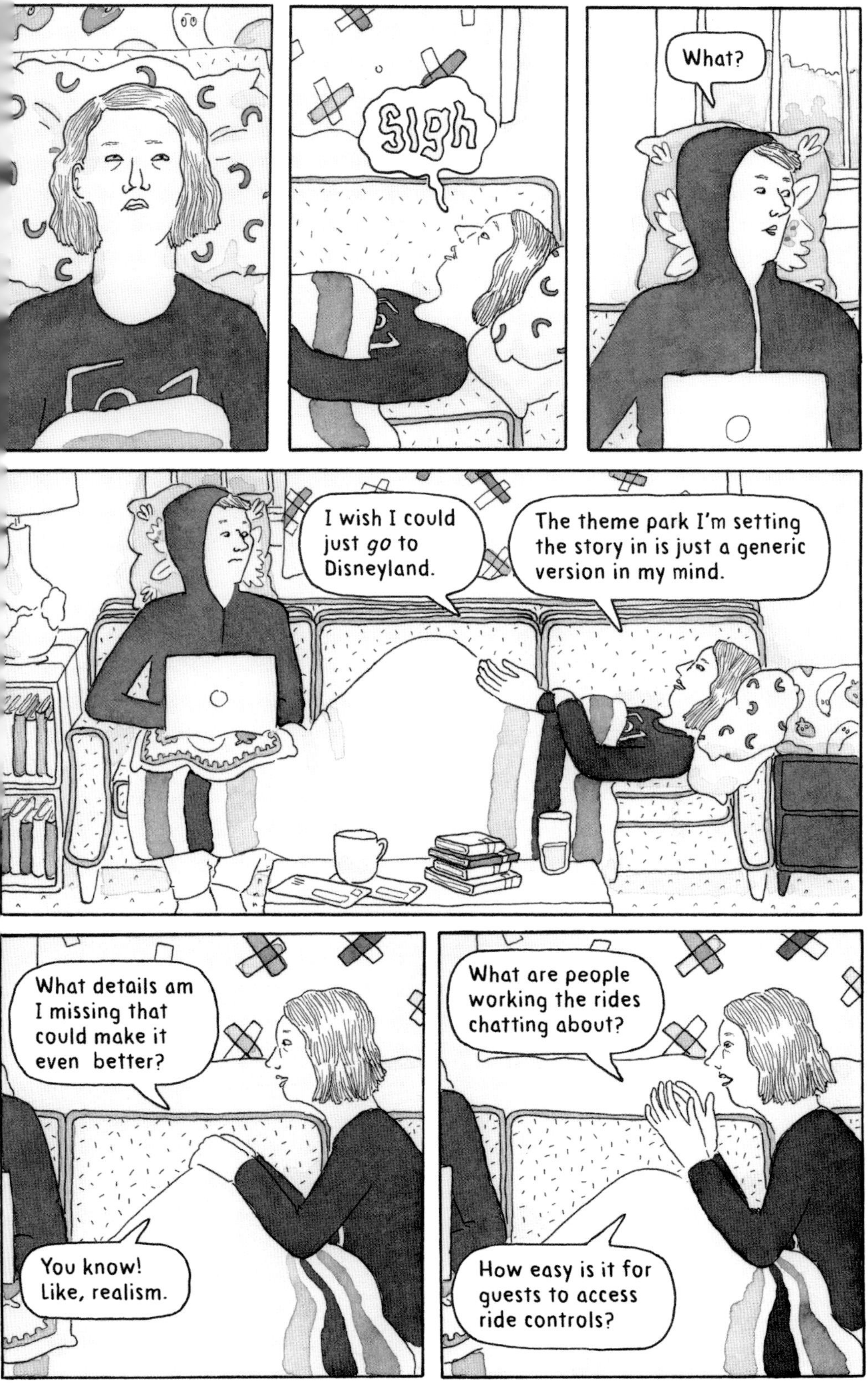
SIGH
What?
I wish I could just *go* to Disneyland.
The theme park I'm setting the story in is just a generic version in my mind.
What details am I missing that could make it even better?
You know! Like, realism.
What are people working the rides chatting about?
How easy is it for guests to access ride controls?

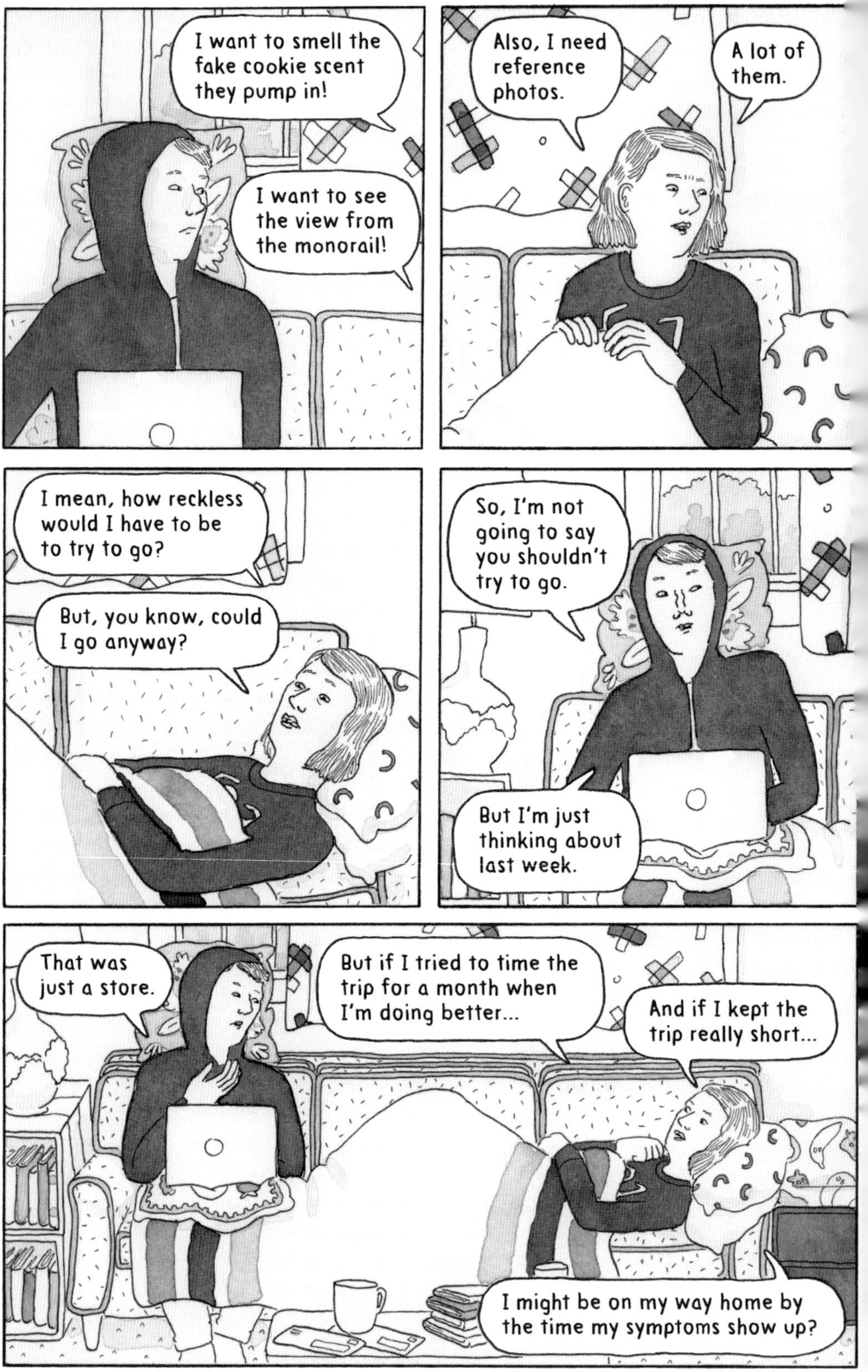
I want to smell the fake cookie scent they pump in!
I want to see the view from the monorail!
Also, I need reference photos.
A lot of them.
I mean, how reckless would I have to be to try to go?
But, you know, could I go anyway?
So, I'm not going to say you shouldn't try to go.
But I'm just thinking about last week.
That was just a store.
But if I tried to time the trip for a month when I'm doing better...
And if I kept the trip really short...
I might be on my way home by the time my symptoms show up?

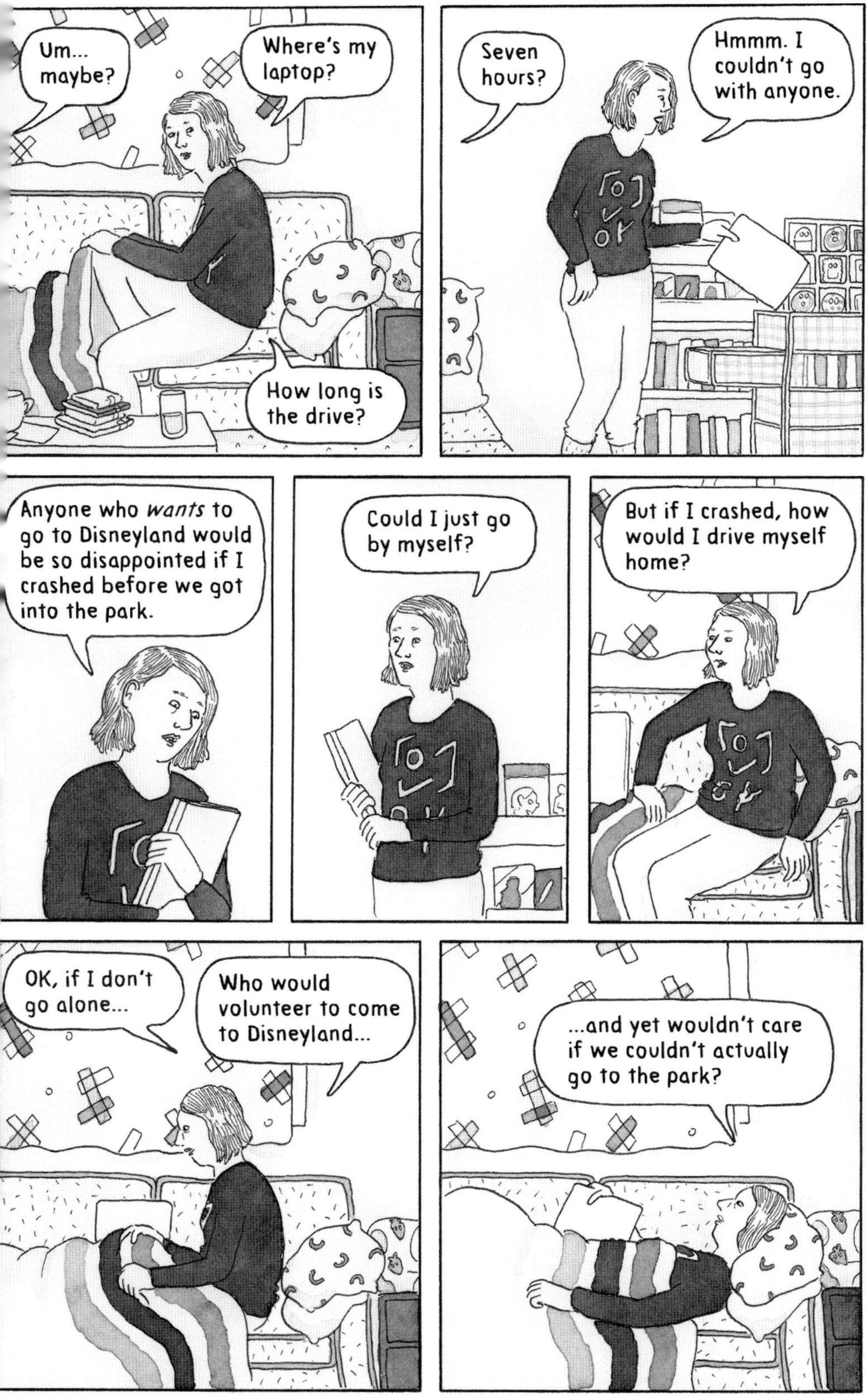
Um... maybe?
Where's my laptop?
How long is the drive?
Seven hours?
Hmmm. I couldn't go with anyone.
Anyone who *wants* to go to Disneyland would be so disappointed if I crashed before we got into the park.
Could I just go by myself?
But if I crashed, how would I drive myself home?
OK, if I don't go alone...
Who would volunteer to come to Disneyland...
...and yet wouldn't care if we couldn't actually go to the park?

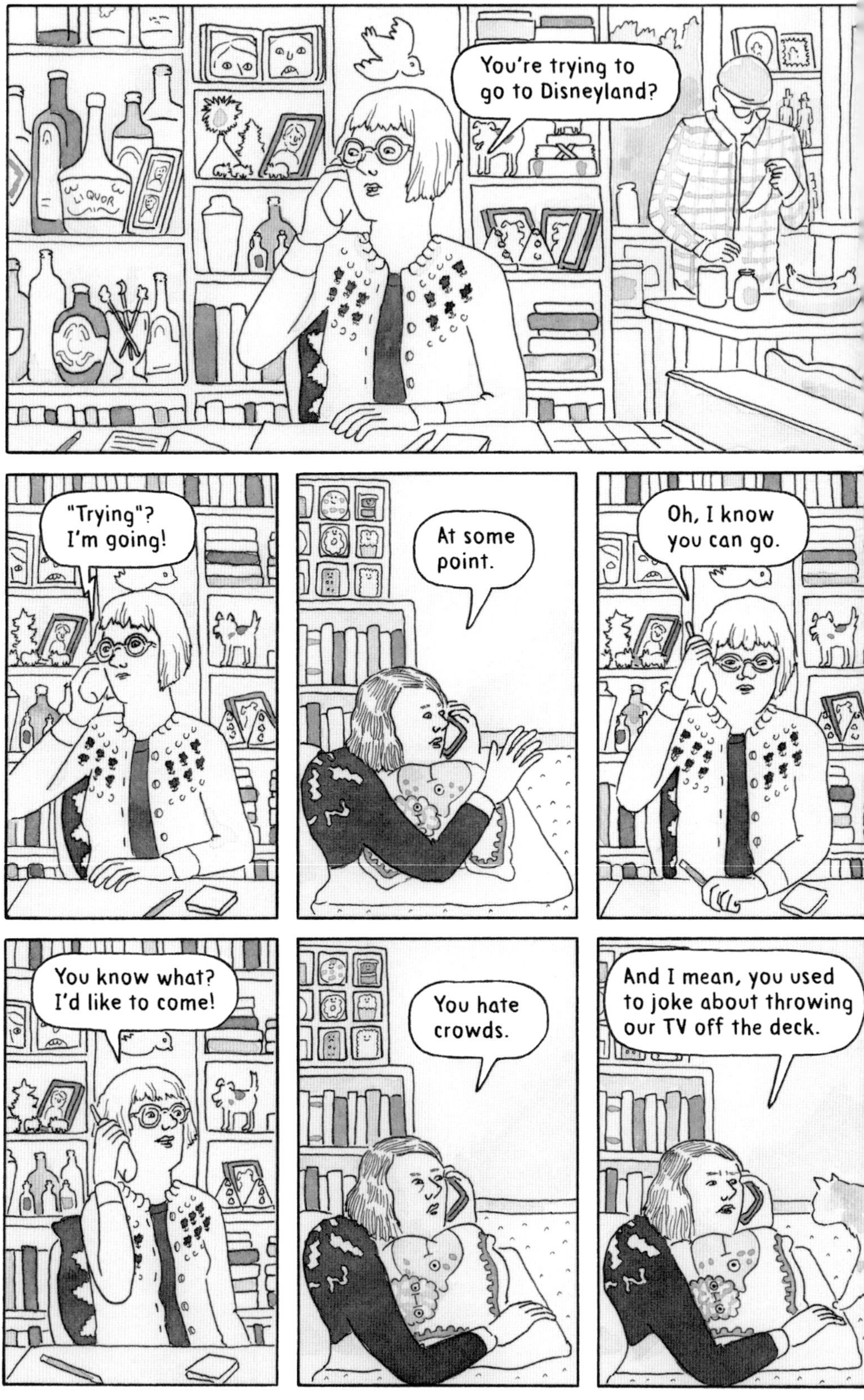

You're trying to go to Disneyland?
"Trying"? I'm going!
At some point.
Oh, I know you can go.
You know what? I'd like to come!
You hate crowds.
And I mean, you used to joke about throwing our TV off the deck.
LIQUOR

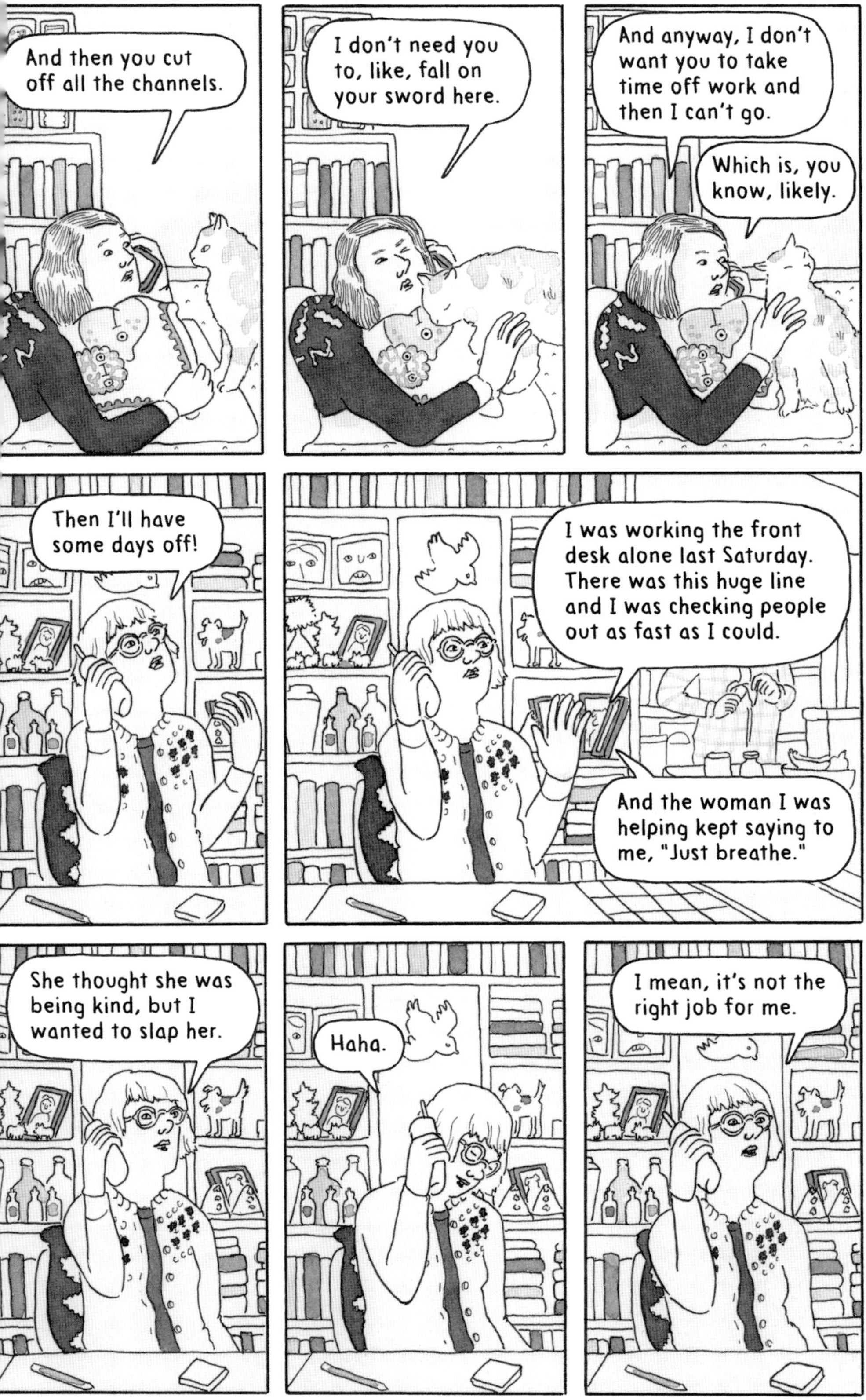
And then you cut off all the channels.
I don't need you to, like, fall on your sword here.
And anyway, I don't want you to take time off work and then I can't go.
Which is, you know, likely.
Then I'll have some days off!
I was working the front desk alone last Saturday. There was this huge line and I was checking people out as fast as I could.
And the woman I was helping kept saying to me, "Just breathe."
She thought she was being kind, but I wanted to slap her.
Haha.
I mean, it's not the right job for me.

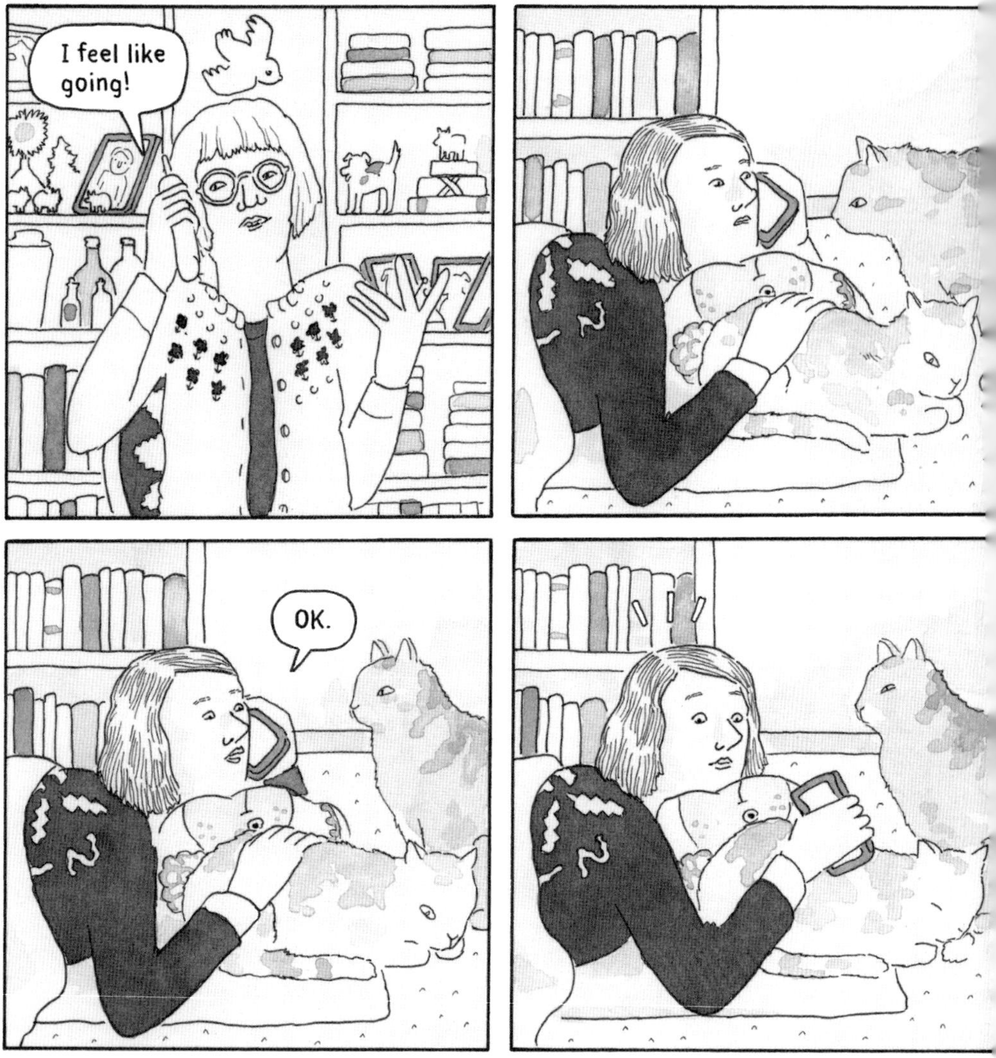
I feel like going!
OK.

However, "just breathe" was good advice for me.

My vigilance around the illness went into overdrive.

I didn't want to ruin my chance.

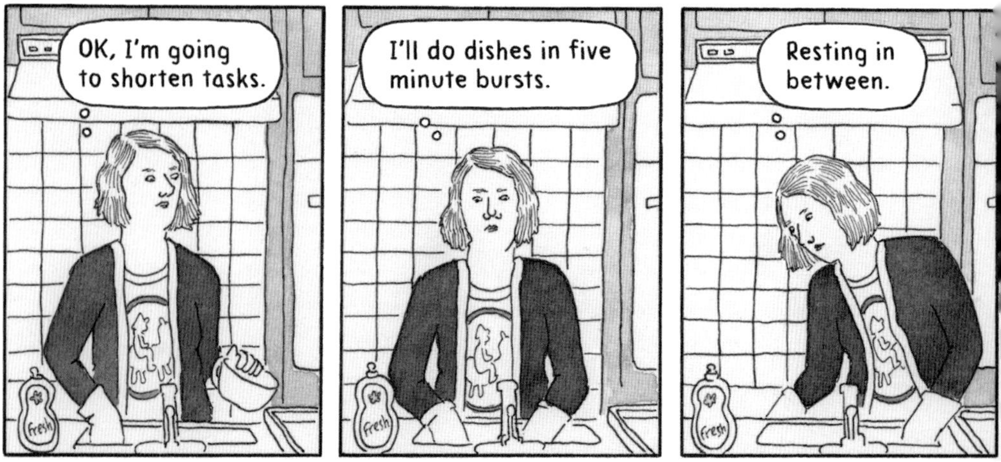
OK, I'm going to shorten tasks.
I'll do dishes in five minute bursts.
Resting in between.

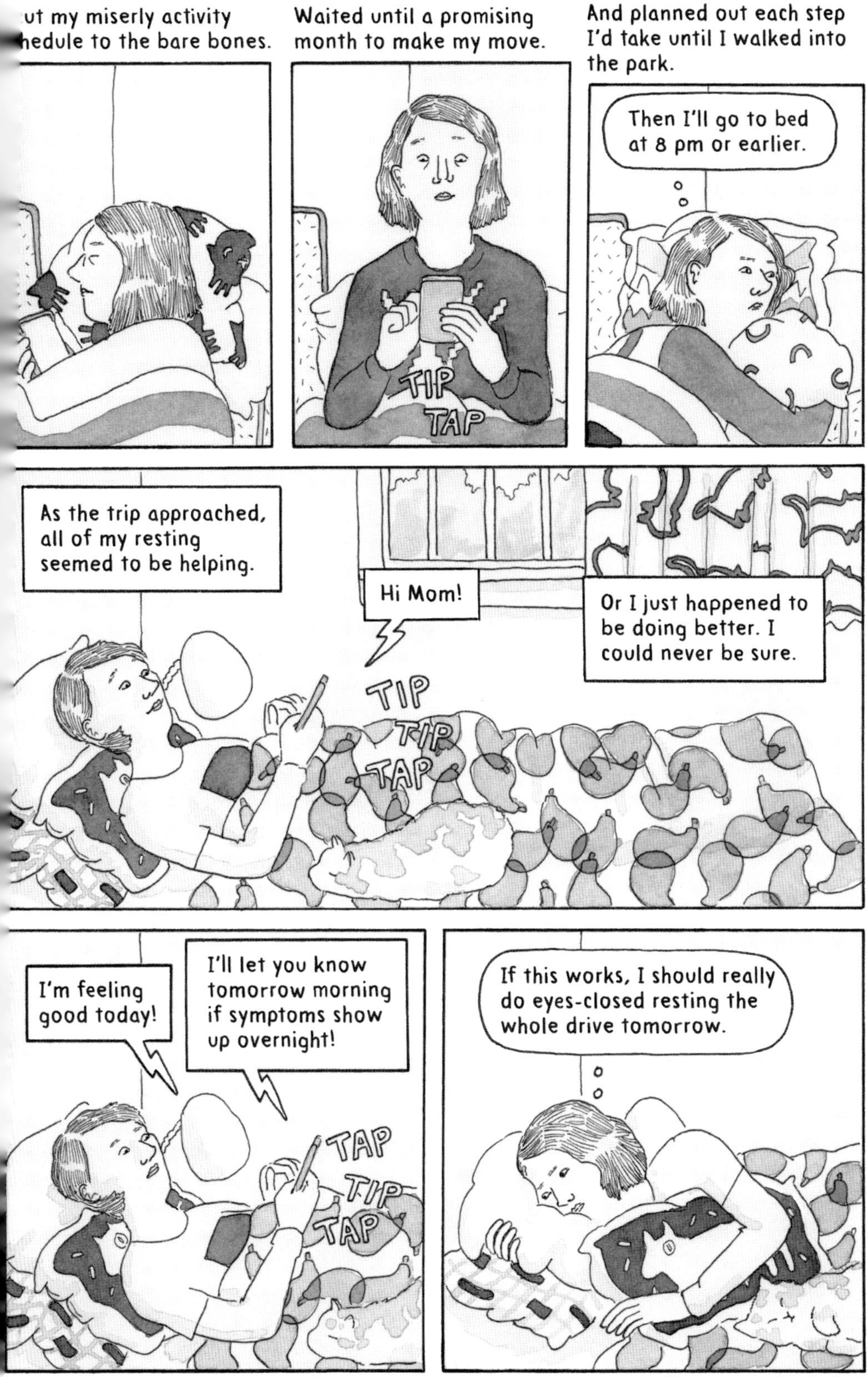

ut my miserly activity
hedule to the bare bones.
Waited until a promising month to make my move.
TIP
TAP
And planned out each step I'd take until I walked into the park.
Then I'll go to bed at 8 pm or earlier.
As the trip approached, all of my resting seemed to be helping.
Hi Mom!
Or I just happened to be doing better. I could never be sure.
TIP
TIP
TAP
I'm feeling good today!
I'll let you know tomorrow morning if symptoms show up overnight!
TAP
TIP
TAP
If this works, I should really do eyes-closed resting the whole drive tomorrow.

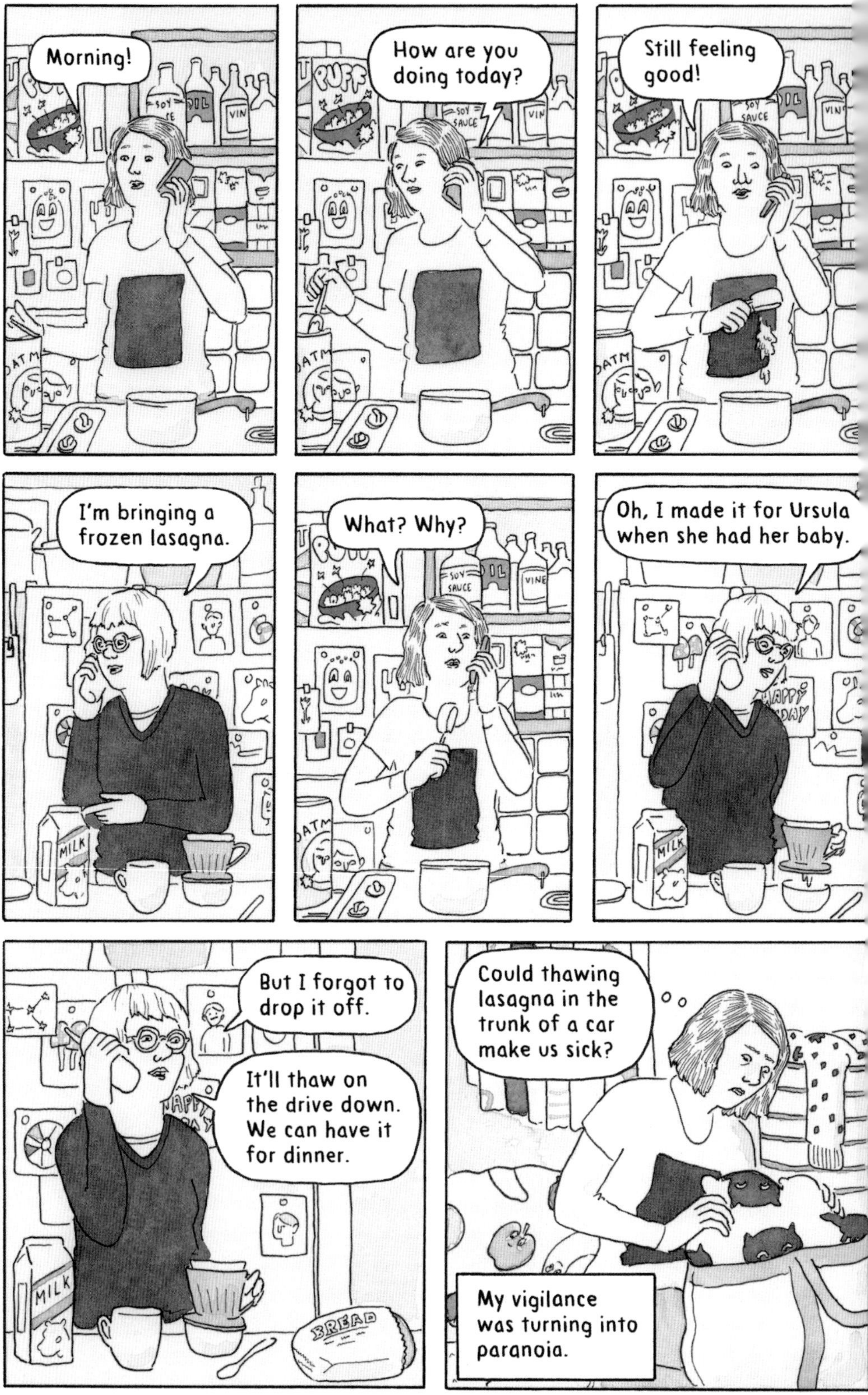
Morning!
How are you doing today?
Still feeling good!
I'm bringing a frozen lasagna.
What? Why?
Oh, I made it for Ursula when she had her baby.
But I forgot to drop it off.
It'll thaw on the drive down. We can have it for dinner.
Could thawing lasagna in the trunk of a car make us sick?
My vigilance was turning into paranoia.

And yet it was no match for my excitement about actually being on a trip.

She's the most Machiavellian dog I've met.

When she put her head on my leg at the shelter, I thought it was so sweet.

But that's just a clueless primate interpretation.

The trainer said she's calculating and...oh, do you want to stop?

FUDGE + PETTING ZOO NEXT EXIT

I shouldn't.

To be fair, it was the first trip I'd been on in five years.

Hello, fluffy.

This wind is cold.

Uh oh. My ears are starting to ring.

I'm being so reckless!

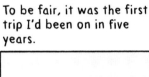

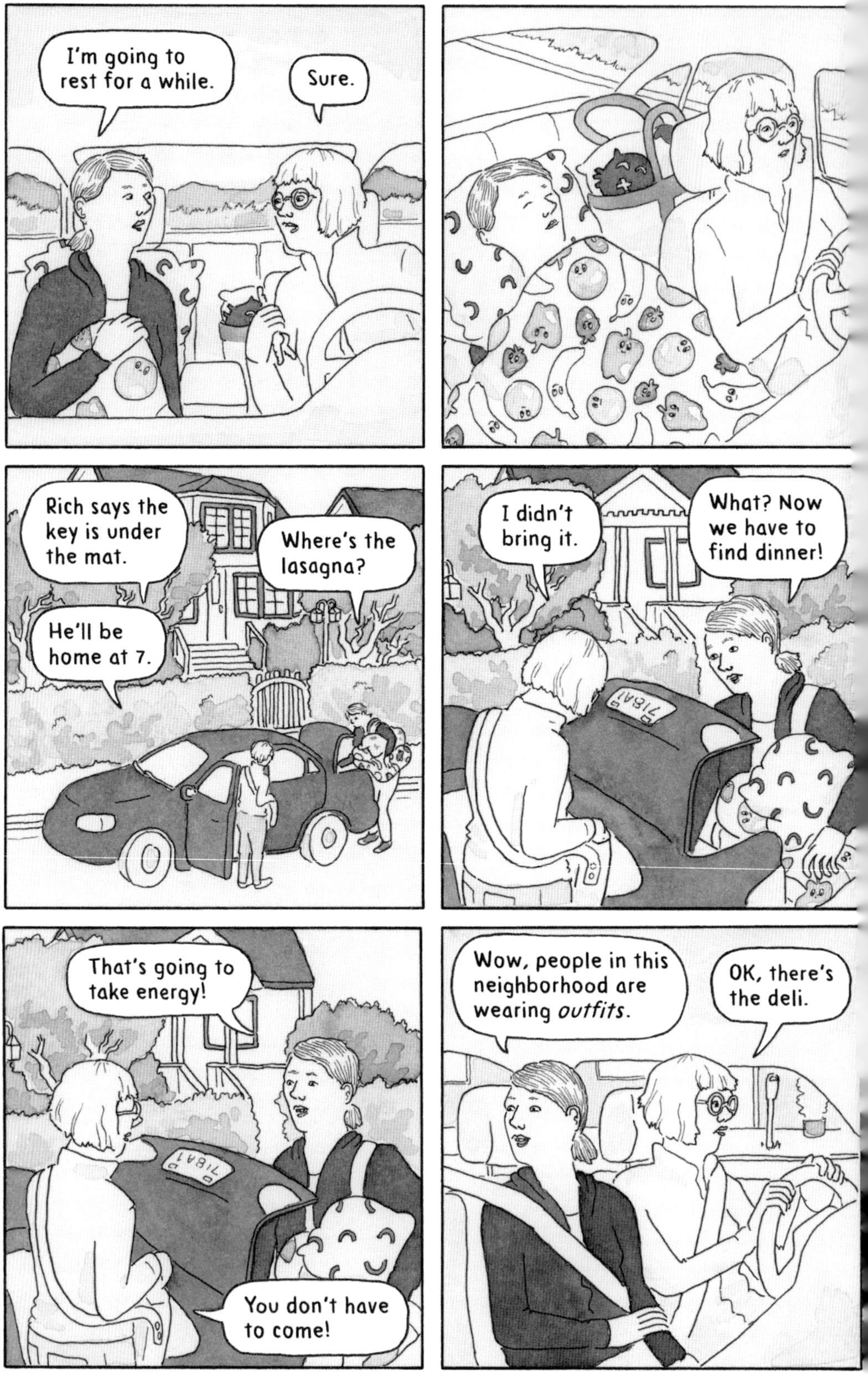
I'm going to rest for a while.
Sure.
Rich says the key is under the mat.
He'll be home at 7.
Where's the lasagna?
I didn't bring it.
What? Now we have to find dinner!
That's going to take energy!
You don't have to come!
Wow, people in this neighborhood are wearing *outfits*.
OK, there's the deli.

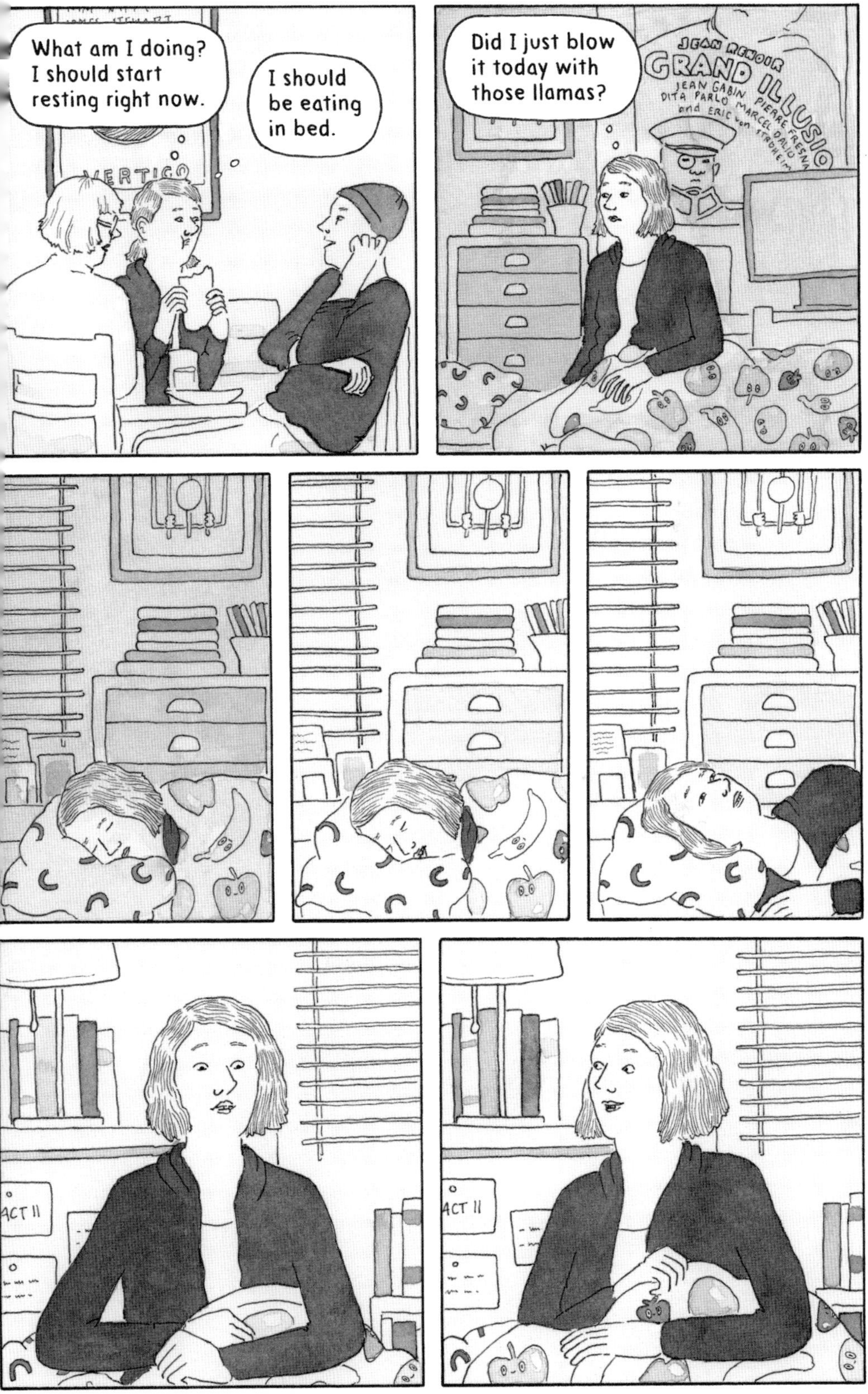

What am I doing? I should start resting right now.
I should be eating in bed.
ERTIGO
Did I just blow it today with those llamas?
JEAN RENOIR
GRAND ILLUSIO
JEAN GABIN PIERRE FRESNAY
DITA PARLO MARCEL DALIO
and ERIC von STROHEIM
ACT II
ACT II

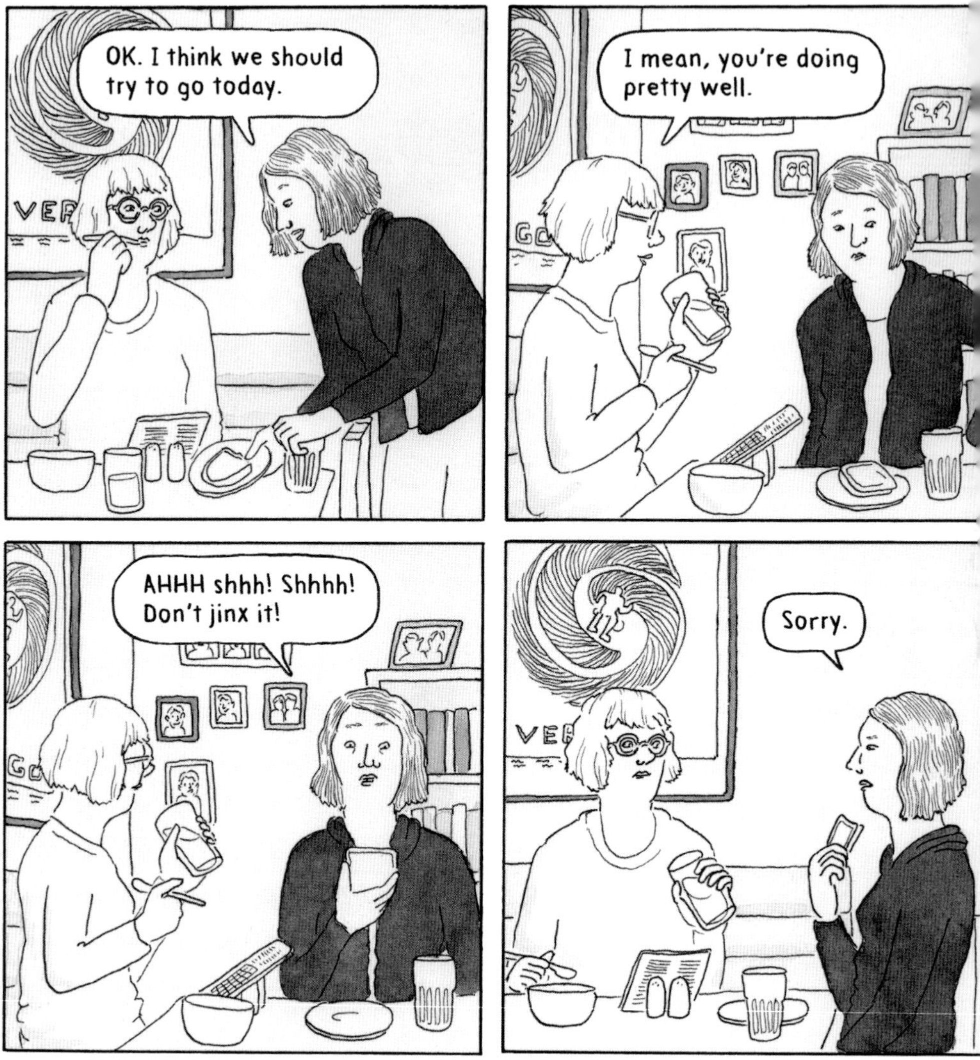
OK. I think we should try to go today.
I mean, you're doing pretty well.
AHHH shhh! Shhhh! Don't jinx it!
Sorry.

It was a dreary, overcast winter day and the adults at the park looked exhausted.

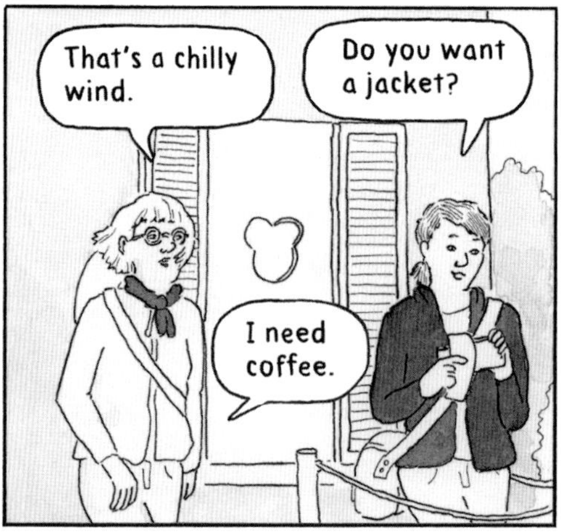
That's a chilly wind.
Do you want a jacket?
I need coffee.

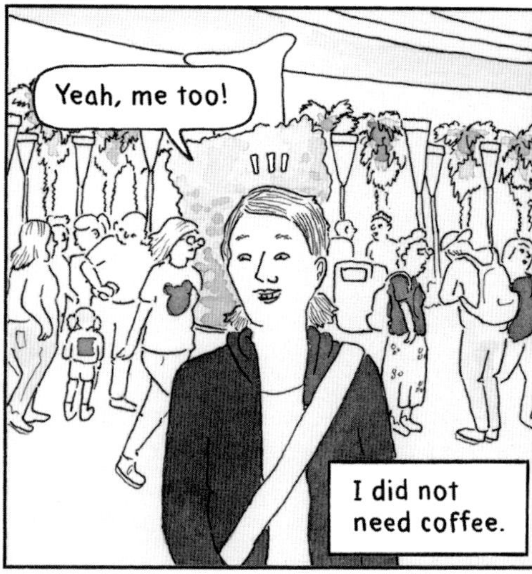
Yeah, me too!
I did not need coffee.

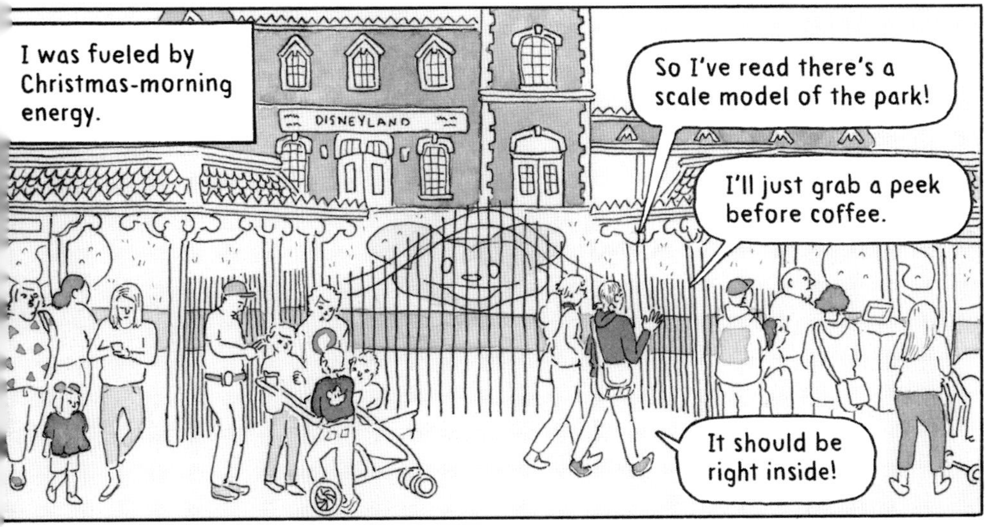
I was fueled by Christmas-morning energy.
DISNEYLAND
So I've read there's a scale model of the park!
I'll just grab a peek before coffee.
It should be right inside!

his was a red-letter day.

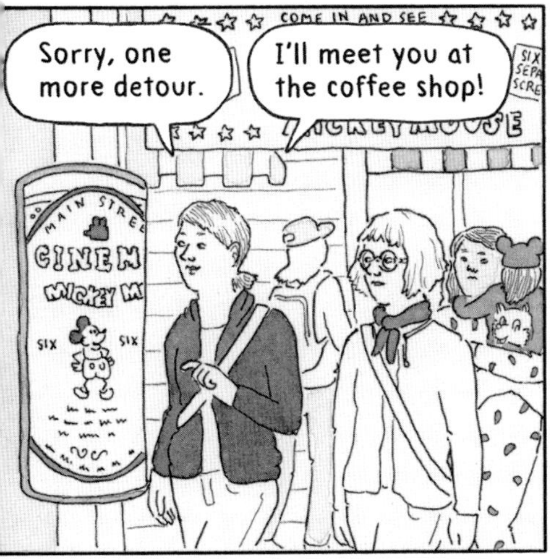
COME IN AND SEE
Sorry, one more detour.
I'll meet you at the coffee shop!

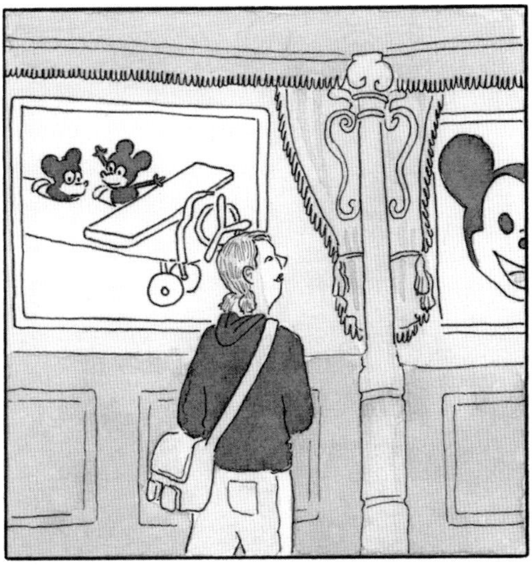

A jackpot that I wanted to spend every penny of before it was taken away.

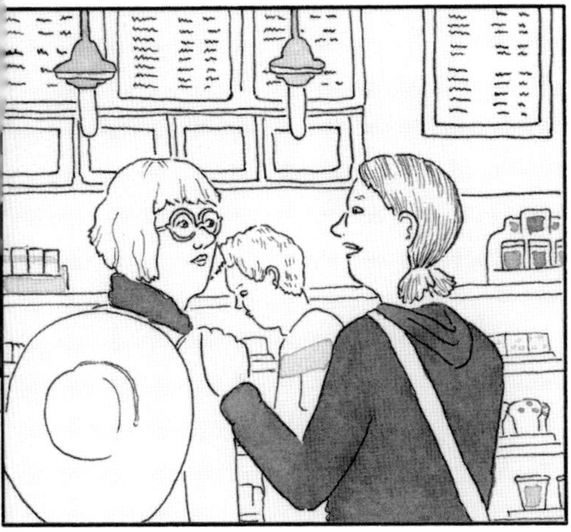

And as soon as we got in the park, I abandoned any pretense I'd had about moderation and being careful with myself.

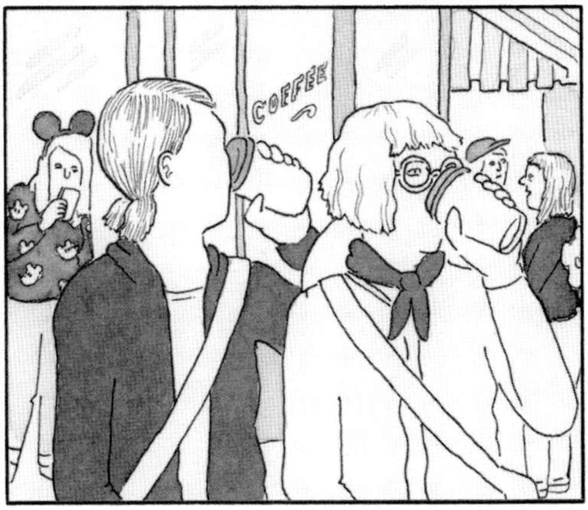
COFFEE

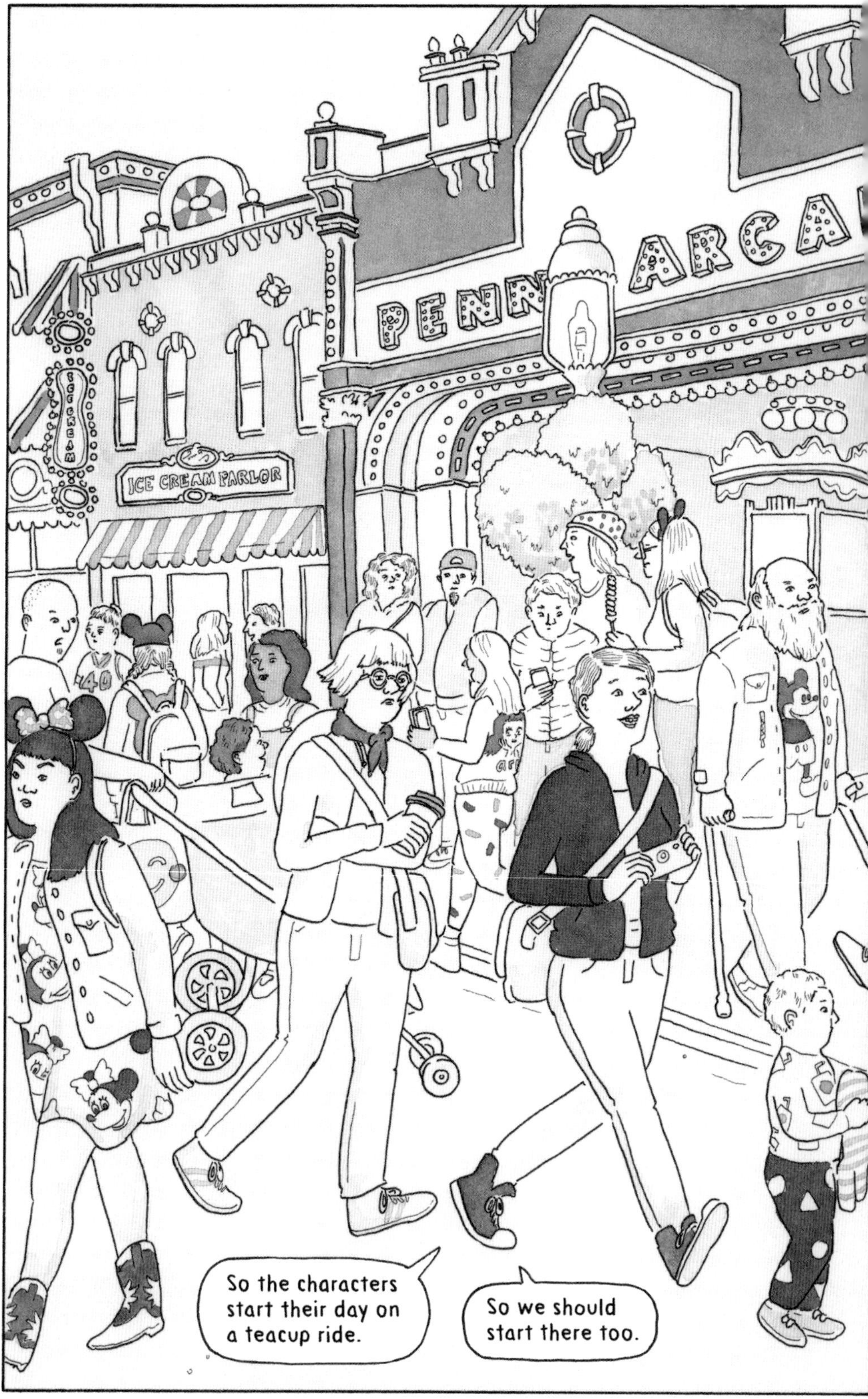
ICE CREAM PARLOR
ICE CREAM
PENN
ARCA
So the characters start their day on a teacup ride.
So we should start there too.

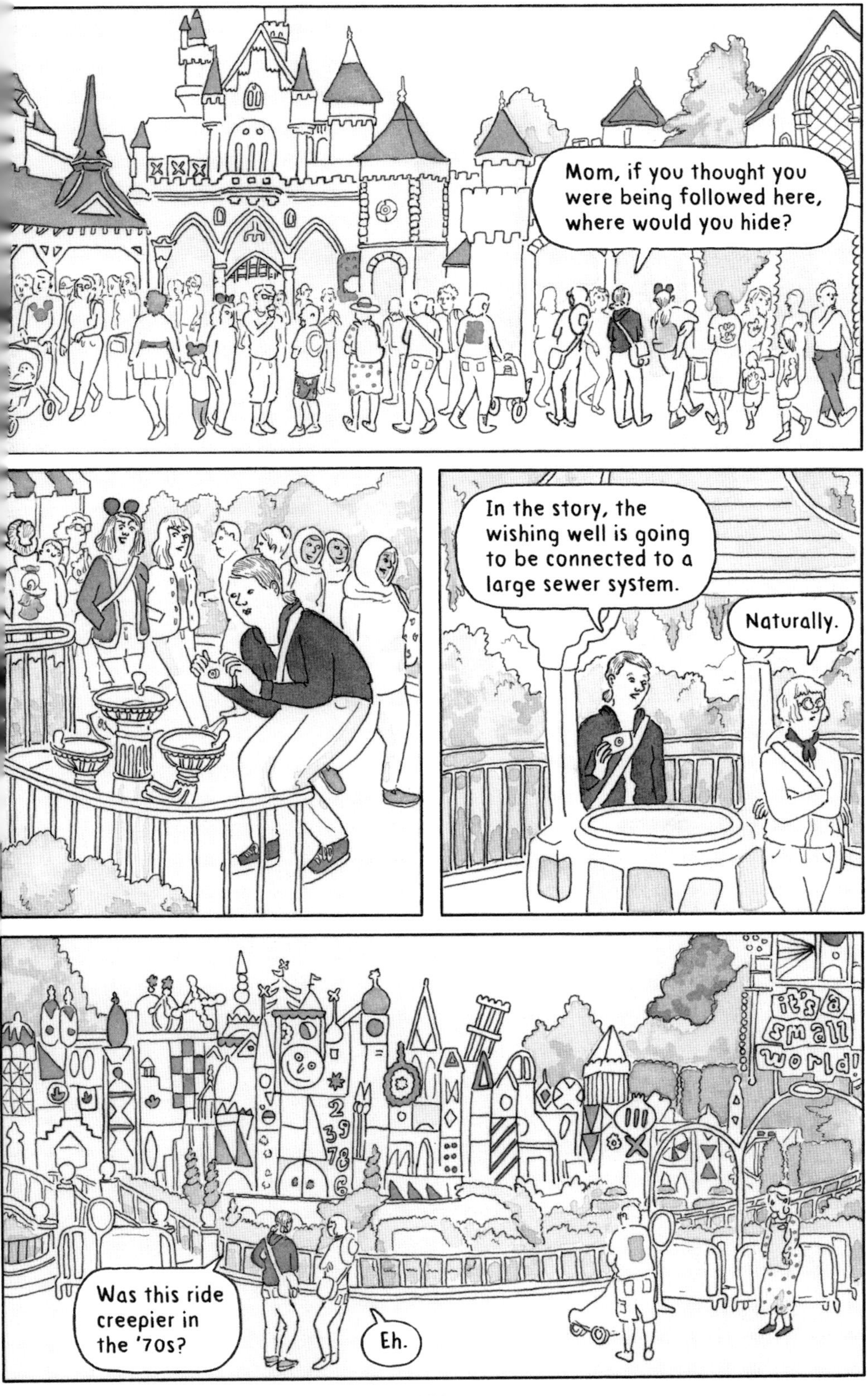
Mom, if you thought you were being followed here, where would you hide?
In the story, the wishing well is going to be connected to a large sewer system.
Naturally.
it's a small world!
Was this ride creepier in the '70s?
Eh.

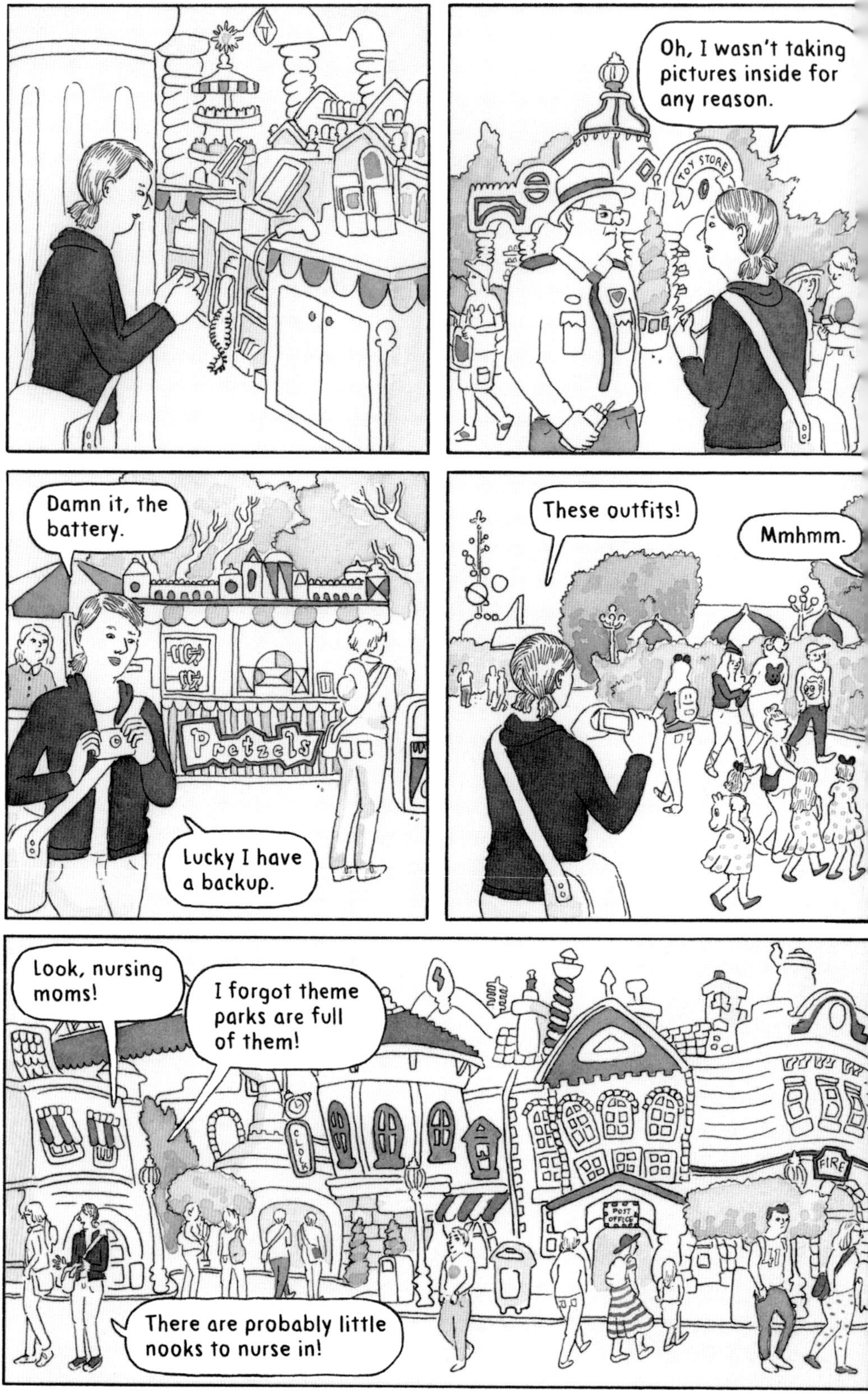
Oh, I wasn't taking pictures inside for any reason.
TOY STORE
Damn it, the battery.
Pretzels
Lucky I have a backup.
These outfits!
Mmhmm.
Look, nursing moms!
I forgot theme parks are full of them!
CLOCK
FIRE
POST OFFICE
There are probably little nooks to nurse in!

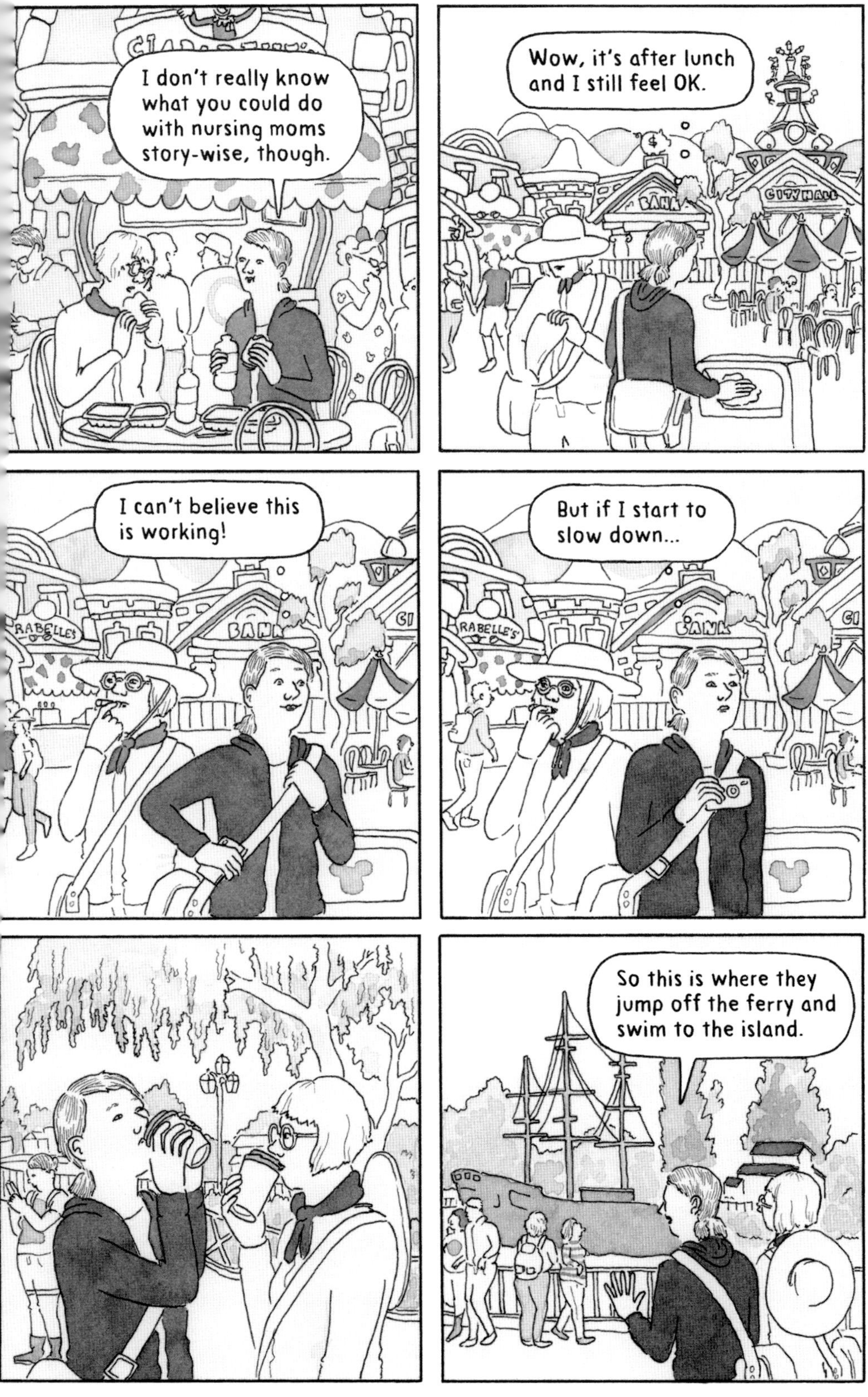
I don't really know what you could do with nursing moms story-wise, though.
Wow, it's after lunch and I still feel OK.
BANK
CITY HALL
I can't believe this is working!
RABELLE'S
BANK
But if I start to slow down...
RABELLE'S
BANK
So this is where they jump off the ferry and swim to the island.

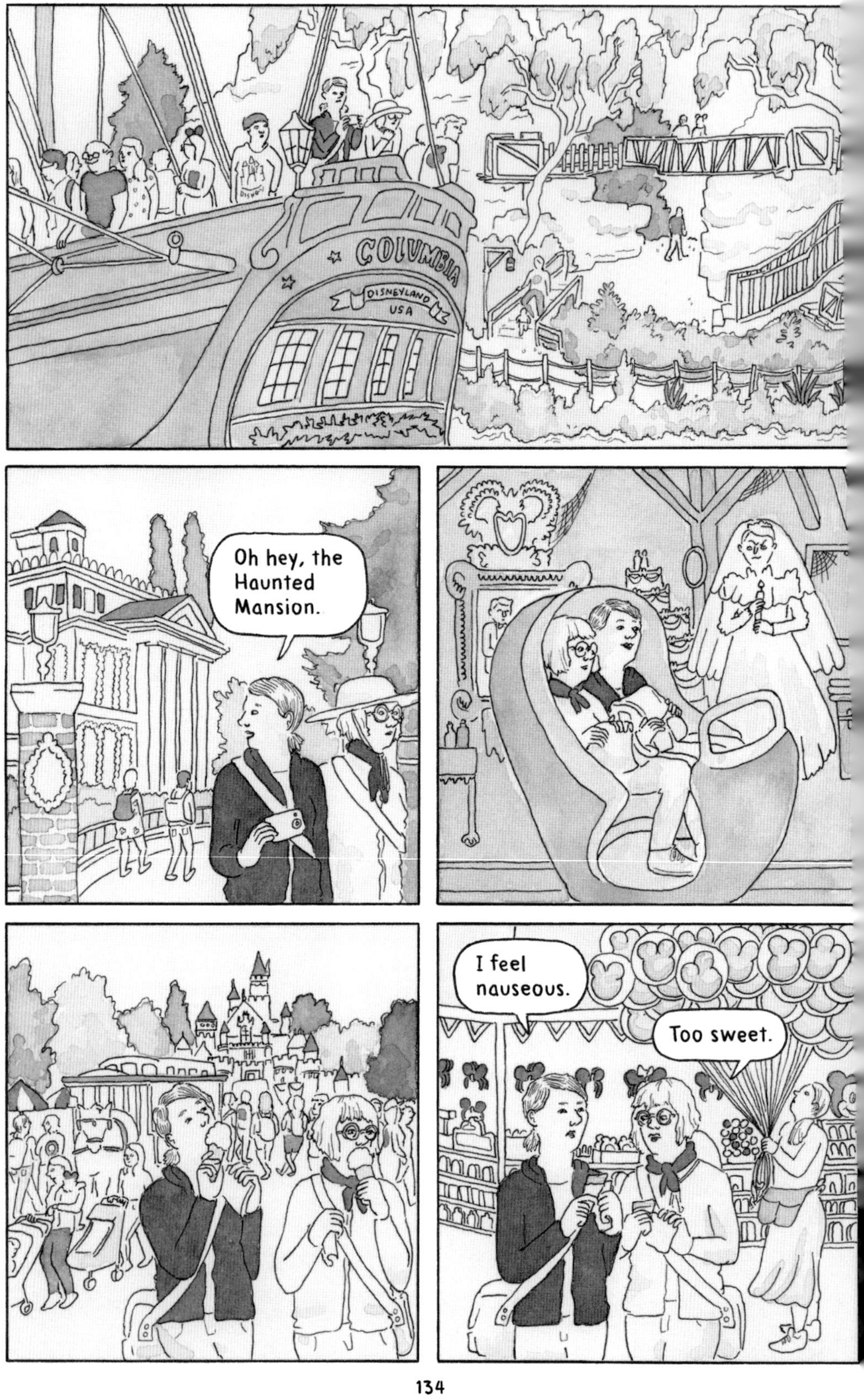
COLUMBIA
DISNEYLAND
USA
Oh hey, the Haunted Mansion.
I feel nauseous.
Too sweet.

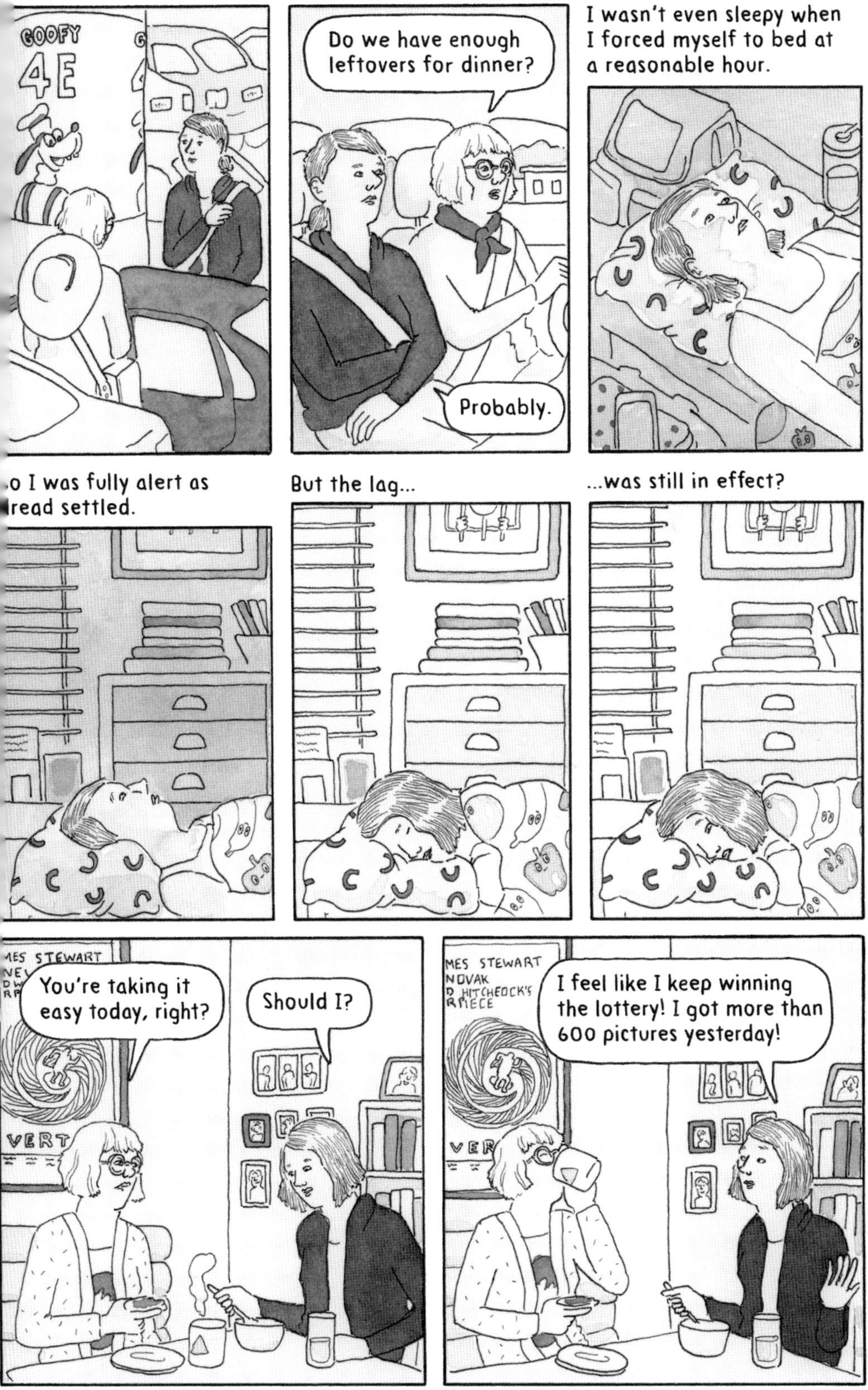
GOOFY
4E
Do we have enough leftovers for dinner?
Probably.
I wasn't even sleepy when I forced myself to bed at a reasonable hour.
o I was fully alert as
read settled.
But the lag...
...was still in effect?
MES STEWART
You're taking it easy today, right?
Should I?
VERT
MES STEWART
NOVAK
I feel like I keep winning the lottery! I got more than 600 pictures yesterday!

I just remember seeing all of these bottoms.

I was sitting on benches a lot, though.

It was nice to see you so happy.

In fact, the lag lasted the rest of the trip.

Predictably.

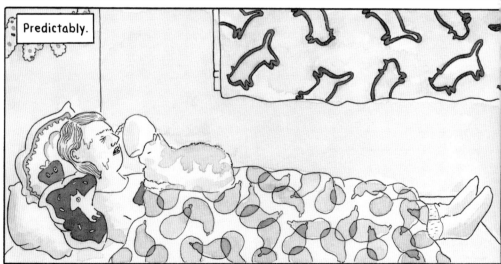

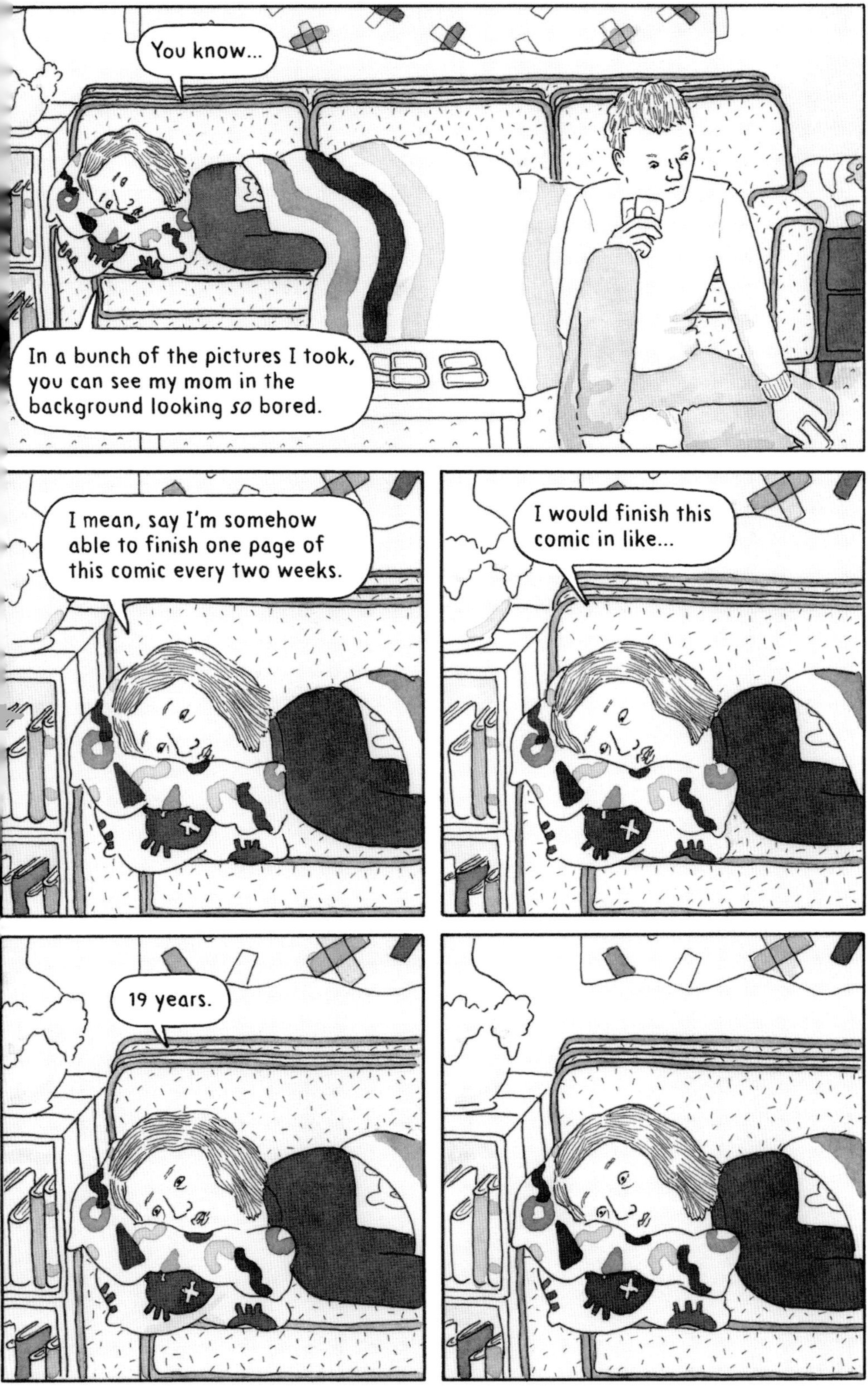
You know...
In a bunch of the pictures I took, you can see my mom in the background looking *so* bored.
I mean, say I'm somehow able to finish one page of this comic every two weeks.
I would finish this comic in like...
19 years.

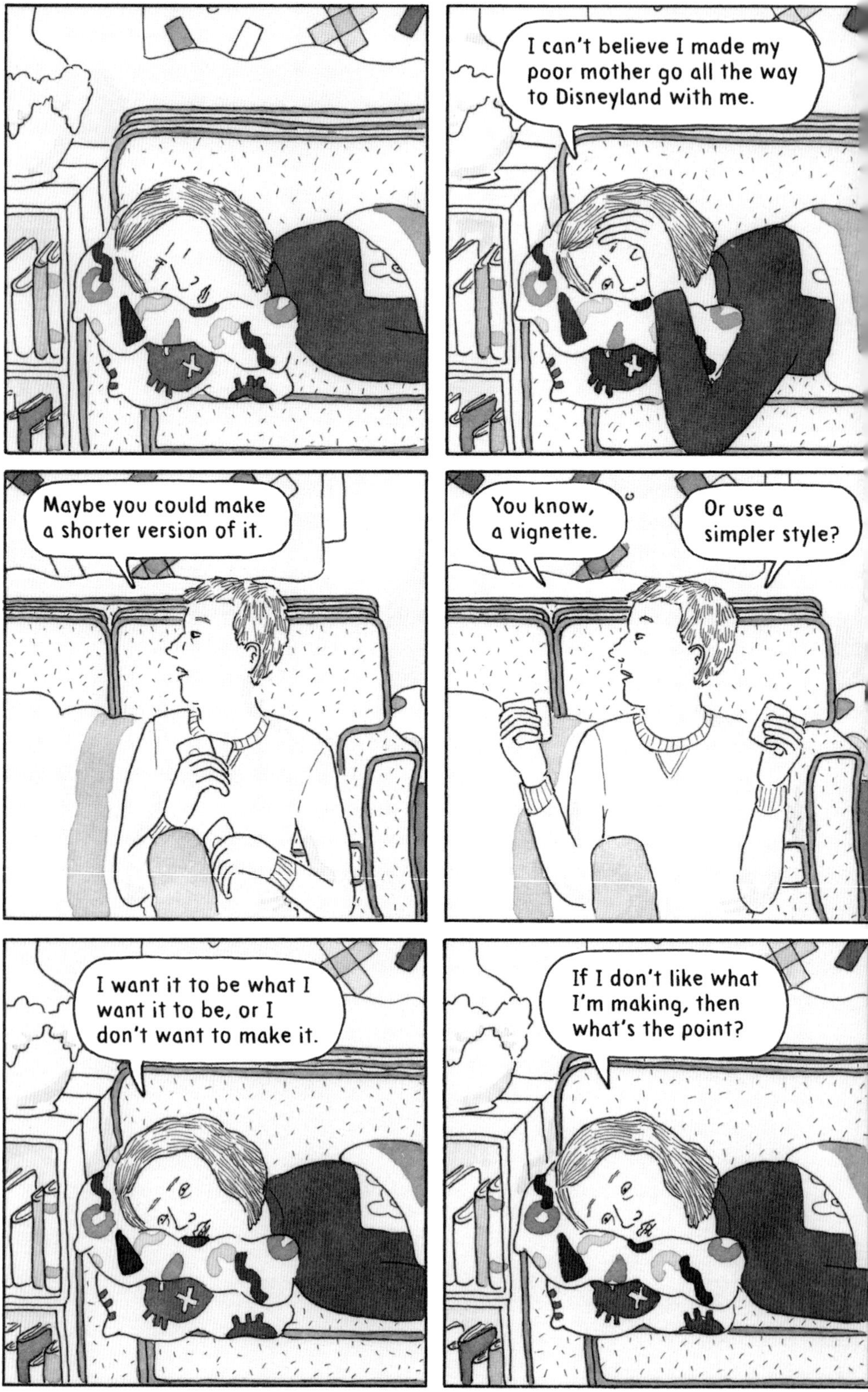
I can't believe I made my poor mother go all the way to Disneyland with me.
Maybe you could make a shorter version of it.
You know, a vignette.
Or use a simpler style?
I want it to be what I want it to be, or I don't want to make it.
If I don't like what I'm making, then what's the point?

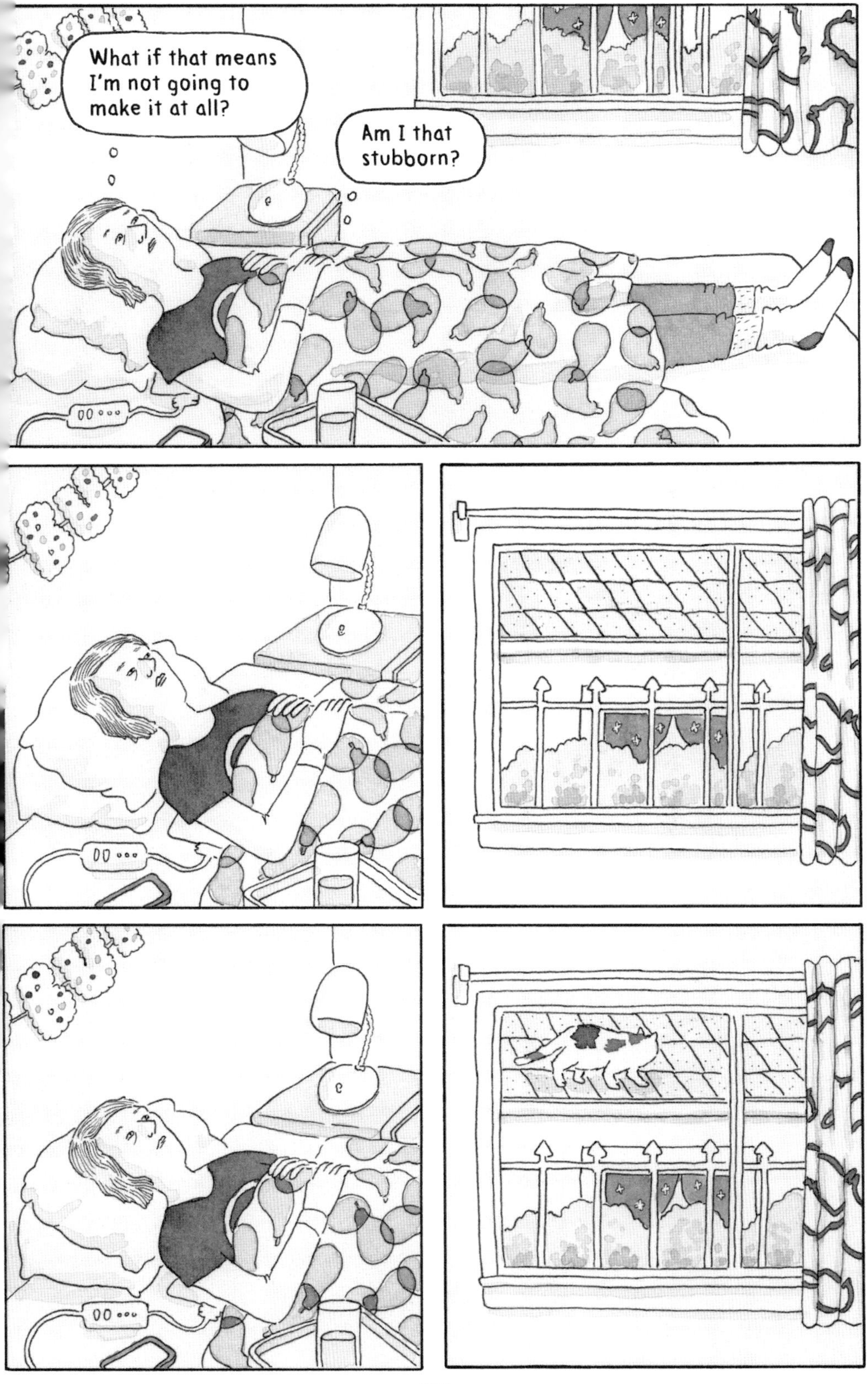
What if that means I'm not going to make it at all?
Am I that stubborn?

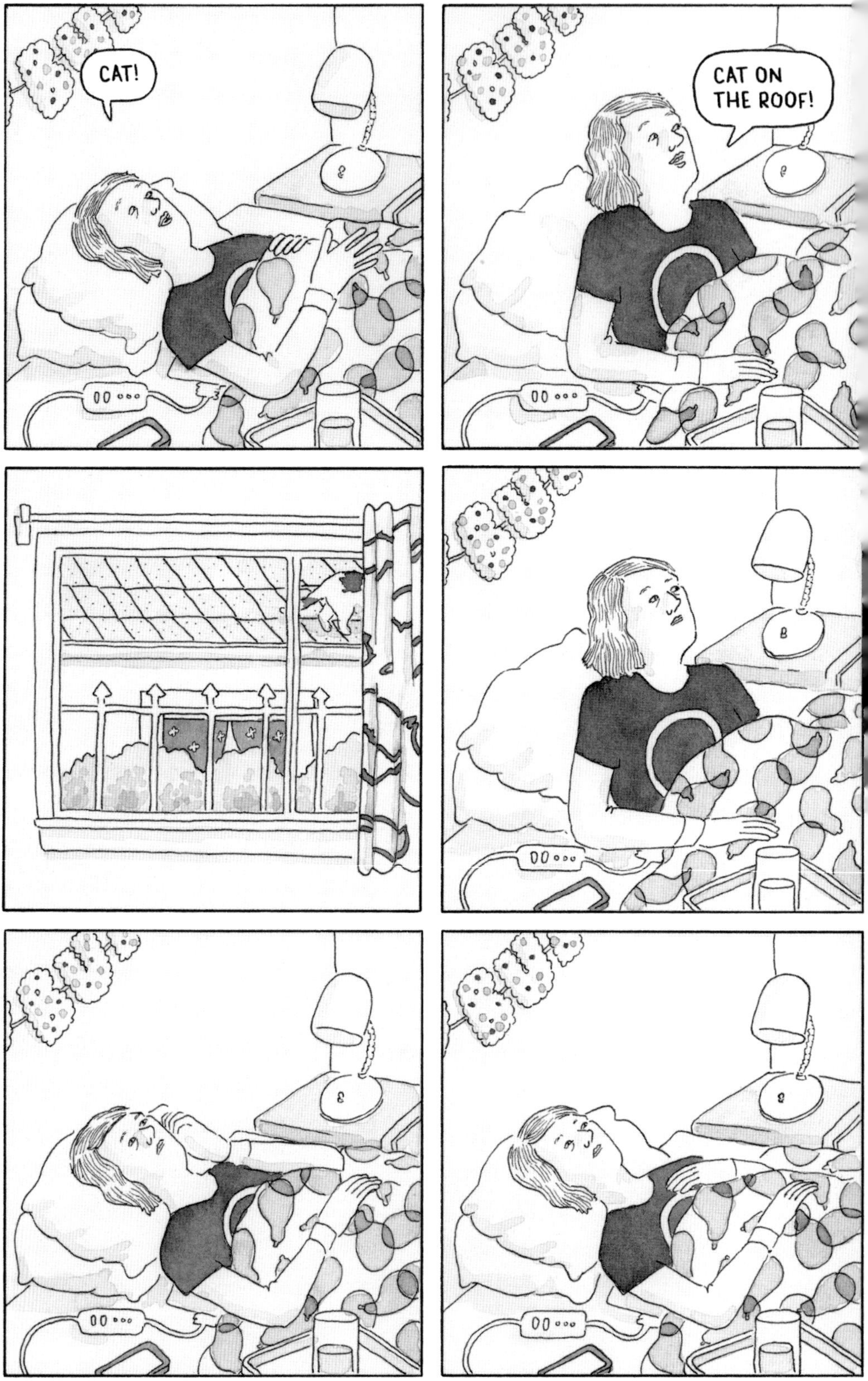
CAT!
CAT ON THE ROOF!

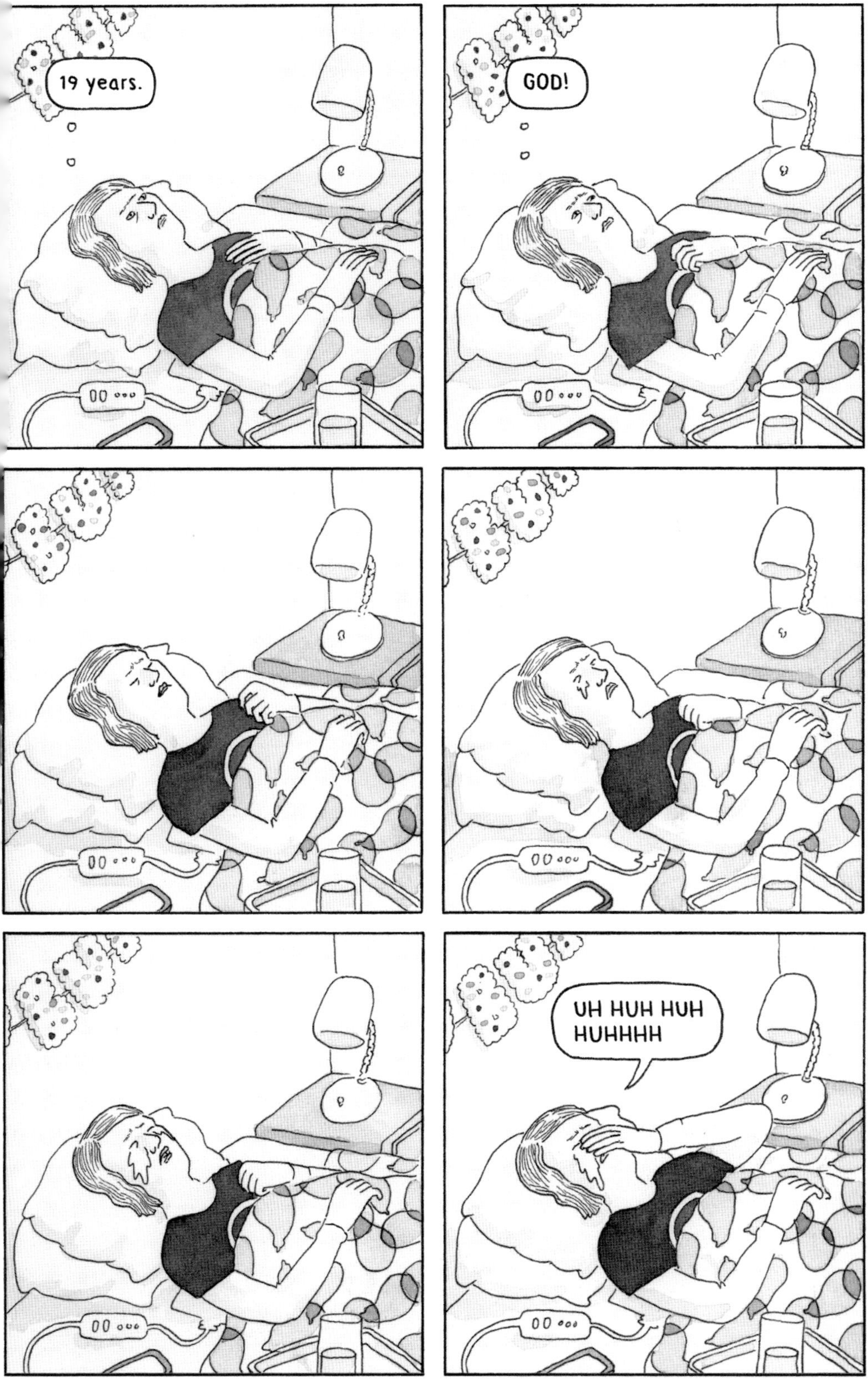
19 years.
GOD!
UH HUH HUH HUHHHH

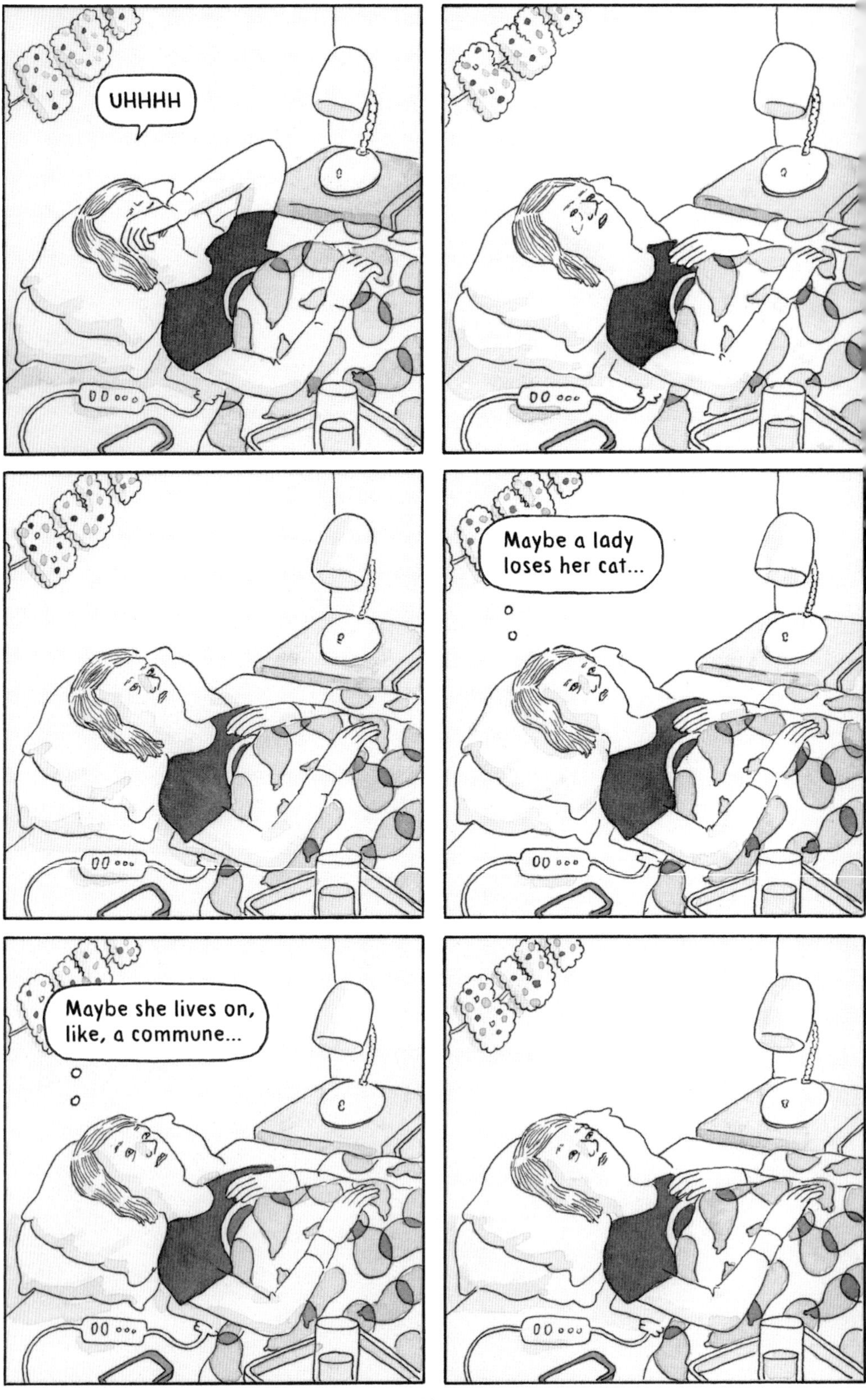
UHHHH
Maybe a lady loses her cat...
Maybe she lives on, like, a commune...

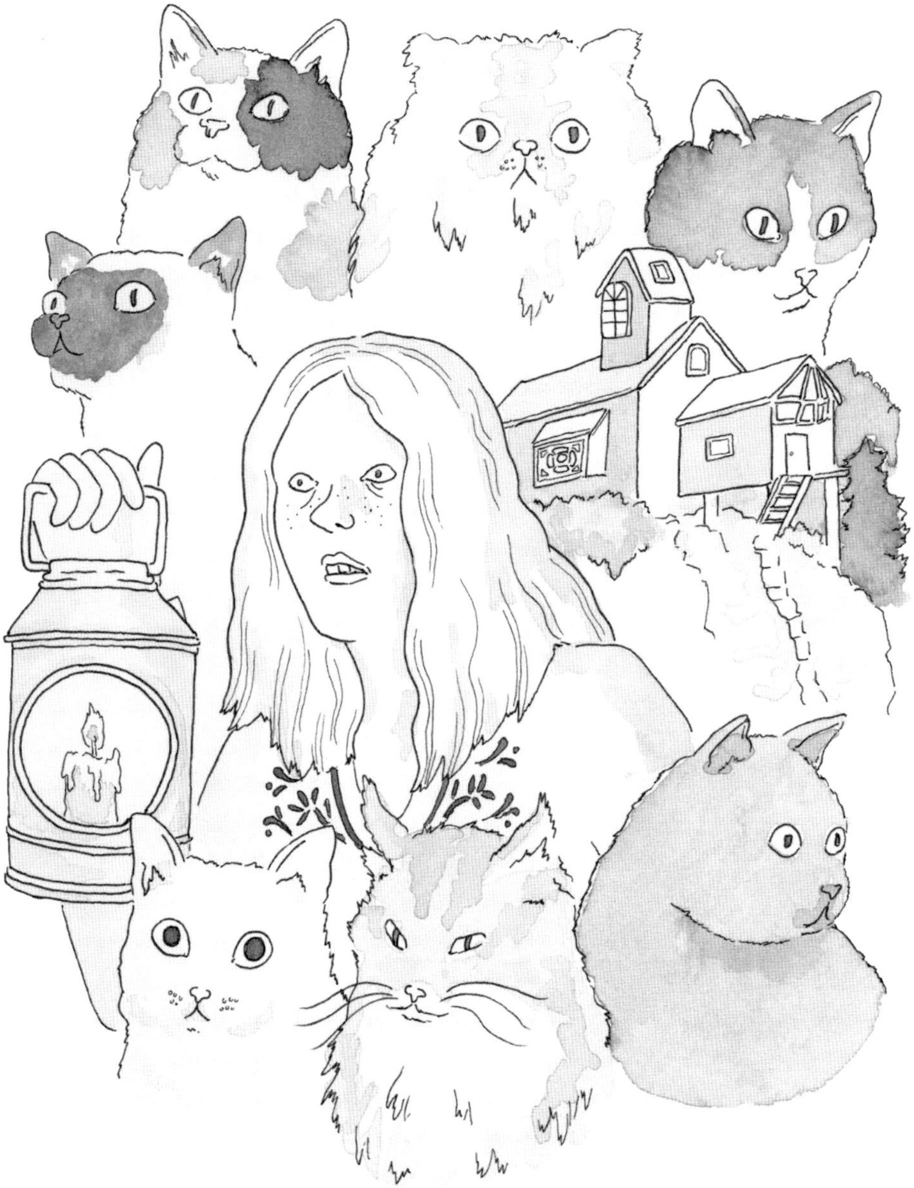

THE COMMUNE

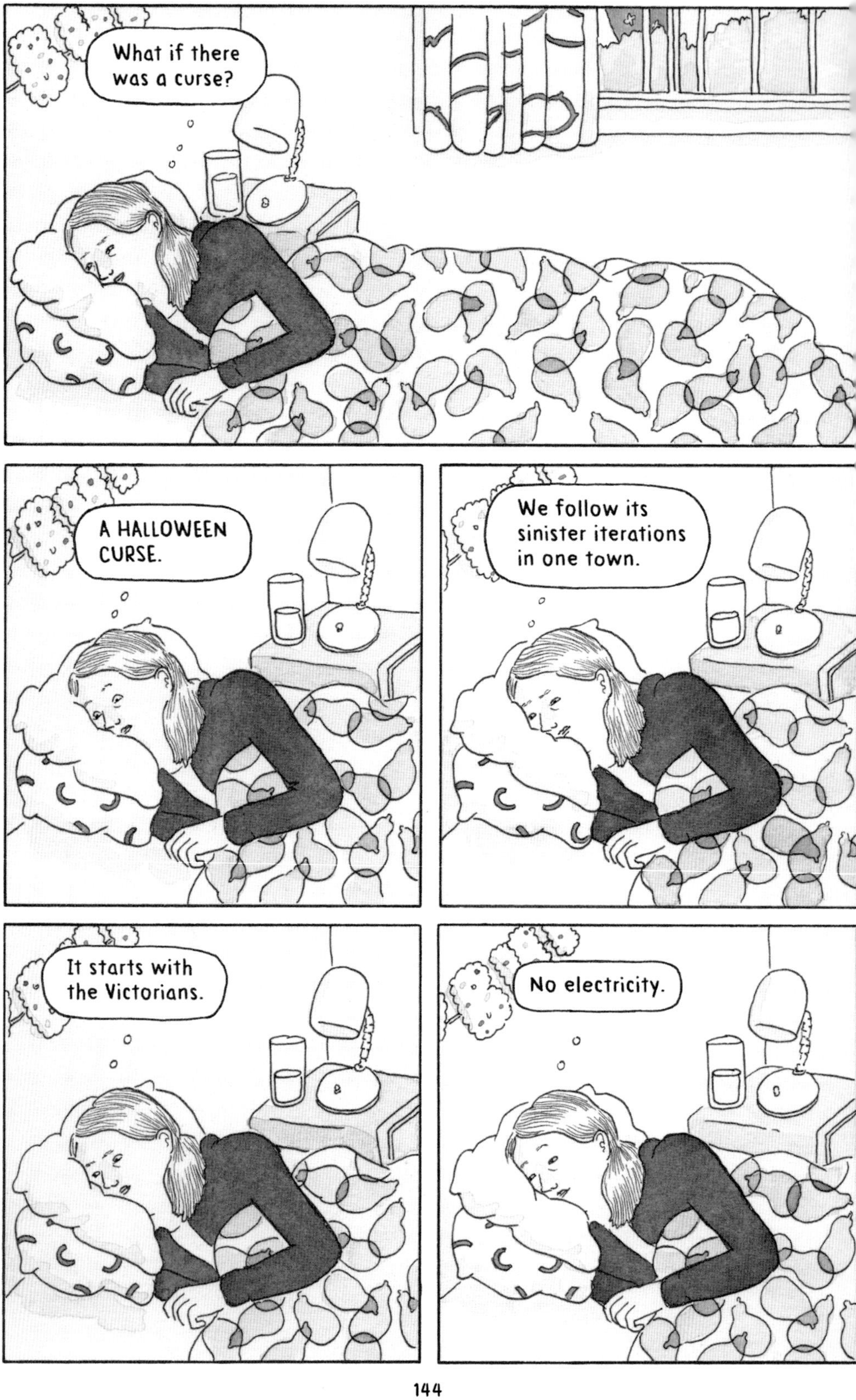
What if there was a curse?
A HALLOWEEN CURSE.
We follow its sinister iterations in one town.
It starts with the Victorians.
No electricity.

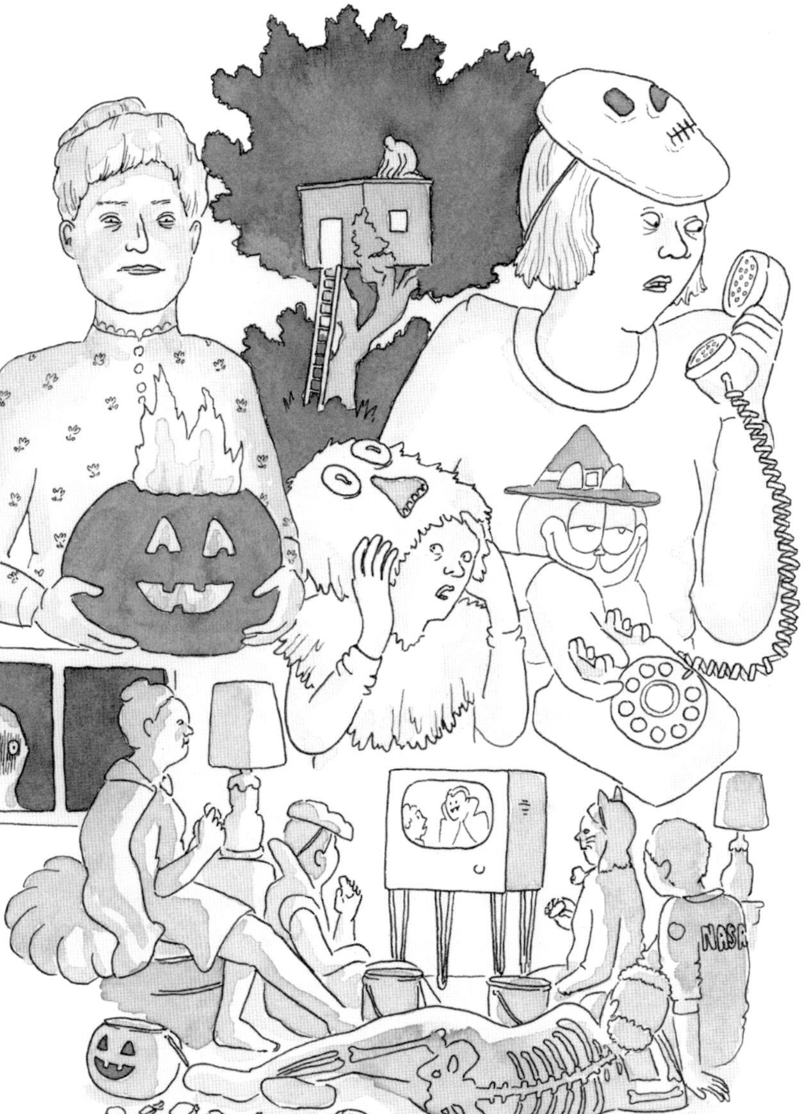
NASA

A History of Halloweens

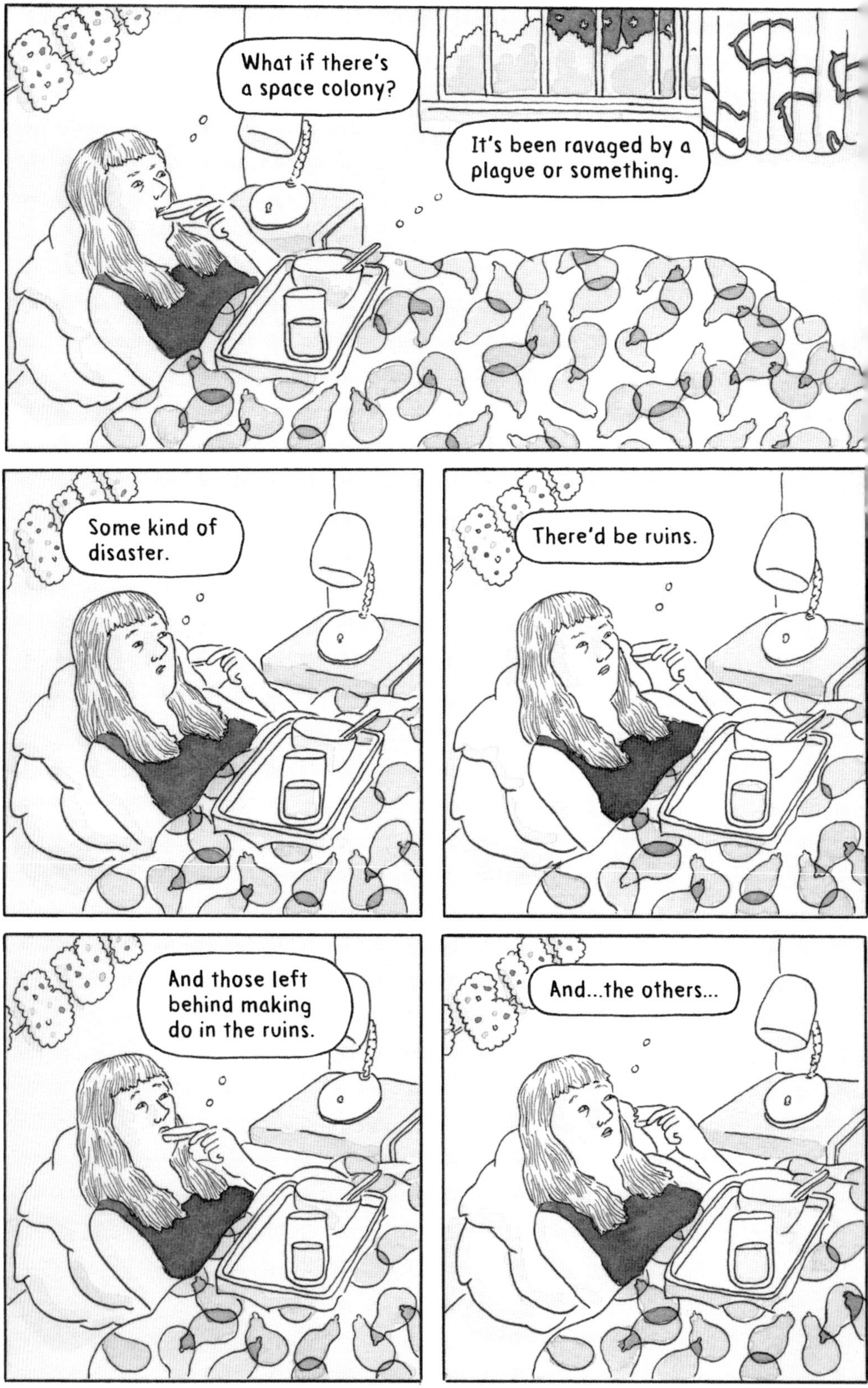
What if there's a space colony?
It's been ravaged by a plague or something.
Some kind of disaster.
There'd be ruins.
And those left behind making do in the ruins.
And...the others...

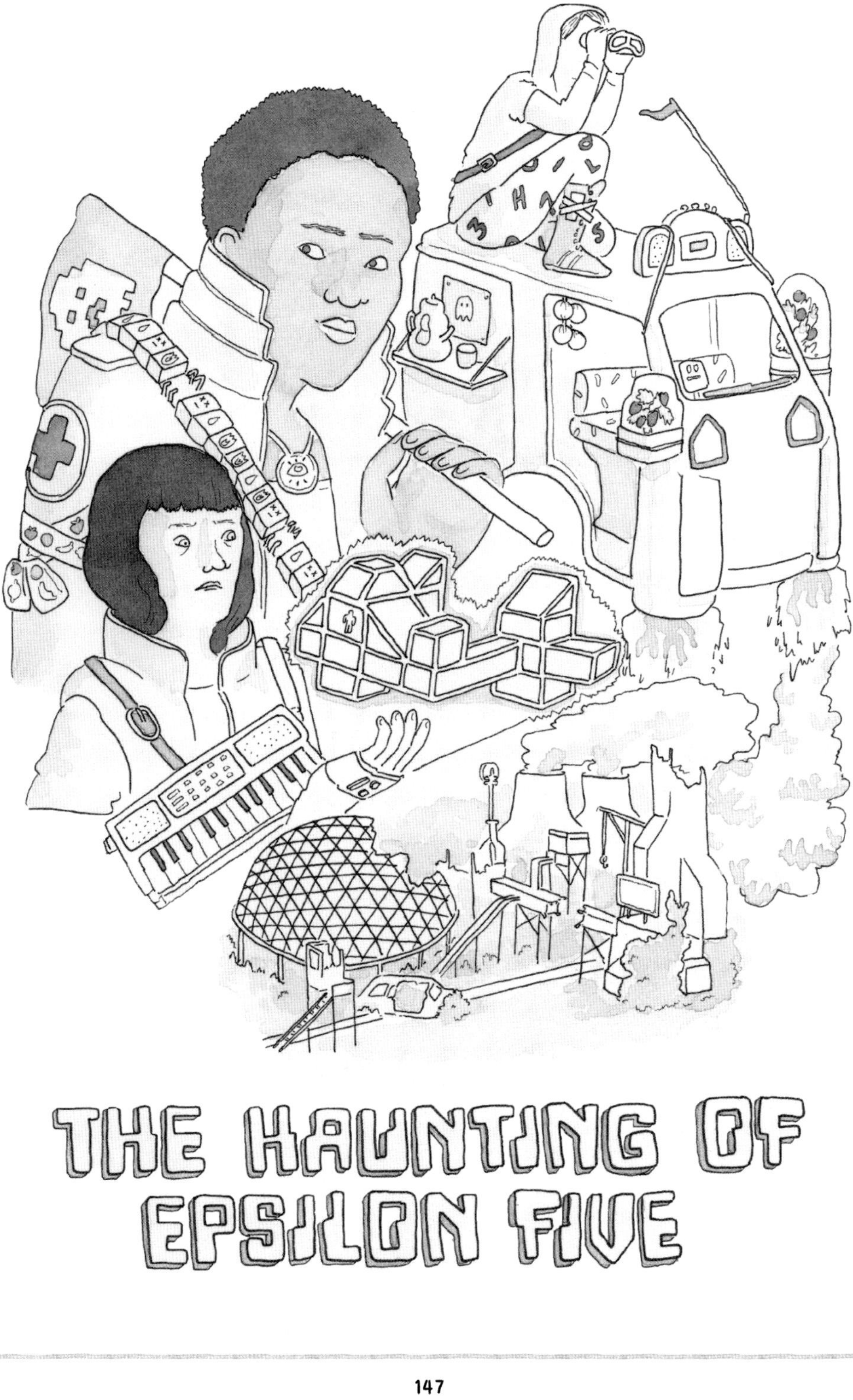

THE HAUNTING OF EPSILON FIVE

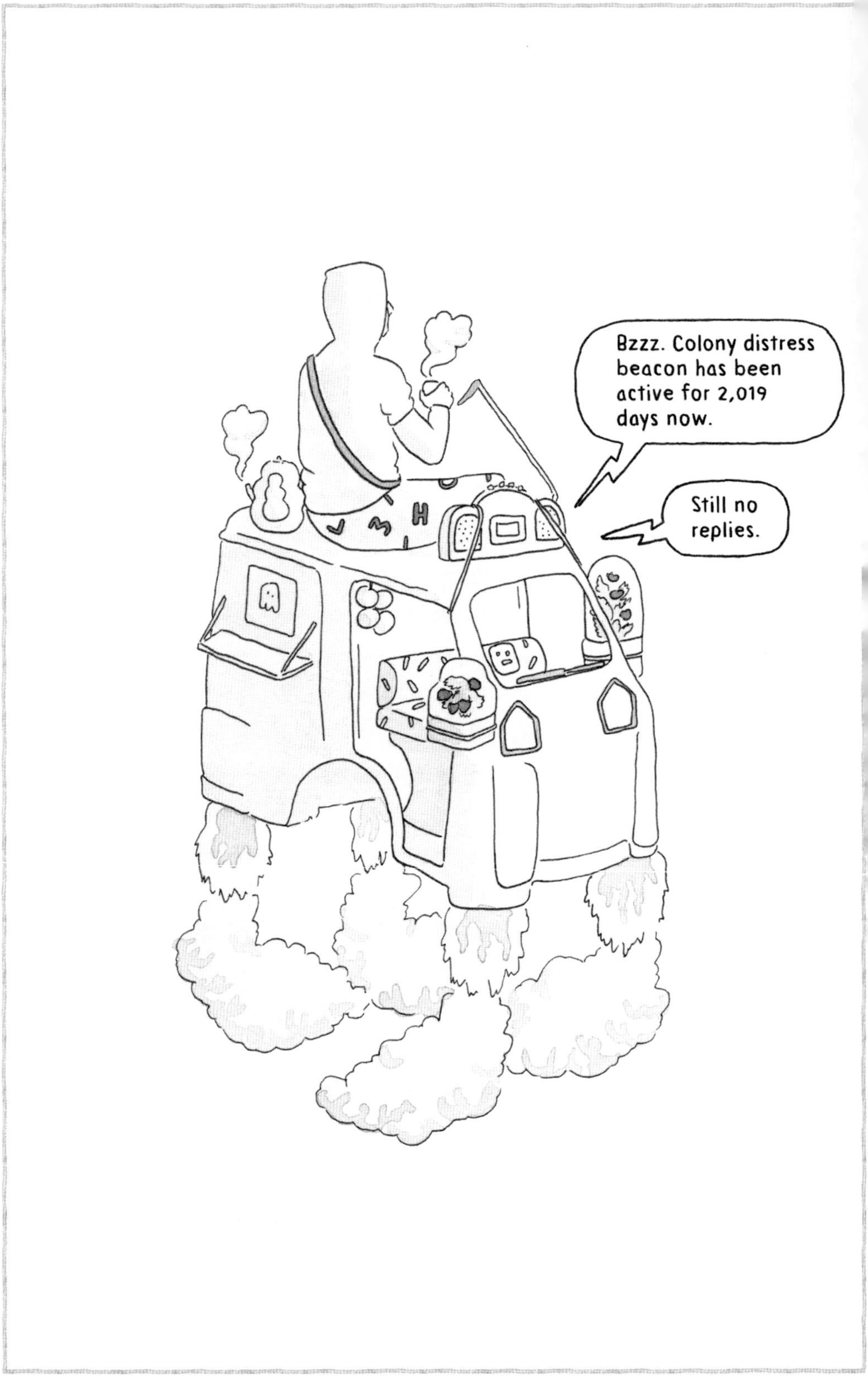
Bzzz. Colony distress beacon has been active for 2,019 days now.
Still no replies.

About the Author

TESSA BRUNTON IS A CARTOONIST from Fairfax, California, whose memoir comics have been nominated for two Ignatz Awards and selected as Notable Comics by the Best American Comics series editors. She currently lives in Richmond, California.

Acknowledgments

MY SPECIAL THANKS TO:

People with ME who researched, experimented with, and shared their own DIY treatments. Copying their strategies helped my symptoms improve, enabling me to make these comics.

The wonderful people who made this book exist: my editor Greg Hunter, book designer Athena Currier, the team at Graphic Universe, and my agents past and present, Trevor Ketner and Maeve MacLysaght.

Jess Wheaton, Amy Martin, Lindsey Simard, Ric Carrasquillo, and Anne Easley, for generously sharing feedback on drafts of these comics (and listening to my hand-wringing).

M.K. Brown, Dylan Williams, and MariNaomi, for helping me along, and my comics friends who've given me so much encouragement.

Brianne Benness, for her help and insight on chronic illness and dynamic disabilities.

Rich, Sara, Finn, Emil, Mom, Dad, and Vivian—what a good bunch. Huge thanks to Finn for crucial help with these comics and for letting me mess around with "Dark Rides" so much.

My deepest and wackiest gratitude to Viv for everything.

And thanks for Disneyland, Mom. ♥

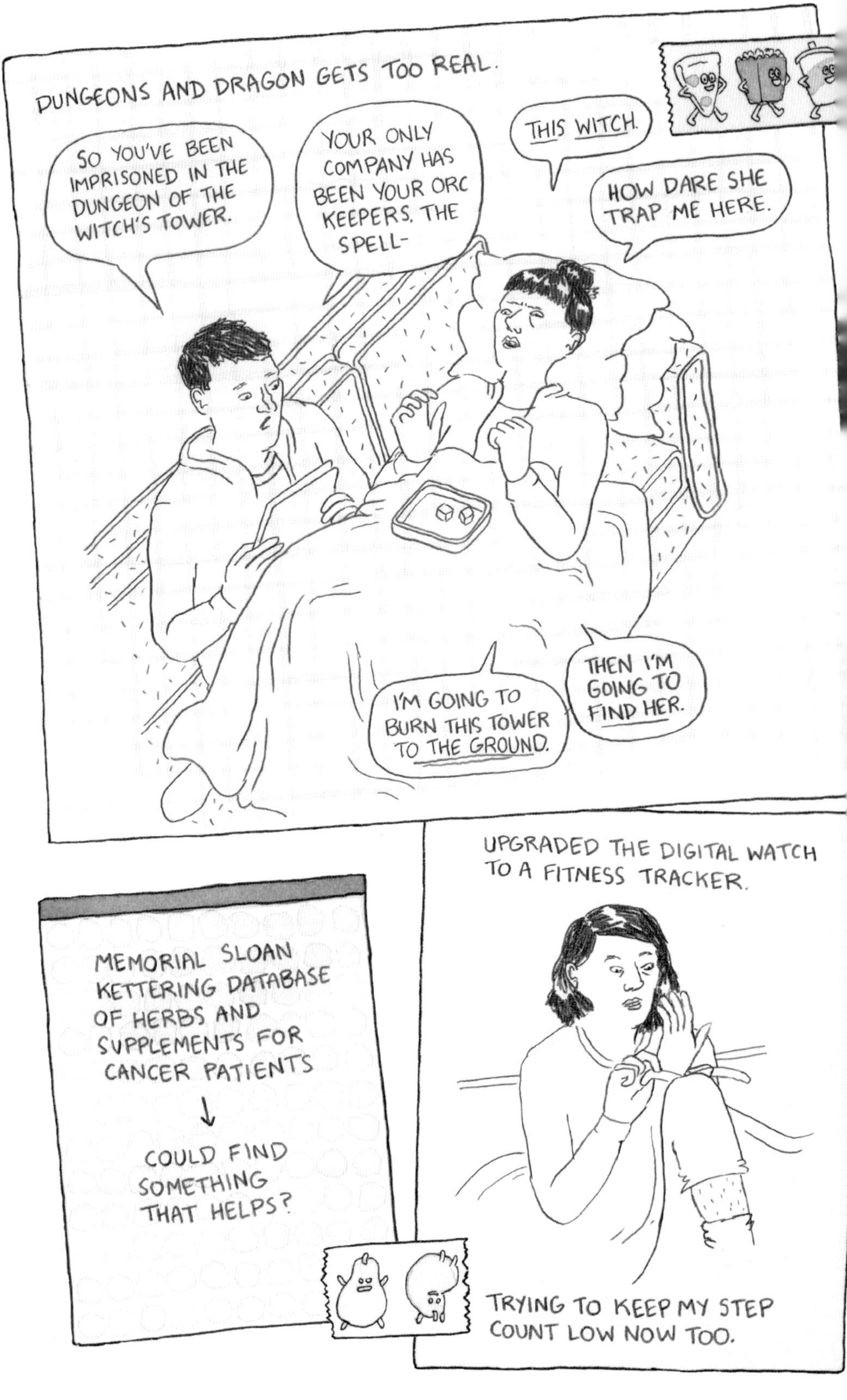
DUNGEONS AND DRAGON GETS TOO REAL.
SO YOU'VE BEEN IMPRISONED IN THE DUNGEON OF THE WITCH'S TOWER.
YOUR ONLY COMPANY HAS BEEN YOUR ORC KEEPERS. THE SPELL-
THIS WITCH.
HOW DARE SHE TRAP ME HERE.
I'M GOING TO BURN THIS TOWER TO THE GROUND.
THEN I'M GOING TO FIND HER.
MEMORIAL SLOAN KETTERING DATABASE OF HERBS AND SUPPLEMENTS FOR CANCER PATIENTS
↓
COULD FIND SOMETHING THAT HELPS?
UPGRADED THE DIGITAL WATCH TO A FITNESS TRACKER.
TRYING TO KEEP MY STEP COUNT LOW NOW TOO.